ADVANCES IN
AUSTRIAN ECONOMICS

Volume 2 • 1995 (PART B)

ADVANCES IN AUSTRIAN ECONOMICS

Volume Editors: PETER J. BOETTKE
New York University

MARIO J. RIZZO
New York University

Series Editors: PETER J. BOETTKE
New York University

ISRAEL M. KIRZNER
New York University

MARIO J. RIZZO
New York University

VOLUME 2 • 1995 (PART B)

JAI PRESS INC.

Greenwich, Connecticut *London, England*

55 Old Post Road, No. 2
Greenwich, Connecticut 06830

JAI PRESS LTD.
The Courtyard
28 High Street
Hampton Hill
Middlesex TW12 1PD
England

ISBN: 1-55938-531-6

Manufactured in the United States of America

CONTENTS

PART B

SECTION II. BOOK REVIEWS

SECTION III. BIBLIOGRPAHY

CONTENTS

PART A

LIST OF CONTRIBUTORS

Frank S. Arnold	Visiting Scholar Environmental Law Institute Washington, D.C.
Peter J. Boettke	Department of Economics New York University
Rueven Brenner	Faculty of Management McGill University
William N. Butos	Department of Economics Trinity College Hartford
Bruce Caldwell	Department of Economics University of North Carolina, Greensboro
Young Back Choi	Department of Economics and Finance St. John's University
Richard M. Ebeling	Department of Economics Hillsdale College
John B. Egger	Department of Economics Towson State University
Roger W. Garrison	Department of Economics Auburn University
Sanford Ikeda	Department of Economics SUNY, Purchase College
Anthony de Jasay	Paluel, France
Don Lavoie	Program on Social and Organizational Learning George Mason University

Peter Lewin	Department of Economics University of Dallas
J. A. H. Maks	Department of Economics University of Limburg
Laurence S. Moss	Department of Economics Babson College
Ralph Raico	Department of History SUNY College of Buffalo
*Murray N. Rothbard**	Department of Economics University of Nevada
Joseph T. Salerno	Graduate School of Business Pace University
Warren J. Samuels	Department of Economics Michigan State University
Hans F. Sennholz	Foundation for Economic Education Irving on Hudson, New York
Charles N. Steele	Department of Economics New York University
Karen I. Vaughn	Department of Economics George Mason University
Martti Vihanto	Department of Economics Turku School of Economics and Business Administration
Lawrence H. White	Department of Economics University of Georgia
Leland B. Yeager	Department of Economics Auburn University

*deceased

ADVISORY BOARD

PREFACE

On February 13, 1995 Israel M. Kirzner reached the age of sixty-five. This special issue of *Advances in Austrian Economics* honors him on that occasion. The articles in this volume either explicitly or implicitly expand themes that he has developed in the course of a very productive career.

Kirzner's contribution to our understanding of the dynamics of capitalist processes is without question. For over three decades Kirzner has striven to refine and deepen our appreciation of the adjustment mechanisms that assure efficient operation of market economies. In particular, in works such as *Competition and Enterpreneurship* (1973), *Perception, Opportunity and Profit* (1979), *Discovery and the Capitalist Process* (1985), and *The Meaning of Market Process* (1992), Kirzner's treatment of the significance of entrepreneurial discovery for the complex plan coordination characterizing smoothly-operating economies has led many to reconsider the modern theoretical formulation of markets. Mainstream treatments have eliminated the entrepreneur from the model of competitive capitalism, and therefore have reduced the professional and public understanding of and respect for capitalist dynamics. The implications of Kirzner's work for economics are vast—even if they are not always heeded within the professional community.

In Kirzner's work we find at least three scientific contributions that are vital to a refined appreciation of the market. They are:

1. *The entrepreneurial function within the market*: The dynamic market adjustment processes articulated in Kirzner's books, particularly *Competition and Entrepreneurship,* provide the disequilibrium foundations of economic analysis. Whereas traditional models of competitive equilibrium are not capable of providing an explanation of how the system would move to the equilibrium in the first place, Kirzner's entrepreneurial theory of the market process attempts to do precisely that. By focusing on the enterpreneur's correction of errors through arbitrage and speculation, Kirzner constructs a theory of how economies could move toward equilibrium. He shows how the often-condemned activities of arbitrage and speculation are actually beneficial to ordinary consumers.
2. *The institutional prerequisites for economic development*: An important implication of Kirzner's work on enterpreneurship is his specification of the institutional prerequisites for unleashing the entrepreneurial spirit and generating a prosperous economic system. This is relevant at both a purely theoretical and a policy level of analysis. The specification of the institutional environment in which enterpreneurship can be encouraged is elucidated in Kirzner's work on development economics, and (via the method of contrasts) in his examination of bureaucracy and regulation.
3. *The examination of distributive justice*: One of Kirzner's most important books, though perhaps his least understood, is his *Discovery, Capitalism, and Distributive Justice* (1989). Rather than argue on the grounds of strictly moral theory—something which he does not wish to do—Kirzner offers an *economic* critique of theories of distributive justice. He argues that standard ethical assessments of capitalism have failed not because of flaws in the ethical arguments themselves, but because they misperceive the nature of market processes, that is, they misperceive the discovery role of enterpreneurs. When entrepreneurs discover, for example, a use of resources, they bring these resources into a new (economic) existence. Accordingly, they have created something *ex nihilo* and therefore are entitled to the associated profit on generally-accepted moral principles.

In addition to these contributions (which do not include his seminal forays into the history of economics in general and of the Austrian School in particular, as well as research in capital theory), Kirzner has been an exemplar of scholarly reasonableness and scientific civility for at least two generations of economists. Seriousness of purpose, deep commitment, and the courage of his convictions, are defining traits of Kirzner's career. Both as a teacher and colleague, he has guided scholars who have embarked upon careers within the economcs profession and the broader intellectual community. As the contemporary leader of the Austrian School of Economics, Kirzner has worked tirelessly to revitalize a scientific tradition that embodies a deep appreciation for market processes and the political, legal, and social framework within which these processes are embedded. Moreover, the collapse of communist regimes in East and Central Europe, and the difficulties associated with transition and development policy, reveal that neoclassical economic theory is ill equiped to provide an understanding of both dynamic processes and the institutional infrastructure required to unleash the entrepreneurial spirit. As the limits of mainstream theory are more widely recognized and admitted, Kirzner's fundamental contributions to economic science will surely grow in influence.

Peter J. Boettke
Mario J. Rizzo
Editors

AN EVALUATION OF ENVIRONMENTAL LIFE CYCLE ASSESSMENT

Frank S. Arnold

As is true of virtually any area of public policy-making, environmental regulatory programs have many critics. Some argue that the nation's pollution-control policies are too lax and thus fail to provide sufficient protection of human health and environmental resources. Others maintain that the stringency of environmental regulations has far surpassed the point at which marginal benefits are worth their costs. Still others suggest that practical environmental policy-making will inevitably be governed mostly by the incentives of the regulatory bureaucracy, which center on administrative process, distributional concerns, and political forces, as opposed to the textbook motivation of enhancing social welfare through internalizing environmental externalities.

While these and many other criticisms may have merit, they mostly focus on the grand posture and direction of environmental regulation. The focus of this paper, however, is on a particular aspect of practical environmental policy analysis that should be of concern to analysts regardless of their views on the broader issues of overall environmental regulation. Specifically, this paper examines a research technique called environmental life cycle assessment,

Advances in Austrian Economics, Volume 2B, pages 241-276.

ISBN: 1-55938-531-6

which seeks to supply individuals with detailed and comprehensive information about the environmental consequences of their consumption and production decisions in the hope that this information will assist consumers and producers in choosing environmentally more benign alternatives.

This paper provides a detailed evaluation of life cycle assessment's practical feasibility and its value in environmental policy-making. A key concern identified here is that life cycle assessment requires analysts to trace economic interactions from a particular product backward through all of the inputs necessary for its supply, and then forward through the product's use and disposal, to identify and measure all of the environmental harms associated with the product's "life cycle." But, as observed many years ago during the Economic Calculation debates, the complexity of modern economies makes this a practical impossibility. Thus, by applying the fundamental insights of market-process economics regarding the central role of prices in solving society's "knowledge problem," this paper concludes that these attempts to substitute data collection and dissemination for the operation of the price system will inevitably be unsuccessful.

I. BACKGROUND

Recent years have seen a surge of interest in conducting analyses commonly referred to as environmental life cycle assessments, which seek to determine which of several products or processes is the "greenest" from an environmental perspective. In the consumer-choice arena, various studies weigh the environmental costs of disposable and cloth diapers, of plastic and paper grocery bags, and of alternative packaging materials, such as foam and paperboard. Life cycle assessment is also used to assist producer decisions about alternative processes and inputs in their attempts to improve industrial environmental performance.

The central motivation of environmental life cycle assessment is the belief that products, processes, and other economic activities cause environmental harms that are not adequately controlled and use natural resources that are not properly priced. Therefore, the goal is to identify and quantify all of the environmental harms associated with alternative products or processes—essentially, to provide environmental "report cards"—so that consumers and producers can choose the environmentally more benign alternative. Pollution in the form of releases of toxic substances to air, water, and land, inappropriate use of natural resources, such as forests and other habitats, and excessive use of energy and water, all are of concern in life cycle assessments.

This study evaluates the theoretical underpinnings and practical applications of life cycle assessment. It is motivated by several observations. One is that life cycle assessment results are the subject of sometimes considerable dispute. Indeed, a study championing one consumer choice for a particular product or activity, such as cloth diapers, seems to be quickly matched by another touting the advantages of the alternative. The apparent lack of robustness of life cycle assessment results may suggest a deeper problem.

More importantly, although life cycle assessments are becoming increasingly complex and costly to perform, the caveats and cautions attached to these analyses do not seem to diminish. It is somewhat troublesome that more and more research resources appear to produce little increased confidence in the results. A perhaps related point is that from a purely theoretical perspective, the task of identifying and quantifying all of the possible environmental harms and natural resource use that could be associated with a product or process seems daunting at best. Hence, this evaluation is motivated primarily by the lack of robustness of life cycle assessment results despite their growing complexity and cost.

Unlike some other evaluations of life cycle assessment, however, this study does not question the central premise that the prices of products, processes, and other economic activities do not adequately reflect their full social costs, particularly their environmental impacts. Whether the environmental problems that motivate life cycle assessments exist is not the issue in this study. Rather, for purposes of this evaluation, it is assumed that many environmental problems are associated with various consumer and producer choices, such as pollution caused by energy use, habitat destruction, occupation of scarce landfill space, and so on. The focus here is on whether life cycle assessments can help to mitigate these environmental harms in practice. From a purely analytical perspective, do (or can) the results of practical life cycle assessments correctly guide individuals' decisions toward environmentally more benign alternatives?

The main body of this paper is organized as follows:

- Section II discusses life cycle assessment's goals and methods, both in the abstract and in practice;
- Section III explores what life cycle assessments must achieve to provide useful guidance to consumers and producers in making environmentally better choices;
- Section IV summarizes the implications of the evaluation for practical life cycle assessment; and
- Section V discusses an alternative to life cycle assessment that is more likely to provide environmental improvement.

II. ENVIRONMENTAL LIFE CYCLE ASSESSMENT: GOALS AND APPLICATIONS

This section first explores the fundamental motivation behind life cycle assessment and its overall analytical goals. Next is a short review of the general condition of actual life cycle assessments in practice. While this section is relatively brief, it is sufficient for the evaluation of life cycle assessment that follows.

A. What Does Environmental Life Cycle Assessment Attempt?

Environmental life cycle assessment grows out of two types of analyses. One is the standard environmental assessment of industrial processes that seeks to identify and, where technically and economically feasible, reduce environmental impacts. The primary concern in these studies is to search out and minimize direct pollution caused by a particular process or economic activity.

The other historical root of life cycle analysis is the studies originating some 20 years ago that sought to measure the full "energy content" of specific products and processes. During the energy crisis, it was held that energy use carried a social cost in excess of its price, so that in addition to the price of a product or process, it was important to know its total energy content as well. Those studies, consequently, sought to identify all of the energy inputs required for a product not only directly, but also indirectly, such as the energy required to produce and deliver the inputs necessary to make the particular product in question.

Environmental life cycle assessment's roots suggest terminology that is useful for the remainder of the paper: environmental problems caused by the particular activity under study, say water pollution from a plant that assembles automobiles, are called *direct* environmental "demerits"; environmental problems caused by any other economic activities necessary to produce the automobile, such as air pollution from electricity generation or water pollution associated with mining and smelting ores to make steel, are called *indirect* environmental demerits. The key distinction between the two sources of demerits is not the type of harm caused, but rather the activities responsible for those harms.

Life cycle environmental assessments are thus the marriage of studies of direct environmental harms and the far more ambitious energy-use life cycle assessments of two decades ago. In essence, environmental life cycle assessment seeks to identify and quantify all of the environmental impacts of a specific product or process that occur both directly and indirectly through inputs to the product and through the product's use and disposal. By summarizing all of these direct and indirect environmental demerits of a product or process, life cycle assessments seek to assist consumers and producers in making environmentally more benign choices.

The literature describes life cycle environmental assessment as consisting of the following three steps:

- Step 1 is a life cycle *inventory* in which possible sources of energy and natural resources use, various emissions and wastes, as well as other factors that could lead to environmental harms, are tabulated;
- Step 2 is a life cycle *impact* analysis in which the actual environmental harms caused and the true value of the natural resources used are determined; and
- Step 3 is a life cycle *improvement* analysis in which changes in consumption or production decisions are defined and evaluated in an effort to reduce total environmental demerits.

Three key features of life cycle assessment are critical for understanding and evaluating it as an analytical and policy tool. The first is obvious, but important enough to repeat—life cycle assessment seeks to identify the total environmental demerits associated with a product or process. Thus, they typically begin with a list of inputs that cause environmental demerits, including the use of energy, water, and renewable and nonrenewable natural resources, air and water emissions, and solid and hazardous waste generation. They then seek to identify and quantify all of the direct and indirect sources of these demerits.

Although it is easy to list many conceivable environmental demerits, it is far harder to measure them accurately, especially the indirect sources. Direct environmental demerits are those visibly caused by the product use or production process, so identifying and quantifying them is conceptually clear-cut, although often difficult in practice. The indirect environmental demerits are harder to identify, for these are, essentially, environmental demerits in other production processes or activities necessary to the product or process in question. Tabulating the indirect demerits first requires that one identify all of these economic activities and then determine whether they cause any environmental problems.

The second central point is that a key goal of life cycle assessment is to evaluate the excess environmental costs of a product or process that are not included in prices, largely because they are not addressed adequately by the environmental authorities. As a result, these assessments seek to measure environmental impacts and damages, not just to tabulate energy consumption, natural resources use, or solid waste disposal requirements. In the parlance of life cycle assessment, to be truly useful to consumers and producers, studies must eventually go beyond the inventory step to the impacts and improvements stages.

The third key point about life cycle assessment important for this evaluation is that sponsors of life cycle studies do not commission them out of idle curiosity. Rather, they wish to use the results to make the best choice from an environmental perspective. Thus, the use to which these studies are put is invariably to juxtapose two sets of environmental demerits associated with two different products or with two different versions of a process. The object is to determine which alternative causes the least net environmental harm. Because life cycle assessments are intended to inform decisions, their value ultimately flows from providing a net decrease in environmental harms by guiding choices to greener alternatives.

To some extent, the life cycle community's definition of the final segment of analysis (Step 3) as the "improvements" stage tends to obscure the fundamental fact that life cycle assessment seeks to help in making choices between competing alternatives. Indeed, the term "improvement" conjures up the image of researchers identifying and mitigating direct environmental harms caused by a product or process, such as reducing direct air or water emissions. This, however, is only part of the story.

Often life cycle assessments explore the tradeoffs between two processes whose environmental differences are largely the result of indirect sources of demerits, not direct ones. One process might use more water and virgin materials, but less energy, than another. Thus, the "improvements" portion of life cycle assessment is really an analysis of tradeoffs involving environmental demerits from both indirect and direct sources. Trading off environmental damages from all sources is very different from attempting to minimize the direct pollution consequences of an activity, as will be shown later in this evaluation.

B. Environmental Life Cycle Assessment In Practice

The purpose of this section is to summarize the state of life cycle assessment in practice to gain some sense of what can be accomplished in reality. Hence, this discussion is not intended to be a review of the literature, only a glance at practical applications of life cycle assessment.

General Approach

Environmental life cycle assessments typically arise from discussions about whether one type of product or process has fewer environmental demerits than another. Probably the most famous are recent studies of the relative environmental demerits of reusable and single-use diapers (which most would refer to as the cloth versus disposables question), paper and plastic grocery sacks, and foam and paperboard food containers. Most life cycle assessments begin with an understandable curiosity concerning which of two (or more) options does the least environmental harm. Of course, the hope is that one can calculate all of the environmental demerits of the options and then select the more environmentally benign one, thereby generating a net environmental improvement.

Life cycle assessments begin by specifying the "system" surrounding the activity or product in question. In general, the system is thought of as one requiring inputs from the earth, for example, energy, natural resources, and so forth, and generating outputs of wastes, emissions of chemicals, and so on. Activities in the system to be studied normally include raw materials acquisition, manufacturing, fabrication, distribution, use and reuse, and waste management. Most of the effort in life cycle studies is on specifying numerous linkages from sector to sector, and activity to activity, to assess direct and indirect sources of environmental demerits.

Practical life cycle assessments use public and private data sources on process technologies and their inputs and outputs, sector-by-sector, to generate a rough sketch of the total "cradle-to-grave" environmental demerits of a product or process. Given the problem's vast complexity, and the nature and aggregation of the available information, life cycle researchers normally can only examine "typical" product manufacturing practices and inputs based on national averages, engineering studies of the processes involved, and a significant amount of professional judgment.

Life cycle assessment inventory results typically list the per unit energy requirements in BTUs, water requirements in gallons, landfilling requirements in cubic yards, atmospheric emissions of chemicals in pounds, and water emissions in various units, including pounds or gallons, oxygen demand, suspended solids, and so on. The stated goal of these studies is to measure contributions to the environmental demerits from both direct and indirect sources associated with the product or process in question.

For the most part, existing life cycle studies indicate that one product may have lower average, or typical, levels of some environmental demerits than another product, but generate higher levels of other demerits. Because efforts so far have only focused on the inventory portion of the assessment, rarely do any of these studies attempt to supply methods for trading these demerits against one another. From the perspective of the three stages of life cycle assessment, tradeoffs must await the "impacts" and "improvements" stages of the analysis.

The Grocery Sack Example

A typical example of life cycle assessment is a recent report on plastic and paper grocery sacks prepared by Franklin Associates.[1] Motivated mostly by reference to scarce landfill capacity, this study sought to inventory all of the energy and environmental inputs of these two types of sacks by performing a cradle-to-grave analysis. The authors explicitly targeted energy use, emissions to air and water, and solid waste requirements. According to the study:

> [t]he analysis involves all steps in the life cycle of each grocery sack, including extraction of raw materials from the earth, processing these materials into useable components, manufacturing the package materials, distribution of the package, and final disposition of the package (whether recycled, incinerated, or landfilled) (pp. 1-2).

In terms of methodology, the study adopts what might be thought of as a process-engineering approach whereby producing each type of sack is conceptualized as a series of processes that lead to the ultimate manufacturing, use, and reuse or disposal of the sacks. Again, quoting from the study:

> [A]ll processes and subprocesses were first considered to be separate, independent systems. For each process or subprocess such as oil extraction or ethylene production a standard unit, such as 1,000 pounds of output, was used as a basis for calculations. A complete materials balance was first performed. If marketable co-products or by-products were produced, the materials inputs were adjusted to reflect only the input attributable to the output being considered. The wastes and energy were adjusted also (pp. 2-3).

Results reported in the Franklin study list the total energy requirements of the two types of sacks at various ratios of polyethylene-to-paper sacks and at different assumed recycling rates. On a "per 10,000 uses" basis, the report lists landfilling requirements, the amount of incinerator ash generated, total energy requirements in BTUs, and the various emissions to air and water associated with the life cycle of making, using, and reusing or disposing of these two types of sacks.

The Franklin study is also only the "inventory" stage of the analysis, which is clear from the following:

> The scope of this analysis is to identify where and what wastes are generated through a cradle-to-grave analysis. No attempt is made to describe what the effects from these wastes may be. In other words, no attempt has been made to determine the relative environmental effects of these pollutants such as fish kills or groundwater contamination as there are no accurate data available (pp. 2-8).

The report goes on to clearly detail the numerous assumptions made and omissions necessary in conducting the analysis.

Observations

In examining actual examples of life cycle assessments, one is struck by the enormity of the efforts required to comprehensively measure the indirect sources of environmental demerits. Numerous complex flow diagrams of industrial systems appear in these studies, along with a host of input data and assumptions, and page after page of numerical results. Sensitivity analyses also figure prominently in life cycle assessments, especially regarding key disputed parameters. For example, in the Franklin study, precisely how many plastic grocery sacks are needed to replace a paper one is very important to the analysis and results. Similarly, exactly how many cloth diapers are needed to replace disposables is critical in that evaluation.

Nevertheless, the picture that recent examples of life cycle assessment paint is one of researchers attempting to compute the total environmental demerits for a product or process to the best of their ability using whatever data are available. It is understandable that their results then reflect the level of aggregation of information realistically available and that various complexities are simply not addressed.

While life cycle assessments seek to be internally consistent and generally attempt to be as comprehensive and detailed as possible within time and budgetary constraints, one aspect of these studies is somewhat troubling, even to the researchers involved. Actual examples of life cycle assessment always seem to contain a long list of caveats acknowledging the limitations of the available data. Repeated attempts to remedy these deficiencies by delving deeper into details and expanding the sets of economic activities incorporated suggest that the results are not robust. That is, it seems easy to find new sources of significant environmental demerits, or to radically alter their magnitude, and thus change the latest "answer," by further expanding the scope of the analysis or by refining and disaggregating the input information.

III. REQUIREMENTS FOR ACCURATE ENVIRONMENTAL LIFE CYCLE ASSESSMENT

To evaluate the prospects for the practical use of life cycle assessment, it is best to return to the fundamental questions these types of analyses seek to answer. Doing so provides a clear sense of the nature of the analytical and empirical efforts required to provide information that is useful to consumers and producers in making environmentally better choices. This section introduces and analyzes several fundamental propositions concerning life cycle assessment which, taken together, point to fairly strong conclusions about the likelihood that these analyses will ever be sufficiently robust in practice.

A. A Single "Correct" Set of Environmental Demerits Usually Does Not Exist

Life cycle assessments are extremely data-intensive tasks, especially in their attempts to identify and quantify the indirect sources of environmental demerits. Understandably, these analyses begin with the information normally available, supplementing this with a variety of different data elements from many sources. Life cycle assessments in practice demonstrate that trying to sketch even a preliminary picture of the total environmental demerits for a typical example of a product or process can be a time-consuming and difficult undertaking.

More Than One "Right" Answer

The natural tendency to use whatever data are available to gain some sense of total direct and indirect environmental demerits has obscured the very important fact that normally there is no single "correct" and complete tabulation of the environmental demerits of a product or process. For example, the correct product decision concerning diapers may be different for people in different situations. The environmental concerns associated with diapers normally are water use, pollution resulting from energy production, and effluent discharges of waste water for cloth diapers, and the use of oil, and the occupation of scarce landfill space for disposable diapers. But the intensities of these environmental harms depend on many different factors, such as the water body into which the effluent is discharged, the type of fuel used to heat the water for washing, the location of the energy production, and the degree to which the social costs of landfill space and water use exceed their prices.

All of the environmental concerns associated with diaper use (and any others one cares to include) may vary significantly by geography and even the time of day, *and* they will change over time. Hence, the relevant question is not "Which diapering choice is better for the nation?," rather it is "Which diapering choice is environmentally better for a particular set of circumstances?" Because the existence, extent, and intensity of the various environmental problems associated with alternative diapering choices can vary so widely, the number of sets of unique circumstances for which the correct choice should then be ascertained is very large. Moreover, the right answer today for a particular person may be the wrong answer tomorrow as economic and environmental circumstances change.

It is easy to see that the correct environmental demerit levels concerning consumer products vary depending on people's individual circumstances. The same is true of producer decisions concerning process changes and other choices. The correct answer for one producer could be different for another in other circumstances. A process that uses less water but generates more solid waste may be best for a producer in the west, but not for one in the east, where landfill space may be relatively more scarce.

Some might argue that the goal of life cycle analysis is not to indicate the "correct" answer, but rather simply to provide extra information to consumers and producers in making their choices. This may be true, but the usefulness of this additional information critically depends on it being correct. Hence, if the actual levels of the various environmental demerits depend on a variety of specific circumstances, then individuals situated in those varying circumstances will need environmental demerit information relevant to them to make correct choices. Seeking a single, national-average tabulation of environmental demerits misses the essential texture of the problem.

Seeking One "Answer" Could Do Harm to the Environment

Clearly, the nature of this limitation is not fully appreciated in the life cycle literature. Providing a single set of estimated environmental demerits when the correct answer really does vary across individuals will suggest the environmentally correct option for some people and the wrong one for others. Where the guidance is wrong, acting on a life cycle assessment's advice will cause increased environmental damages. Yet, it is tempting to argue that overall, the net impact on the environment will be positive even though the single set of estimated environmental demerits will be correct for some people and incorrect for others. That is, surely we will not do net damage to the environment if the national average levels of demerits point to one product over another.

Unfortunately, it is possible that this focus on estimating a single set of environmental demerits for a product or process could actually harm the environment, not help it. The key issue here is that one should not compare the overall environmental consequences of everyone choosing one product with those that would result if everyone chose the other. Rather, one should compare the environmental effects of any life cycle assessment-induced changes in consumer or producer decisions with the environmental effects of their current choices.

To illustrate the importance and implications of this problem, consider the following highly simplified example of the diaper decision. Table 1 lists the levels of environmental demerits caused by two different people's decisions about diapers. Mary, who uses disposable diapers, owns an electric washer and dryer system in an area where water tends to be relatively more valuable than is reflected in its price, and power generation involves relatively more pollution than in other locations. John, who uses cloth diapers, lives in a crowded eastern city where the main problem is the high social cost of solid waste disposal. As the entries in the table indicate, each of these individuals currently makes the environmentally-correct choice for her or his circumstances, Mary electing to use disposables and John cloth.

Table 1. Environmental Demerits and the Diaper Choice Hypothetical Numbers of Demerits

	Mary		*John*		*National Average*	
Category	*Cloth*	*Disposables*	*Cloth*	*Disposables*	*Cloth*	*Disposables*
Energy/Air	20	5	10	5	15	5
Virgin Materials	5	20	5	20	5	20
Water	20	0	5	0	12.5	0
Effluent	10	5	10	5	10	5
Solid Waste	5	10	10	50	7.5	30
Totals	60	40	40	80	50	60

Note: Example assumes that the results of a life cycle inventory can be translated to a common metric through an impacts assessment. This may not be at all easy in practice.

Now suppose a life cycle assessment produces environmental demerit results for typical, or national-average cloth and disposable diapers, and concludes that one of these options is more environmentally benign. In this example, averaging the environmental demerits for both Mary and John over the two alternatives yields a score of 50 for cloth and 60 for disposables, so such a study would recommend cloth over disposables. Clearly, starting from a situation in which both Mary and John are already making the environmentally correct choice (by accident or otherwise), if they both follow the advice of the study, one will switch from making the right choice to the wrong one, as Mary would here.

The example generalizes to situations with more than two people, and of course, one can alter the assumptions to show that in other circumstances, acting on the advice of a life cycle assessment's single list of environmental demerits enhances environmental quality. Yet, the essential point is that it is possible for a one-size-fits-all life cycle assessment recommendation to increase environmental harms. Even worse, there is no way to know whether a life cycle study that reports a single list of the environmental demerits will lead to overall environmental improvement or harm unless the details of specific circumstances are explored. In the example, the life cycle researcher does not know the specific environmental demerits for Mary and John individually, only the national average information is estimated. Hence, unless the specifics of different individuals' circumstances are investigated, it is not clear that the net environmental effects of a life cycle study will be beneficial.

Observations

The fact that the actual environmental demerits of a product or process depend on a variety of factors that vary across the country and change over time helps to explain some of the frustration many life cycle researchers have experienced in recent years. In many examples of these analyses, the "answer" tends to shift from one product or practice to the other when sometimes small assumptions are altered and if more detail and disaggregated input data are used. Given that there isn't one right answer, however, this should not be at all surprising.

Unfortunately, the tendency in the life cycle research community has been to continue to assume that a single tabulation of environmental demerits for a product or process will suffice, rather than many sets that reflect varying circumstances. Life cycle assessment researchers further suggest that by using common rules and data sets, everyone will arrive at this single answer for a particular product or process. Codifying rules to obtain consistency is unproductive for it seeks to define a single correct set of inputs for the analysis, not to determine what the correct levels of environmental demerits are in different specific circumstances.

Some reluctance to recognize that there isn't one correct set of environmental demerit levels in most life cycle assessments is understandable. Once this is admitted, the number of different times the same products and processes, such as diapers and packaging, must be studied to account for location and other significant determinants of actual environmental harms becomes large and potentially open-ended. Even worse, however, is that as environmental and economic linkages evolve over time, all of these studies must be repeated.

Pursuing a single list of environmental demerits despite the fact that this conceals the true magnitude and complexity of the problem also has been viewed as satisfactory because of the lack of disaggregated information required to tailor the analysis to specific circumstances. Because tracing the indirect environmental demerits for a product even at a highly aggregated level is a challenging task, life cycle researchers have more than enough complexity to handle already, and they can generate large amounts of information. Thus, what really amounts to a fundamental methodological problem is converted to just one of the many standard limitations and qualifications of life cycle assessments in practice.

Some might argue that the inventory stage of life cycle assessment supplies information that can then be applied in a disaggregated way by users of the studies to reflect their particular circumstances. This is a plausible idea, but ultimately not realistic. It is conceivable, for example, to imagine that consumers and producers could try to attach their own locality's environmental demerits associated with solid waste disposal to the reported landfilling requirements. It is harder, but still possible to imagine them determining the actual environmental impacts of their specific energy use and adjusting the life cycle assessment's results accordingly.

But these are the easiest problems people would face in trying to tailor life cycle assessment conclusions to their specific circumstances. The hallmark of life cycle assessment is in cataloguing all of the indirect sources of environmental demerits of products and processes. These could well vary across individual consumer and producer circumstances in ways completely unknown to the users of life cycle inventory results, and involve demerits from activities that take place in locations far removed. Thus, to fine-tune a life cycle assessment's results to one's specific circumstances essentially requires one to trace all of the indirect environmental demerits again—which is, of course, another life cycle assessment itself.

B. Life Cycle Analyses are Prohibitively Costly Without Reasonable Boundaries

Most of the examples of life cycle assessments discussed so far are highly simplified to illustrate some basic analytical points. Yet, accurate life cycle assessment for a given product or process that would correctly guide consumer or producer choices can be extremely complex and costly. A researcher contemplating conducting a life cycle assessment is confronted by numerous details, all of which are difficult to ignore given that the goal is to measure total environmental demerits, both direct and indirect. Moreover, as just demonstrated, the efforts necessary to define a product's environmental demerits for a particular set of circumstances will have to be repeated for the many different situations in which individuals interested in the product's demerits find themselves.

Life Cycle Assessment is Expensive and Complex

A useful example of how life cycle assessments can become very complex is provided by a discussion of setting boundaries for such analyses contained in EPA's *Life-Cycle Assessment: Inventory Guidelines and Principles.*[2] On page 20 of that report, a figure (reproduced here) appears indicating an initial attempt to define the system's boundaries for a life cycle assessment of a bar of soap. The flow diagram lists a variety of activities related to soap manufacturing including grain production, cattle raising, meat packing and tallow rendering, salt mining, caustic manufacturing, paper production, and post-consumer waste management. It is worth quoting from the ensuing advice in the guidance document on defining appropriate boundaries.

> [The Figure] shows an example of setting system boundaries for a product baseline analysis of a bar soap system. Tallow is the major material for soap production, and its primary raw material source is the grain fed to the cattle. Production of paper for packaging the soap is also included. The fate of both the soap and its packaging end the life cycle analysis of this system. Minor inputs could include, for example, the energy required to fabricate the tires on the combine used to plant and harvest the grain (p. 20).
>
> If the life cycle inventory were intended to analyze whether bar soap should be manufactured using an animal-derived or vegetable-derived raw material source, the system boundaries and units of analysis would be more complicated. First, the system flow diagram would have to be expanded to include the growing, harvesting, and processing steps for the alternative feedstock. Then the performance of the finished product would have to be considered (p. 20).
>
> Suppose an analyst wants to compare bar soap made from tallow with a liquid hand washing soap made from synthetic ingredients. Because the two products have different material sources (cattle and petroleum), the analysis should begin with the raw materials acquisition steps. Because the two products are packaged differently and may have different chemical formulas, the materials manufacturing and packaging steps would need to be included. Consumer use and waste management options should also be examined because the different formulas could result in varying usage patterns. Thus for this comparative analysis, the analyst would have to inventory the entire life cycle of the two products (p. 20).
>
> However, if the liquid hand soap also had a skin moisturizer in its formula, the analyst would need to include a moisturizing lotion product in the boundaries of the bar soap system on two conditions. The first condition would apply if the environmental issues associated with this component were germane to the purpose of the life cycle assessment (p. 21).

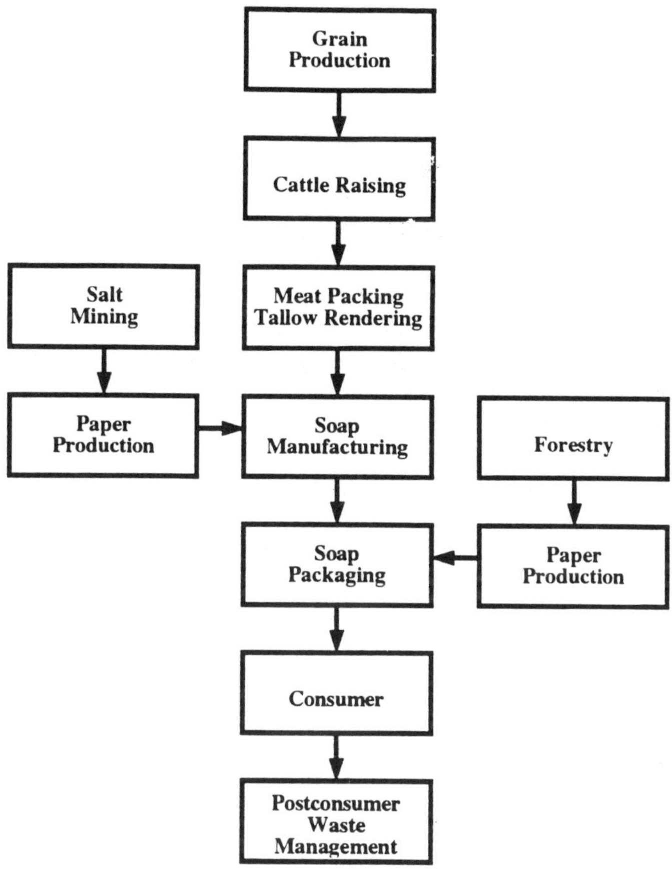

Example system flow diagram for bar soap

Source: Reproduced from Vigon et al. 1992, p. 20.

Figure 1.

Even in this simple example, the complexity of life cycle assessment is obvious. Many items of potential importance, such as whether the two soap products require different amounts of transportation or water, were not even explicitly mentioned. Moreover, the statement concerning the energy necessary to make the tires on the combine that harvests the grain to feed the cattle whose tallow is used as an input to soap manufacturing should give one pause. The complexity of the analysis appears to be limited only by the ingenuity of the researcher and his or her research resources.

Thus, what at first seems to be a simple tallying of environmental demerits instead escalates into a major data-intensive investigation. First, one specifies the list of potential environmental demerits, which normally consist of a variety of pollution possibilities typically associated with energy use, chemical emissions, primary resource extraction, natural resources use, and waste generation and management. These demerits are assumed to be generated at a variety of points in the entire economic system.

Next, the really hard work begins. As suggested in the guidance document's example, the analyst must work backward from the product or process in question through its inputs and the activities necessary to make those inputs, pausing along the way to measure any environmental demerits. It is useful to think of this process as one in which the economic activities associated with the product or process and its inputs "fan" outward to more and more distant processes, each of which causes indirect environmental demerits through energy use, natural resource use, chemical emissions, and waste generation. Of course, not only the nature of these activities and their potential demerits are important, but their locations are as well, for the intensity and damages of the various environmental demerits can depend on many site-specific factors.

The analysis also must investigate indirect environmental demerits that might be caused by activities "downstream" from those specifically under study, such as a product's use, and reuse or disposal, because these activities could also create environmental demerits. In most cases, a number of layers of activities may happen sequentially before matters finally end, so the same "fanning out" of possible activities occurs here as well. Similarly, the intensity of the environmental demerits caused by use, and reuse or disposal, will generally vary by location and other factors, so this also must be taken into account in the tabulation.

Actual Demerits Caused is the Goal

Obviously, the life cycle assessor faces a daunting challenge in tracing through from activity to activity to identify and measure indirect sources of environmental demerits. Yet, another hurdle exists that is often ignored in the life cycle literature. Specifically, it is not enough to identify environmental demerits "associated with" products or processes. Instead, one must conceptualize altering a consumer's or a producer's choice, deciding between plastic or paper grocery sacks for example, and then determine to what extent the environmental demerits change in response. This is not an easy task because often the actual changes in economic activities that result, and the environmental demerits caused by them, may be different from what one might expect based on casual analysis, and require significant detailed information to predict.

For example, if a less energy-intensive product is selected over a more energy-intensive one, less power will be required. But exactly what fuel will be saved and what environmental demerits will be avoided are difficult to determine. Electric power is routinely traded across transmission grids, so it is not clear precisely where less electricity generation will occur much less what environmental harms will be avoided. Worse still is the fact that sometimes the energy use reduction is in the home, say, hot water heating in the case of diapers. Here, because the environmental demerits of electricity and other fuels, such as natural gas, are different, one needs to know what type of hot water heater is used to estimate the reduction in environmental demerits.

A similar complication is that sometimes the reduction in an environmental demerit promised by a life cycle assessment doesn't actually materialize. Suppose significant environmental demerits are the land erosion and water quality effects of logging in the United States. But if the U.S. timber industry sells into a large international market, shifting consumer choices toward products that use less virgin timber will not necessarily reduce the amount of U.S. logging and its associated damages. Under plausible conditions, the same amount of U.S. logging continues regardless of any changes in consumer and producer choices guided by life cycle assessments. Thus, predicting what will actually happen to the levels of economic activities remotely connected to the decision under study, and the environmental demerits they cause, can be a very tricky business.

Life cycle analyses in practice are thus confronted with numerous conceivable sources of environmental demerits associated with a product or process, including indirect ones that can be quite remote. The length of the list of environmental demerits of concern, along with any reasonable estimate of the number of economic activities conceivably associated with the product in question, require setting reasonable boundaries to make life cycle assessment practical, otherwise these studies face enormous difficulties. From an epistemological point of view, identifying and measuring all possible changes in environmental demerits, especially indirect ones, caused by changing a consumer or producer product or process decision is "knowable." Actually "knowing" them all, however, would involve a preposterous level of effort.

Complexity is Unavoidable

That seeking to catalogue all (or at least "enough") of a product's direct and indirect environmental demerits is complex and costly should not be surprising.

Life cycle assessors essentially seek to develop an information system that provides the same type of data normally communicated by the price system. Prices of economic goods and services summarize the costs of their supply regardless of how remote those costs are from the product or service in question. As goods move through the chain of production and commerce, the cost of the primary inputs (labor, capital, land, and raw materials) incorporated at successive stages of a product's supply are added to its price. All of this information transmission is accomplished without the guidance of any single entity, but as the result of the anonymous functioning of the market and the price system.

Life cycle assessments, however, are motivated by a fundamental belief that many environmental demerits are not adequately captured in prices, or at least that social concern for these environmental harms and natural resources use surpasses merely their prices. As a result, they must attempt to trace from products and processes back through layer upon layer of other economic activities associated with them to identify and quantify indirect sources of environmental demerits.

Thus, the real problem for life cycle assessment is not just measuring environmental demerits for known processes and activities, for one can reasonably expect that once the activity, its location, and other relevant features, are specified, experts can judge whether it causes significant environmental degradation or other harms. Instead, it is the need to trace through so many of the economic activities connected to a product or process, stopping to determine whether demerits exist at each point, that makes life cycle assessment so complex and difficult.[3]

Central Tension of Setting Practical Boundaries

Clearly, life cycle assessments must set reasonable boundaries in order to be at all feasible in practice, for the pursuit of indirect sources of environmental demerits cannot extend to every conceivable economic activity even remotely associated with the product or process being studied. The central issue here is the ability to establish practical boundaries for these analyses within which the conclusions reached can be considered robust, so that one has confidence that they will not be overturned easily.

The acknowledged necessity of establishing boundaries to avoid being overwhelmed by complexity and details has created a serious tension in life cycle assessment today, one that pits the detail, scope, and accuracy of such studies—which determine whether their results have any real value—against the cost and feasibility of conducting them—which govern their practicality.

On the one hand, practical life cycle assessment researchers labor hard to incorporate whatever details and complexity they can, and generate large amounts of information. Despite the inevitable caveats, limitations, and omissions, it is assumed that what can be (or, perhaps, might be) accomplished in practice still has value to consumers and producers in helping them choose environmentally more benign products and processes. This is the sense conveyed by many statements concerning boundary setting in the life cycle literature. For example, in the section pertaining to the raw materials and energy component of life cycle assessment in SETAC's *A Technical Framework for Life Cycle Assessments*,[4] the following discussion is revealing:

> A fundamental concept that must be accepted by anyone undertaking an inventory is that the raw materials acquisition system not only extends all the way back to the source for each primary raw material, but also extends laterally to include all inputs of energy, materials, and equipment necessary for executing each step of acquisition. Obviously such an analysis soon becomes intractable without some methodology for screening insignificant contributions. It may be necessary to extend the analysis of material inputs beyond the first level to second or even multiple levels to identify all significant contributions. In some cases such secondary contributions are the source of the most crucial impacts of all.
>
> The issue from an analytical point of view is how to define the criteria that will determine what is insignificant and can be discarded or ignored. In the absence of superior logic, an analyst must rely on professional judgement or must establish an arbitrary threshold (e.g., components comprising less than 5 percent of the inputs will be ignored) (p. 34).

On the other hand, the guidance literature states that setting arbitrary boundaries in life cycle assessments imposes limitations on the accuracy and comprehensiveness of their results. Therefore, when arbitrary boundaries are set, one cannot make statements about the total level of, or change in, any environmental demerit categories that might be affected outside the system examined. For example, EPA's *Life-Cycle Assessment: Inventory Guidelines and Principles* states the following:

> Depending on the goal of the study, it may be possible to exclude certain stages or activities and still address the issues for which the life-cycle inventory is being performed. For example, it may be possible to exclude the acquisition of raw materials in a life cycle inventory without affecting the results. Suppose a company wishes to perform an internal life-cycle inventory to evaluate alternative drying systems for formulating a snack food product. If the technologies are indifferent to feedstock, it is possible to assume the raw materials acquisition stage will be identical for all options. If the decision will be based on selecting a drying system with lower energy use or environmental burdens, it may be acceptable to analyze such a limited system. However, with this system boundary, the degree of absolute difference in the overall system energy or environmental inventory cannot be determined. The difference in the product manufacturing stage, although significant for the manufacturer, may represent a minor component of the total system. Therefore, statements about the total system should not be made (p. 19).

The source of the tension is obvious. What can be done in practice necessarily involves setting limitations on the study's boundaries, reining in the scope, and neglecting the immense complexity and details of the real world. Still, one would think that what can be done in practice, albeit imperfect, is still valuable. However, if one cannot make statements about total changes in the levels of particular environmental demerits if some of those changes occur outside the boundaries set for the study, what does this mean for the value of practical life cycle assessments? Can nonarbitrary and defensible boundaries be defined to make life cycle assessment both practical and accurate?

C. Setting Boundaries that Ensure Practicality and Accuracy May Be Impossible

The key issue in setting analytical boundaries for a life cycle assessment is whether in doing so, one has any confidence that the excluded elements, or lack of disaggregation and detail, could harbor environmental demerits great enough, or sufficiently different, that consumers and producers would wish to know them before revising their product or process decisions. Of course, questions concerning what level of disaggregation and degree of detail are required to be confident that the results are robust are common ones for all economic analyses.

Analytical Boundaries in Principle

The intellectual process of how one decides the scope and depth of conventional analyses is important to appreciate. Ordinarily, decisions about whether further disaggregation of input data or additional analysis of certain aspects of a problem are worthwhile are guided by balancing the value of the extra information gained against the costs of acquiring it. In conventional analyses, the magnitude or importance of the additional information one could obtain through more study is generally correlated with elements of the problem that are known.

For example, one might decide not to disaggregate an industry sector in calculating compliance costs for a regulation because the likely variation in costs across individual firms is small based on inherent similarities of their activities. Hence, having started by investigating first the broad determinants of the total regulatory costs, additional disaggregation is not likely to significantly alter the results. The key to this process is that one begins with what one already knows are the largest determinants of the answer—economic size, activities subject to the regulation where compliance will be particularly costly, economic costs of the regulated activity relative to the total product, and so forth—and works down a list to less and less significant factors.

Of course, surprises can occur in the process, just as statistical confidence intervals allow for small probability events in the tails of their distributions. Nevertheless, the defining feature of conventional information gathering and analysis is that decisions about levels of disaggregation and further data collection can be made rationally on the basis of an observable set of factors that help predict the influence and importance of elements not yet investigated.

Boundaries in Life Cycle Assessment

There is a subtle difference between ordinary analyses and life cycle assessment, however, that makes it far harder to set boundaries that are both feasible and defensible for the latter. The critical element that makes setting boundaries problematic for life cycle assessment has to do with the information the researcher can use to establish rational expectations regarding the potential influence on the results of adding details and expanding the scope.

The fundamental problem is that there is no a priori basis for assuming that the elements excluded from the assessment are necessarily smaller than those included. This is because the indirect sources of demerits that life cycle assessment seeks to quantify usually are not incorporated into prices. Hence, economic measures of remote or small activities related to a product do not translate directly into conclusions about the significance of the environmental demerits associated with those activities.

It is therefore much harder to safely ignore details and remote activities in life cycle assessments because the researcher has no clear basis for assuming that accounting for them will not reveal substantial environmental demerits, or levels of demerits significantly different from those already estimated. For example, while it is true that the amount of electricity used in an activity very remote from the product or process in question will be a small input, it still might not be safe to exclude it from the analysis. The ultimate demerit of interest is not the electricity use per se, but the environmental damages it causes. It is entirely possible for an activity that constitutes a small portion of the overall cost of a product to harbor a particular environmental demerit of great significance, indeed, far out of proportion to the activity's cost contribution to a product.

Hence, the essence of the problem in using practical boundaries to make life cycle assessments feasible is that one generally does not know whether exploring a set of activities currently excluded, or disaggregating and developing location-specific information, will not uncover environmental demerits of sufficient importance to warrant their inclusion. Measures of small and remote inputs based on cost or other information known to the researcher do not provide a logically sound basis for assuming that the possible environmental demerits associated with that input are small as well. Since what is sought is not signaled by elements of the problem known to the researcher, such as costs, it is difficult to decide rationally when to exclude sectors from the analysis or when to cease disaggregating information.

In light of this difficulty, boundaries that render life cycle assessment feasible in practice will generally be far more restrictive than those necessary to inspire confidence that the details ignored and the elements excluded from the analysis will not harbor environmental demerits significant enough to warrant inclusion. Because the levels of environmental demerits caused by activities many steps removed are not known or necessarily signaled to the researcher through prices or costs, it is hard to defend their omission from the analysis. But practical life cycle assessments must satisfy realistic constraints on funding, so they will always be haunted by unexplored details and hidden indirect sources of environmental demerits that could be important to the results.

The problem of boundary setting, or deciding the degree of disaggregation, is not simply an academic one in life cycle assessments, for it largely explains the character and results of practical attempts to conduct them. For example, several recent reports[5] assessing the relative life cycle environmental impacts of cloth and disposable diapers devote considerable effort to tracing the indirect impacts of each alternative in greater depth than previous studies, although they arrive at mixed and different conclusions. Moreover, the study prepared for the National Association of Diaper Services, which concludes that the overall environmental impact of cloth diapers is less than disposables, devotes nearly six pages (out of a total of 40 pages in the summary report) to describing why its results are superior to previous attempts—because its boundaries are more expansive than earlier assessments.

Another anecdote on the diapers controversy is illuminating. According to one observer of the debate, researchers investigating cloth diapers are said to have used the national average amount and value of water required to grow cotton, which is a major input for cloth diapers. Yet, according to this source, the cotton required to manufacture cloth diapers is a particular variety grown only in the southwestern United States. The social cost of water in this region is presumably far higher than in the nation as a whole, so the environmental demerits of cloth diapers were probably severely underestimated.

This also illustrates not only the difficulties of setting study boundaries and levels of aggregation, but also how life cycle assessment differs fundamentally from ordinary analysis. In conventional studies, one might seek to measure the divergence of the social and private costs of water use. Common sense suggests that examining these conditions in the desert southwest would clearly be one of the top empirical priorities. In life cycle assessment, however, what turns out to be a very significant determinant of cloth diaper environmental demerits is several steps removed from the diapering decision itself, and would not be known without explicitly investigating cotton growing specific to diaper manufacturing.

Observations

It might be pointed out that it is possible to construct cases in which a life cycle assessment's practical boundaries based on feasibility are sufficiently wide to impart robustness to the results as well. Just as it is epistemologically possible to imagine conducting a "perfect" life cycle assessment, there is no reason to doubt that one can imagine cases in which practical life cycle assessments are also accurate and robust. Nevertheless, the fact that one can construct such hypothetical conditions and circumstances does not mean that reality will conform to them. Most life cycle assessments target consumer and producer decisions that are connected to a wide variety of activities that potentially cause environmental demerits. These are not the types of situations one imagines when constructing hypothetical situations in which feasible life cycle assessments also provide robust results.

Some might also argue that surely the probability of excluding an environmental demerit of sufficient importance to the analysis falls as one successively analyzes smaller and smaller sectors ever more remote from the product or process in question, or when one continues to further disaggregate and incorporate more details into the analysis. Assuming one starts with a perfect and complete life cycle assessment—one that accounts for every nuance and detail, and for all of the many ways in which indirect environmental demerits can arise—it does seem reasonable to think that excluding a few minor elements might not substantially alter the results.

The relevant question, however, is not so much the theoretical possibility of conducting less-than-perfect life cycle assessments that are still robust, but instead whether one can rationally and safely establish boundaries for these analyses given where life cycle studies really begin. That is, the central issue is whether the boundaries necessary to make life cycle assessments feasible in practice can be justified on the basis of well-founded expectations about the impact on the results of excluded sectors or added details. In general, life cycle assessments encounter the financial, analytical, and informational constraints of practical analysis long before they reach the point at which one has much confidence that added details and expanded boundaries will not substantially affect the results.

This problem is especially acute in light of the results normally generated in life cycle assessments. Most products studied are connected to a wide variety of activities, most of which use energy, involve a large set of emissions to air and water, require use of natural resources, and generate wastes. When comparing which version of a product to use, what type of diapers for example, both alternatives generally have many direct and indirect demerits, with some higher for one version and others higher for the alternative. One decides which of the two "evils" to select by netting the demerits out and trading off higher and lower levels of specific environmental problems. For practical life cycle assessments, it is highly likely that additional disaggregation or including more sectors and activities could alter the estimated levels of demerits for one or the other product enough to tip the balance. Indeed, this is exactly what happens in practice.

Life cycle researchers are aware that using practical boundaries based on real-world feasibility raises the issue of accuracy. Indeed, recent guidance documents have sought, but failed to find, rules for determining study boundaries that will make them feasible in practice but not sacrifice confidence at the same time. In light of the key points raised in this evaluation, this is not surprising.

A careful reading of the guidance literature thus reveals considerable hesitancy in establishing and defending rules of analytical boundaries. In a sense, the search for rules to limit life cycle boundaries seems to be motivated mainly by unanimous agreement that without them, these studies are not feasible, rather than by the belief that such rules are rational and defensible. For example, in EPA's *Life-Cycle Assessment: Inventory Guidelines and Principles*, the following statements are interesting:

> A theoretically complete life-cycle system would start with all raw materials and energy sources in the earth and end with all materials back in the earth or at least somewhere in the environment but not part of the system. Any system boundary different from this represents a decision by the analyst to limit it in some way. Understanding the possible consequences of such decisions is important for evaluating tradeoffs between the ability of the resulting inventory to thoroughly address environmental attributes of the product and constraints on cost, time, or other factors that may argue in favor of a more limited boundary. Too limited a boundary may exclude consequential activities (p. 19).
>
> In a traditional inventory, a material contributing less than 1% by weight of the total system typically contributes less than 1% of to the total emissions of a particular inventory item and can be omitted from the inventory. The "less than 1%" effect is generally considered insignificant. This approach is based on many years of conducting such studies and not on statistical or technical grounds. However, it does not make any assumptions regarding the environmental significance of the emission. Thus, one problem with a blanket application of this approach is that toxic materials could inadvertently be eliminated from the inventory analysis even though they present a serious potential environmental impact (p. 69).

Thus, the central problem with setting feasible boundaries in a life cycle assessment on the activities to be included, or failing to disaggregate to account for important details, is that this tends to rob them of robustness. Given the boundaries normally required to make life cycle assessments feasible in practice, it is hard to know the potential magnitude of what has been ignored because the sizes of the environmental demerits sought are not explicitly signaled by information known to the researcher. This leads to the unusually awkward result that one cannot exclude sectors and activities, or ignore details and complexity, unless one has verified that it is "acceptable" to do so. This verification, however, is very close to what it would take to actually include these details and sectors.

IV. IMPLICATIONS FOR ENVIRONMENTAL LIFE CYCLE ASSESSMENT

A number of critical issues have been raised concerning the ability of practical life cycle assessment to provide accurate and useful results. Taken together, they point to an unsettling conclusion. Nevertheless, it is never easy to reach conclusions about the practical viability of a research program in which accuracy and usefulness is theoretically possible. Many analytical pursuits are difficult, so expense and a lack of rigorous results should not themselves cause one to conclude that these research activities are not worth continuing. Yet, to decide that a research program will eventually yield useful results requires more than simply the belief that what is sought is an epistemological possibility. Unfortunately, while life cycle assessment's underlying motivation is understandable, and researchers are capable of generating large quantities of numbers, the view that life cycle assessment can provide accurate advice for consumers and producers at practical levels of effort is really just a hope based only on remote theoretical possibility, not on any real evidence of practical feasibility.

Realistically, in light of the current state of life cycle assessment—seeking a single set of demerits when there are multiple ones, seeking demerits "associated with" rather than "caused by," setting boundaries based on practical feasibility rather than on the belief that a wider scope is not necessary for robust results, and so forth—additional research using this approach is unlikely to result in any increased confidence in the results. It is not so much any one problem facing life cycle assessment that makes this type of analysis impractical. For example, if there really was a single correct set of direct and indirect environmental demerits for a product, and these did not change over time, and if it was not too costly to identify and quantify them, one might think that conducting such a life cycle assessment might be worth the cost.

The reality is that there generally is no single correct list of direct and indirect environmental demerits for a product or process—there are many applicable to specific circumstances in our complex economy, and they will change over time as environmental and economic linkages evolve.[6] Moreover, the level of detail and the inclusiveness of study boundaries required to inspire confidence in a life cycle assessment's results are generally far beyond those feasible in practice.

Hence, future life cycle assessments will become increasingly complex and expensive, but will never really deliver on their promise to confidently guide consumer and producer choices toward environmentally more benign alternatives. To be sure, more details will be included, and more pages of results will be generated, but the sense that any significant progress has been made toward conclusive, widely-applicable, and durable results of value to consumers and producers will be an illusion.

A recent report on packaging prepared by the Tellus Institute is a case in point.[7] Obviously this was an expensive and time-consuming study. Indeed, in the Acknowledgements section, the report states that "(d)ozens of people have worked hard over the past three years to make this study possible" (p. i). A study of this magnitude and duration is representative of what can realistically be achieved even with large levels of effort. The Tellus researchers are to be congratulated for their tenacity and attention to details.

Unfortunately, it is not so much what is in the report that counts, it is rather what is not. Even a study of this magnitude still must admit that it is far from complete and accurate. Some of the limitations described in the report include out-of-date information, omission of the package forming, filling, and transportation stages, omission of the industrial solid waste sector, absence of the plastics recycling sector, and no explicit accounting for habitat destruction, old-growth forest cutting, and other considerations related to timber production. Regarding logging and other aspects of virgin materials use, the report suggests that "(r)eaders who are concerned about virgin materials depletion should consider that factor in addition to the analysis presented here, when evaluating materials recycling options." One wonders how the reader is supposed to do this if the voluminous and expensive study in his or her hands failed to do so.

The point is that even an expensive and extremely data-intensive effort summarized by the Tellus report cannot arrive at the level of detail and comprehensiveness necessary to give consumers and producers definitive information to improve their choices, and the Tellus effort is still only the inventory stage of the analysis, so the impacts and improvements stages still remain. To be sure, the report contains a very large set of results, and even attempts to monetize impacts.[8] But given the omissions and other limitations of the study, if one were to make different choices based on the study there is a good possibility that rectifying these shortcomings would provide new information important enough to cause one to reconsider.

Of course, the Tellus report does not claim to offer information that can conclusively guide consumers and producers to the environmentally correct choice. The report merely states that "(w)e believe that we have advanced the state of knowledge on packaging materials, raised a number of previously hidden issues that require discussion, and given the best answers possible based on the available data and resources. We are well aware that we are offering the first word, not the last, on these topics. We hope that our current study will be followed by further refinement and development of research tools and publicly available databases in this area" (p. 5).

Ultimately, the problem is not that nothing can be done within the practical limitations of financial feasibility, for the reams of results life cycle assessments can generate are a testament to the creativity and commitment of these researchers. The main problem is that what generally can be done within practical levels of effort does not provide conclusive results of any use in guiding consumer and producer choices. Instead, life cycle assessments generally show that all products and processes are potentially associated directly and indirectly with a host of environmental demerits at various levels, so that making choices between alternatives is already problematic. They then so severely qualify the results with caveats, limitations, simplifications, and other potential problems, that one has no confidence that more details and wider boundaries will not reveal more environmental demerits of substantial importance.

Some might protest that life cycle assessment should be evaluated only in terms of how well it identifies and tabulates environmental demerits of a product or process, not whether a consumer or producer can use that information to arrive at an environmentally correct choice. That is, despite admittedly inadequate data and scarce financial resources, surely the efforts of these researchers can provide interesting information about products and processes of use to someone.

Again, there is every reason to study product manufacturing and use to identify and minimize direct pollution and other environmental harms. To the extent that life cycle assessments do, so much the better. Seeking to minimize direct environmental consequences is socially beneficial, analytically coherent, and eminently reasonable in practice. But, this is not the underlying motivation of life cycle assessment, which is to tabulate the indirect sources of environmental demerits as well. Trying to quantify the indirect sources of environmental demerits of a product inevitably involves endless and detailed searches for remote sources of environmental impacts, and difficult to defend limitations on the boundaries of the study.

Similarly, there is nothing in this evaluation of life cycle assessment that indicts individuals' everyday common sense attempts to avoid harming the environment. Reducing litter, reusing resources such as grocery sacks and aluminum foil, and conserving energy and other natural resources to minimize one's direct contribution to harming the environment, are all laudable and worthwhile pursuits. Traditional notions of environmentally-friendly consumer behavior are uncomplicated and are likely to result in the environmental benefits that motivate them.

It is the extension of this notion to product choices not involving obvious differences in direct environmental demerits that causes problems. As soon as consumers try to purchase greener products based on both their indirect and direct sources of environmental demerits, they are confronted with a host of competing claims and counterclaims. Aware that "green" is also profitable, marketers then begin to expand the environmental and analytical criteria by which products are evaluated. Claims about the indirect environmental characteristics of products then become the weapons with which an expensive war is waged for the consumer's environmental conscience (and dollar).

Of course, all of this provides a perfect garden for a classical "prisoners' dilemma" to grow, one in which a manufacturer who does not engage in studies to prove the environmental friendliness of his or her product will be at a disadvantage relative to competitors who do make these claims. Unfortunately, these parties probably all know that these green claims are on shaky ground, but they nevertheless must defend themselves.

Finally, some might argue that economists undertake projects that involve "mapping" the economy, sector-by-sector, in estimating input-output matrices for production. Hence, why is it not worthwhile to conduct similar analyses for life cycle assessments? While it is true that those who perform economic input-output analysis are attempting to trace economic activities to and from many different sectors, life cycle assessment is not quite the same exercise. In particular, input-output analysis can define for itself the level of aggregation sought, can rely on market transactions to provide the data required to perform the analysis, and is completely disinterested in where and how the various economic activities summarized in the ultimate matrix are carried out. Life cycle assessment's goals, however, do not allow self-defining disaggregation decisions, cannot permit arbitrary limitations on scope, require measurement of events and consequences largely not included in market transactions, and necessitate a careful focus on the specifics of an activity that determine the extent and magnitude of the actual environmental harms caused.

Thus, input-output researchers find it hard enough to trace and catalogue an economy's interdependencies even given their advantage of seeking national averages, relying on observable market transactions, and so forth. Life cycle researchers have none of the advantages enjoyed by input-output modelers, and face a task with a far larger scope, and a less well-defined set of concerns to measure that are poorly documented by the market.

In the end, whether the attempts of practical life cycle studies to explore the indirect environmental demerits of a product or process have value to society independently of their use in improving the environmental results of consumer and producer choices is not clear, for it is not obvious from what source that value might flow. One might plausibly argue, for example, that the process of evaluating indirect environmental demerits of a process might happen upon a particularly acute problem that has eluded other attempts at environmental management and stewardship. But one could reply that a random search of different economic activities might provide the same probability of such a discovery at a lower cost.

It is conceivable there might be good reasons for conducting life cycle assessments, perhaps on a limited basis and in certain very specific and important circumstances. This evaluation, however, focuses on whether practical life cycle assessments can generally be relied upon to provide information that really can be used to confidently guide consumer and producer choices toward environmentally more benign alternatives. As a general matter, the answer is no.

The life cycle research community appears to be on the verge of realizing the conclusions reached in this evaluation. Indeed, the current debate about the possibility of establishing boundaries for practical life cycle assessments suggests that at least some practitioners are aware of the underlying problems. There is a vague sense of frustration that ever increasing levels of effort devoted to more and more detailed life cycle analyses that yield non-decreasing lists of limitations and caveats. Establishing research rules and protocols, and seeking agreement on what are ultimately arbitrary limitations on life cycle assessment boundaries, however, are not the answer.

V. IS THERE ANOTHER APPROACH?

The conclusions reached in this evaluation of life cycle assessment are essentially that conventional studies of direct pollution caused by economic activities can help to improve their environmental performance, but that life cycle assessment's attempt to go beyond direct environmental demerits to incorporate indirect sources as well is unproductive. Unfortunately, this seems to leave these researchers without any recourse for addressing the environmental problems they consider so serious and widespread.

For several reasons, this conclusion may seem somewhat depressing. First, and probably most obvious, is that the hope that life cycle assessment will generate meaningful and accurate guidance for consumers and producers, at least at some point in the future, will never be fulfilled. It is difficult to accept that all of the honest and diligent efforts to improve life cycle assessment techniques, data, and results will not yield beneficial results.

The evaluation's findings are all the more troubling because life cycle assessment might be viewed as the culmination of what has been a long process of public education and awareness concerning the environment. The past several decades have witnessed a significant change in public attitudes about the natural world and the impact of human activities have on it, during which many environmental improvements, great and small, have occurred. Life cycle assessment's ultimate motivation is to empower individuals so that they can help the environment by altering their choices. That life cycle assessment cannot fulfill that goal is sad, but true.

One should be cautioned against viewing the strong conclusions about life cycle assessment reached in this paper as any statement whatsoever about the underlying value of the attitudes and concerns that motivate life cycle assessment in the first place. This evaluation focuses on life cycle assessment as an analytical tool intended to help people achieve their goal of acting in environmentally more benign ways. The fact that life cycle assessment does not advance those goals says nothing about the underlying motivation for this sort of inquiry.

The other, more subtle way in which some might find the conclusions of this evaluation depressing is the possibility that if life cycle assessment cannot help to address the environmental problems that motivate these analyses, perhaps we can do nothing at all about them. This would indeed be a most unfortunate outcome from an environmental perspective.

A. A Viable Alternative

Fortunately, there is an alternative approach for addressing these environmental harms, one that avoids the insurmountable difficulties of tracing and tabulating the economic activities remotely associated with a product or process. While this alternative approach can successfully begin to address the environmental problems that motivate life cycle research, it nevertheless will not provide detailed environmental and natural resources information about products to consumers and producers.

This more productive approach for addressing the environmental problems that motivate life cycle research is simple and quite conventional: Attack the environmental harms and inappropriate resource uses of concern where they occur, using the variety of tools at the disposal of the environmental authority. That is, if one believes that these environmental demerits exist, they should be identified and corrected with the arsenal of regulatory and nonregulatory approaches normally used to correct or control pollution problems.

For example, if one of the important environmental demerits of concern is habitat destruction, erosion, and turbidity caused by logging forests, the suggested approach calls for developing regulatory policies that strike at the heart of the problem directly. Limitations on logging, standards for cutting and preservation, even taxes on the damaging consequences of logging, all might be considered good candidates for addressing these problems. The result of directly applying corrective environmental regulations of one sort or another will be both a reduction in the actual damages caused by logging and, in general, an increase in the costs and prices of products for which logging is an input.

Similarly, if another environmental demerit of concern is potential harms to human health and the environment caused by over-using fertilizers and pesticides, the traditional approach would suggest attacking these problems at their sources by developing stronger regulatory and other programs to limit these risks. These might include additional restrictions on pesticide application procedures, limitations on using certain types of fertilizers and pesticides in particular areas or in certain circumstances, and so forth. Again, the result of these direct approaches would be a reduction in the environmental harms caused and increased costs and prices for items whose supply causes the pesticides and fertilizer use in the first place.

B. Advantages of the Alternative

Of course, the suggested approach offers no magic wand that will easily wipe away the nation's environmental problems. It is no more and no less than the traditional recommendation that successful environmental management and stewardship generally flow from clear problem definition and careful development and application of regulatory and nonregulatory mechanisms to address these concerns. But the advantages of the suggested strategy are many.

First, it immediately focuses efforts directly on the problems of concern in life cycle analysis—supposed widespread environmental harms and inappropriate or underpriced natural resource use. Practical life cycle assessments never really arrive at the ultimate harms of concern. Instead, all of the resources are expended in attempting to trace particular consumer and producer decisions back through the almost infinitely complex interconnections of the economy to those harms, and then hoping that the responses to the answer generated will wend their way back to the problems exactly as predicted. There are obvious advantages of beginning with the environmental problems to be solved rather than leaving their identification and measurement for later.

Identifying, quantifying, and mitigating specific environmental problems directly where and when they occur offers a second benefit. Under this approach, the costs of the controls used to reduce environmental damages caused by even remote economic activities, and the damages that remain if these are priced through, say, environmental taxes, will be reflected in prices faced by consumers and producers. Moreover, these costs will end up being embodied in the prices of all products and processes that are associated with those environmental demerits, not just the few consumer and producer decisions that life cycle researchers elect to examine.[9]

Third, as actual sources of environmental demerits are identified and successfully addressed, the underlying need to assist consumers and producers in making the best environmental choice among products and processes will fade. Bolstering the public's confidence that environmental problems are being addressed and that the consequences of doing so will be incorporated into prices will ultimately eliminate the original motivation for conducting life cycle assessments.

Fourth, the information requirements for the suggested approach are a small subset of those needed for accurate and definitive life cycle assessments. The traditional approach requires the environmental authority to locate and quantify environmental harms and inappropriate resource use. Armed with this information, regulators then can promulgate rules of whatever type seem appropriate to address these problems.

Life cycle assessment, on the other hand, requires that the innumerable interconnected activities of the economy be traced and retraced periodically, location-by-location, and that the ultimate environmental harms of concern be identified and quantified in order to provide useful information to consumers and producers. In practice, the task of even crudely tracing all of these economic activities and linkages consumes all of the resources in a life cycle assessment. The result is that practical life cycle assessments never really arrive at the environmental harms that motivate them in the first place.

Finally, the suggested approach allocates responsibilities for environmental stewardship more appropriately than does life cycle assessment. In essence, the traditional approach charges individuals—in their roles as consumers and producers—with ensuring that they cause as little direct environmental damage as is feasible. Thus, individuals should strive to reduce the environmental problems they cause directly based on their specific situations and activities. Contrary to the distrust of prices and the market that motivates life cycle assessment, consumers and producers under the suggested approach should accept prices of inputs and goods at face value in making their choices. To do otherwise throws one into the world of life cycle assessment, a world in which neither prices nor lists of environmental demerits can be trusted to guide one to environmentally more benign alternatives.

The inability to make rational choices in a world in which one does not trust prices is a particularly important point to understand. Suppose one identifies a cost-saving change in an industrial process that also reduces its direct environmental damages. Ordinarily, this would be a clearly desirable process change to make. But suppose further, as does life cycle assessment, that there are many indirect environmental demerits that are not accounted for in prices. In this event, one cannot decide rationally that changing the process change will reduce total environmental demerits. Presumably the process change will affect many other activities throughout the economy, so until one investigates these indirect sources of environmental demerits, the conclusion that it will be environmentally beneficial overall cannot be supported. Of course, this is a ridiculous situation, but precisely what results from a lack of confidence in prices.[10] Hence, the role allocated to individuals under the suggested approach allows them to trust prices.

Under the traditional approach, the environmental authority is charged with ensuring that people actually do act in environmentally responsible ways. Its obligation is to correct failures of the market to adequately protect the environment or to price natural resources to reflect their full value to society. If the environmental authority successfully accomplishes its part of the task of managing the impacts of humans on the environment, it will validate the trust that individuals must place in prices.

C. Observations

Several objections might be raised to abandoning life cycle analysis in favor of the more traditional approach to environmental regulation and stewardship advocated here. One is that it is difficult to attack the environmental demerits of concern via the traditional approach, so life cycle studies represent an alternative to doing nothing about them. This objection is understandable because it may indeed be difficult to address many of these environmental harms directly. Similarly, some regulators argue that the causes of the environmental demerits of concern are beyond their regulatory authority, so that life cycle assessment is viewed as their only available means of doing something about these harms.

Nevertheless, life cycle assessment is not really a viable analytical or policy making alternative because practical analyses do not provide robust or useful results at justifiable cost levels. Moreover, without knowing it, practical life cycle assessments might be doing more harm than good for the environment. Hence, it does not seem reasonable to continue to allocate more and more funds to life cycle assessment with only the vaguest hope that someday they will generate reliable and robust results, especially if one suspects that they probably will not satisfy that goal. This might be true even if there was no alternative for addressing the environmental demerits that motivate life cycle research, but it is certainly so if there are other ways to try to address these problems.

Another objection is that it is probably not possible to correct environmental problems perfectly using the traditional methods, hence the recommended alternative is also not perfect. This may be true, but perfection is not a requirement of the traditional approach to environmental regulation and stewardship. Real environmental problems are complex, difficult to identify and quantify, and controversial to correct. But even imperfect strategies for addressing these environmental harms can provide clear social benefits. The same cannot be said for life cycle assessment, which generally yields large sets of results with no guarantee that any changes in consumer and producer decisions based on them will be environmentally beneficial.

One final objection to discarding life cycle analysis and undertaking the difficult, but ultimately more productive, traditional approach is that doing so still does not give consumers and producers information about the environmental "content" of the products and processes they choose. This complaint goes to the very core of the motivation of life cycle assessment. Proponents of life cycle analysis assume that prices do not reflect many environmental harms and inappropriate natural resource use, so they seek to provide this information in parallel with the price system. Taken literally, the belief that prices cannot be trusted to reflect the full social costs of products and processes indicts all economic decisions, not just the few that are commonly the subject of life cycle assessment. That is, no economic decisions can be trusted to be socially correct if the prices upon which they are based do not reflect vital information about costs.

Unfortunately, it is not possible in practice to provide accurate information on the environmental inputs to processes and products or, for that matter, for any set of economic inputs. One can collect and disseminate information about the nature, seriousness, and extent of the environmental problems of concern. Indeed, environmental performance data are very useful, for they direct efforts to monitoring, measuring, and perhaps mitigating actual environmental harms at their sources. Recent attempts to supplement the national income accounts with information on the change in the nation's stock of natural and other environmental resources represent productive first steps in this direction.

What is not feasible in practice is to analytically allocate these environmental problems to particular products and processes, which is the goal of life cycle assessment. Some may think this an unfortunate limitation of reality. Perhaps so, but it is the inevitable result of the complexity and diversity of modern economies in which, fortunately, the price system communicates necessary information efficiently, rapidly, and anonymously. Indeed, it is perhaps the most profound benefit of the price system that it coordinates actions by transmitting remotely and diversely held information, for this could not be feasibly accomplished by a single entity.[11]

While there is no analytical way to trace from products back through the virtually endless complexity of a modern economy to the environmental demerits of concern, there is one conceivable way to provide this information to consumers and producers. Suppose that, for some reason or another, using energy causes environmental damages that are not incorporated in its price, and assume that this harm is the same regardless of the type of the energy. If, on pain of death, one had to supply information to consumers and producers about the amount of energy (and, hence, the damages of concern) embodied in specific products or processes, the only feasible way to do so would be to establish two colors of money, say, red and green. Red money would be the only currency accepted for purchasing energy and green money would be used for all other goods.

Under such a system, all goods and services in the economy would end up with two prices—a red price summarizing energy inputs and a green price reflecting all other factors of production. This approach could be extended to other environmental harms by simply expanding the number of colors of money, where each color would be used for a specific environmental demerit. In the end, products would have many prices, one for each color of money and its associated environmental demerit. This would supply the detailed environmental information desired.

It is noteworthy that the somewhat fanciful multiple-currency method of obtaining this information still fundamentally relies on the price system, not analysis of the economy and its interrelated sectors. It also emphasizes the fact that doing anything to mitigate environmental demerits requires one to begin with the sources of the harms themselves, not with consumer and producer choices about products and processes. It further reveals that, at its core, the ultimate solution to the environmental problems that motivate life cycle researchers lies not only in attacking these harms directly, but also in restoring confidence in prices. As shown above, if one does not believe prices, it is difficult to make any rational choices, environmental or otherwise.

Finally, some might argue that recommending to consumers and producers that they accept prices as the basis for making choices still seems less than satisfying. Indeed, one might assert that the regulatory authorities cannot be relied upon to address the many environmental problems that still exist. This is a valid concern, but it still does not point to life cycle assessment as the solution because, in practice this approach will not reliably advance those goals. Hence, those who hold this view should consider other ways to affect policy outcomes, for these are more likely to result in environmental improvement than conducting life cycle assessment.

ACKNOWLEDGMENT

Visiting Scholar, the Environmental Law Institute, Washington, DC. This research was supported in part by Cooperative Agreement CR-820539-01 provided by the Economic Analysis and Innovations Division, Office of Policy Analysis, U.S. Environmental Protection Agency. The views expressed are those of the author. This paper is based on material that appears in Arnold (1995).

NOTES

1. Franklin Associates, Ltd (1990)
2. Vigon et al. (1992).
3. The central difficulty in life cycle assessment is the process of trying to obtain detailed information about environmental demerits in possibly far-flung locations and activities. Somewhat ironically, this is precisely the same problem that the Austrian economists Ludwig von Mises and Friedrich Hayek considered to be the critical reason for the inability of socialist planners to direct economic activities in the absence of a price system. Both von Mises and Hayek considered it a practical impossibility for a single mind to obtain and process all of the information necessary to make rational and even remotely efficient choices for an entire society given the complexity of modern economies. See, for example, Mises (1935). Although motivated by a different set of concerns than central planners, life cycle researchers face the same sort of data collection task in a world of arguably greater complexity and interconnectedness of economic processes than 70 years ago.
4. Society of Environmental Toxicology and Chemistry and SETAC Foundation for Environmental Education, Inc. (1991).
5. Lehrburger, Mullen, and Jones (1991) and Franklin Associates (1992).
6. Hayek emphasizes changing conditions in explaining the central role of the price system in organizing and coordinating economic activity. See Hayek (1948).
7. Tellus Institute (1992).
8. Essentially, the report uses regulatory control costs for monetization. This is very different from actually measuring real environmental harms, as the report admits, and it is far from obvious that this shortcut is analytically sound.
9. A related point is that life cycle assessment today is concerned with environmental issues. Twenty years ago the focus was on energy use. Tomorrow, however, the concern could be safety or other problems of particular social importance. In any case, focusing directly on the problems,

regardless of their nature, tends to address them with greater certainty and to price activities related to them more appropriately.

10. Once again, this point has its roots in the Austrian tradition. Mises (1935, note 3, p. 104), argues that "...as soon as one gives up the conception of a freely established monetary price for goods of a higher order, rational production becomes completely impossible." The observation here is that distrusting prices has functionally the same impact on the ability to engage in rational action as having no prices at all.

11. Hayek (1948, note 6) is careful to point out that the price system does not communicate all information to everyone. Instead, prices summarize important facts and conditions for decision makers thereby economizing on the amount and type of information individuals require to make rational choices, and this is an advantage of the price system, not a deficiency. Hayek argues that those who criticize the price system because it does not make all information available to everyone fail to recognize "...the fact that the method by which such knowledge can be made as widely available as possible is precisely the problem to which we have to find an answer" (p. 81). Evaluated in these terms, life cycle researchers' goal of obtaining and disseminating to potential purchasers information on all of a product's environmental demerits might be considered inherently misguided.

REFERENCES

Arnold, F. S. 1995. *Economic Analysis of Environmental Policy and Regulation.* New York: John Wiley and Sons, Inc.

Franklin Associates. 1992. *Energy and Environmental Profile Analysis of Children's Single Use and Cloth Diapers.* Report prepared for the American Paper Institute and the Diapers Manufacturers Group, May.

________. 1990. *Resource and Environmental Profile Analysis of Polyethylene and Unbleached Paper Grocery Sacks.* Prepared for The Council for Solid Waste Solutions, June.

Hayek, F. A. 1948. "The Use of Knowledge in Society." In *Individualism and Economic Order*, edited by F. A. Hayek. Chicago: Henry Regnery Company.

Lehrburger, C., J. Mullen, and C. V. Jones. 1991. *Diapers: Environmental Impacts and Lifecycle Analysis.* Report prepared for the National Association of Diaper Services, Philadelphia, PA, January.

Mises, L. von. 1935. "Economic Calculation in the Socialist Commonwealth." In *Collectivist Economic Planning*, edited by F. A. Hayek. London: Routledge and Sons.

Society of Environmental Toxicology and Chemistry and SETAC Foundation for Environmental Education, Inc. 1991. *A Technical Framework for Life-Cycle Assessments*, January.

Tellus Institute. 1992. *CSG/Tellus Packaging Study.* Prepared for The Council of State Governments and the U.S. Environmental Protection Agency, May.

Vigon, B. W., D. A. Tolle, B. W. Cornaby, H. C. Latham, C. L. Harrison, T. L. Boguski, R. G. Hunt, and J. D. Sellers. 1992. *Life-Cycle Assessment: Inventory Guidelines and Principles.* Prepared for U.S. Environmental Protection Agency, November.

METHODS AND METAPHORS IN CAPITAL THEORY

Peter Lewin

I. METAPHOR AND ECONOMIC THEORY

> *Capital: L. Capitalis*, f. *Caput*—head. Relating to the head.... 5. Of funds, stock, etc. original, serving as a basis for commercial or financial operations.
>
> —Oxford English Dictionary

There is a growing recognition that (as Donald McCloskey has so persuasively taught us) economics, like all scientific endeavors, makes widespread use of metaphors and that this is more than simply ornamental. As one recent commentator has put it:

> Metaphors are more than similes... metaphors are central to reason... the use of metaphor involves interaction, by invoking and filtering different but associated conceptual systems. The interaction generates a novel semantic context, and goes beyond the literal meaning of the terms of the metaphor itself (Hodgson 1994, p. 19; see also McCloskey 1985, pp. 74-79, 1990, chapter 1).

Advances in Austrian Economics, Volume 2B, pages 277-296.

ISBN: 1-55938-531-6

Metaphors are implicit analogies. They involve the comparison of two phenomena, the one under discussion (the subject) being implicitly compared to something else (the modifier). The properties of the latter are used to shed light on the hitherto unseen properties of the former. In this way a kind of "cross fertilization" occurs.

Economics is suffused with metaphorical reasoning at various levels, some metaphors being embedded within others. The predominant metaphor in economics is the mechanism. The economy is implicitly likened to a mechanical device. This is seen in the widespread use of mathematical methods borrowed from classical mechanics. This metaphor bolsters the belief that the goal of economics is the construction of mechanical models that allow prediction. The specification of initial conditions and trajectories allows the calculation of resultant positions. Also, the impact of changes on the system can be precisely calculated. Metaphors embedded within the predominant one are seen in the use of concepts like "equilibrium," "optimal growth," "fine tuning," "efficiency" and many others.[1]

It is an interesting question as to how one should judge the value or validity of various metaphors. Clearly much of the complex and voluminous discussion about methodology implicitly involves this question. It is one, however, that lies largely beyond the scope of this paper. Perhaps McCloskey is right when he argues that the best metaphor is the one that is most persuasive, the one most likely to illuminate the world in which we live. An understanding of the ubiquity and importance of the use of metaphor in economics suggests, at the very least, that we should be more self conscious of the metaphors that we use (and abuse), more inclined to examine their appropriateness in the light of whatever evidence we deem to be decisive.[2]

Doubts about the value of the mechanism metaphor spring from what may generally be called the arrow of time:

> We are all aware of the irreversible flow of time which seems to dominate our existence, where the past is fixed and *the future open*. We may yearn to turn back the clock, to undo mistakes or to relive a wonderful moment. But alas, common sense is against us: time and tide wait for no man. Time cannot run backwards (Coveney and Highfield 1990, p. 23, italics added).

In particular, the discovery that even well specified interactive (not necessarily very complicated) systems do not contain sufficient information to yield knowledge of their developments over extended time, has led to a search for new methods of reasoning and analysis. For example, economists are making increasing use of simulation as a technique for exploring possible outcomes where once this was thought to be methodologically out of bounds (Day and Chen 1993). Biological as opposed to mechanical analogies are used with increasing frequency (Hodgson 1993) and there is increasing deference paid to "bounded rationality" (Sargent 1993).

Over the last decade or so even some of the luminaries in the field have begun to feel that there might be some validity to the criticisms of the mechanistic method.[3] This breakthrough did not come from a realization finally of the correctness of the Austrian or any other economic critique. Rather it is to developments in the fields of chaos, complexity, nonlinear mathematics, and related subjects that one must look for the source of the current flurry of activity that is occurring on many fronts (Day and Chen 1993; Sargent 1993; Waldrop 1992).[4] Perhaps, however, it does signal a new openness to alternative ideas.[5]

Capital theory probably has more than its fair share of metaphors, mechanistic and otherwise. Witness Knight's Crusonia plant, Dorfman's bathtub, Wicksell's aging wine, Clark's woodlot, not to mention "putty clay," "input-output" and "stock flow." The variety of metaphors in capital theory is probably testimony to the difficulty that economists have had with the subject. While acknowledging the importance of an understanding of capital and its functioning in the economy (how could it be otherwise in *Capital*istic economies?), economists have not been able to agree on its essential nature (i.e., on what it really is)[6] and have had difficulty integrating it into their essentially mechanistic framework. The problem has been solved by basically ignoring it. In macroeconomics, Keynes's work suggested that the flow of investment funds was the important thing and that we need not bother with the nature of capital. In microeconomics, the neoclassical paradigm reduced capital to a category of homogeneous inputs alongside labor whose relevant characteristics were fully described by the "production function." Development economics and growth theory for the most part followed the lead that the microeconomists had provided. The result was that capital theory all but disappeared with the neoclassical and Keynesian revolutions.

There were notable exceptions. One was the short work by Israel Kirzner entitled *An Essay on Capital* published in 1966 (Kirzner 1966)[7]. In this work Kirzner seeks to provide an "insight into those economic processes in which capital emerges, and which capital theory hopes to illumine" (p. 2). Though it is his work on the nature and function of entrepreneurship for which Kirzner is justifiably noted, this examination of capital theory is, in this author's estimation, one of the finest pieces of economic writing in existence. As noted earlier, the subject matter is intrinsically difficult. Kirzner's purpose is to "sort it all out," to provide any reader with an interest in discovering what the talk in capital theory is all about with a clear road map. And in just four short chapters, each a sort of mini essay, he cuts through the maze of complexity and confusion. It is a testimony to the power of sustained and careful reasoning, and of lucid, eloquent writing.[8]

An Essay on Capital involves a careful examination of the prevailing metaphors in the capital theory literature. In examining the images used by capital theorists, Kirzner questions their ability to illuminate the role of capital in the real world economy. In so doing he is obviously concerned to offer and defend his own opinion, his own metaphorical vision, of how it is that we should understand capital. The recent openness to new ideas, noted earlier, may provide an opportunity for a fruitful reexamination of this work and of the relevance of capital theory in general. The next two sections examine aspects of Kirzner's work on capital. The subsequent and final section attempts to relate these aspects to the recent literature on human capital.

II. KIRZNER AND ROBINSON CRUSOE

We begin by asking: why do we care about capital?

> Consider the state of an economy at a particular point in time. An examination of the economy reveals the existence of numerous, heterogeneous tangible things. Since we confine our observations to a single instant, this is all that can be observed. How are we to interpret the significance of a particular set of such tangible things? What does the existence of the set tell us about the history of the economy? What basis does it provide for a prevision of the future (Kirzner 1966, p. 33).

So, we are interested in capital theory, firstly, in order to understand how the capital items, those "tangible things" existing in an economy, function in the overall economic process. More obviously, we all know that the nature and quality of our everyday lives depend on these things. We ought to be able to say how. We ought to be able to say why and in what way our lives in America are different from the lives of human beings in Poland or in Ethiopia and how capital fits into this. How apt are the alternative metaphors for this purpose?

Another way to look at the role of metaphorical reasoning in economics is to note that we proceed in economics by constructing *conceptual economies*. These take different forms. Sometimes they are formal mathematical models, sometimes they are sustained or passing verbal constructions. Whichever it is, when we use them we are, in effect, saying that the real economy is in some relevant sense like the conceptual one. In other words, we are talking metaphorically. Now, another important feature of economic reasoning is that these conceptual economies can be generally distinguished on the basis of what individuals in them are assumed to know and how they are assumed to act on the basis of this knowledge. For example, in a rational expectations economy economic agents are assumed to act rationally and to have mutually consistent perceptions about the environment. Dissatisfaction with this construct has prompted a search for better ones.[9] Similarly, neoclassical microeconomics assumes that agents have sufficient knowledge to behave like calculus students in finding local (and sometimes global!) maxima and minima, implying that real world economic agents behave *as if* they do as well. The establishment of equilibrium in these conceptual models depends upon the knowledge assumptions, which in turn depends upon the degree of stability of the environment assumed in the model. So, a dissatisfaction with equilibrium theorizing probably reflects the judgment that the environment in the real world is less stable than that assumed or implied by the model.

In capital theory different models (metaphors) have vied for attention. Kirzner examines and contrasts the various alternatives subjecting them to careful, reasoned scrutiny, attempting to ascertain whether they further our ability to understand capital. In the first chapter Kirzner introduces the major theme: capital can be profitably understood only in terms of its relationship to human plans. "The identification of a 'resource' as distinct from other physical things, cannot be made without reference to human purposes" (p. 38). All capital goods are, in effect, "unfinished plans" (this is also the title of the first chapter). The plans are unfinished because the economic process is ongoing and plans are continually being implemented and revised. The economic rationale of those "tangible things" is simply that they contribute in one way or another to the fulfillment of human consumption plans and, therefore, to human satisfaction.[10] Any explanation of capital that fails to refer to this will omit a crucial feature of the real world.

To understand this better begin, as Kirzner does, with Robinson Crusoe. Robinson Crusoe is an individual isolated from the world. His economy is completely autarkic. Yet he still faces crucial economic choices. He must decide how to allocate his time and the resources at his disposal. Any decision involves the sacrifice of the fruits of alternative decisions. This is the cost of any decision. Also, any decision involves planning the use of resources in such a way that no conflicts are implied. Resources must be made to cooperate with one another in a feasible way if the plan is to succeed. "The essence of a plan is that each of the activities embraced in the plan is coordinated with the other planned activities. Each portion of the plan 'fits in' with the other portions: it depends on their fulfillment, and their fulfillment depends on its fulfillment"(p. 6). For example, assume Crusoe decides to make a fishing net in order to improve his yield of fish and so improve the quality of his life by adding to the quantity and perhaps variety of fish as well as to his time available for doing other things including resting. In order to do so he must plan to devote considerable time to the construction of the net and this means providing for his sustenance in the interim. He must also ensure that he has the raw materials and tools necessary to accomplish his task. Any particular plan that Crusoe makes must involve this sort of multi-period perspective. This is typical of all planning. "Plowing now, is required if the sowing and harvesting planned for the future is to be able to be carried out. And the current plowing is undertaking only on the assumption that future sowing and harvesting will in fact be undertaken as well"(pp. 6-7).

Crusoe's position can be examined from three alternative points in time: *before* the plan is implemented, after the plan is completed, and at some point during the implementation of the plan. From the perspective of a point of time before the plan is implemented, all aspects of the plan are prospective. Crusoe is aware of the significance of the resources that are at his disposal in terms of the role that they play in the plan. Their value to him is derived from that role. Their cost is assessed in terms of their perceived alternative uses. Kirzner is careful to point out that an outside observer may well arrive at a different assessment of the cost and value of these resources, but that the process of evaluation must necessarily refer to Crusoe's plan. From this perspective at the start of the plan, the plan will be deemed profitable if the expected combined value of the resources it uses, including Crusoe's own time, exceeds their estimated value in any viable alternative.

From the perspective of a point in time *after* the completion of the plan, all aspects of the plan are retrospective. Crusoe is aware of the significance of the resources that were at his disposal in terms of the role that they have already played in the plan. He is in the position of having to engage in historical speculation. The value of the resources used in the plan is derived from his assessment of their performance in terms of fulfilling the plan. Their cost is assessed in terms of the perceived value that they might have had in alternative uses. Kirzner is careful to point out that an outside observer may well arrive at a different assessment of the cost and value of these resources, but that the process of evaluation must necessarily refer to Crusoe's plan. From this perspective at the end of the plan, the plan will be deemed to have been profitable if the combined value of the resources it used, including Crusoe's own time, exceeded their estimated value in any viable alternative. "He will judge himself to have gained, if the alternatives which (hindsight shows that) he rejected, appear less important than the results actually achieved by his adopted project. He will judge himself to have suffered loss if the achieved results rank less important than these rejected alternatives"(p. 9).

A crucial implication of this simple exercise is that the two perspectives, before and after the implementation of the plan, will yield the same assessment of the plan if the plan is successful. The most likely outcome however is that, having arrived at the end of the plan's implementation, Crusoe will find that in some respects the plan turned out differently from what he expected and that this has affected (either positively or negatively) his overall assessment of the plan. Or, to put it another way, he will come to the conclusion that if somehow he could turn back the clock and go back to the beginning of the plan he would do it differently in some respects knowing what he does now. In fact, the most likely situation is one in which some way through the implementation of the plan Crusoe decides to change some aspects of it. In effect Crusoe is in the process of continual planning, since the identification of the start and finish of a plan is complicated by its continual revision. Even if we could somehow identify the end point of a plan, we must acknowledge that the resources available at that point of time, including any relevant fruits of the plan itself, are available for Crusoe to begin another plan. Whether we consider him to be at the beginning of one plan and at the end of another or in the middle of a larger multi-period plan involving both sub-plans is surely a matter of semantics. We might as well regard Crusoe always in the midst of "unfinished plans."

What does matter, however, is that, as mentioned, in general a backward looking perspective will yield different results from a forward looking one. Only in the case where no unexpected events occur, no events that cause Crusoe to revise his plan in any way, will it not matter which point of time is chosen for assessment. In general, history matters.

It is probably no exaggeration to say that, in Kirzner's hands, this case captures all of the essential aspects of capital. The fish net is a capital good whose value to Crusoe at any time is given by its ability to yield fish in the future and whose historical significance can only be understood in terms of Crusoe's plans at various points of time. In arriving at any point of time at a value for his net (or any other resources) Crusoe must take full account of the fact that the yields will occur at different points of time in the future. At each point of time the fact that Crusoe must wait in order to enjoy the fruits of applying his resources, will be reflected in the value that he attaches to the resources at his disposal—they reflect his time preference. It is important to note that the individual physical items in the plan may be called capital goods and that these are to be distinguished from the general term "capital." The latter refers to the value of a group of capital goods. It has no independent existence apart from those goods and apart from the production plan incorporating them. This perspective is to be contrasted with those that see "capital" as some sort of disembodied, fungible substance.

It is crucial to Kirzner's vision that when we extend our focus from an isolated Crusoe to an individual in a market economy, we find that nothing essential is affected. An individual in a market economy faces exactly the same type of situations in all respects that matter for an understanding of capital. In other words, individuals in market economies, when it comes to understanding capital, are like Robinson Crusoe. There are, of course, differences and these are didactically as important as the similarities:

> In a market economy an individual is able to make multi-period plans with a greater range of freedom than was possible for Crusoe... The individual in a market economy can make plans which call for the employment of resources which he does not now possess, and which he does not expect to come directly into his possession at all... because he is able to exchange in the market the resources which he does expect to come directly into his possession, into the other resources required for the execution of his plans. A special, very important example of this, arises from his ability to *borrow* the means to acquire the resources he needs... Nevertheless, when an individual considers a particular plan of production, he must

> still at some stage in his calculations, deal with it at a technological level. While calculation can now be carried on in a monetary terms, the alternative plans being weighted still involve the same real elements that were relevant to Crusoe (Kirzner 1966, pp. 23-25).

The most important aspect of the Crusoe metaphor is that of the individual plan. Crusoe faces an uncertain future for which he plans. His plan is often, perhaps always, disturbed in some way by unexpected events. If this is true for Crusoe it is true *a fortiori* for an individual in a market economy whose plans depend crucially on the plans of others. "Crusoe had first to construct an oven, to grow, harvest and grind grain into flour, and finally to bake bread. In a market economy these various steps in the long process of production leading to bread are broken up into separate self-contained processes... Taken together the plans tend to fit into an integrated pattern. But no single mind has formulated any such overall integrated plan. It is enough for the oven maker to know that there are men willing to sell him iron, that there are men willing to buy ovens from him. And so on" (Kirzner 1966, p. 28). In the market economy individual plans interact in a way that introduces both additional opportunity and additional uncertainty. It is the market process that tends to remove the latter by coordinating plans. "This way of looking at things emphasizes the most fundamental of the insights into the market-system that economic analysis has been able to supply-the perception that the plans made in a market interact in a manner that tends to bring about a system of *interlocking* plans... At the same time economic analysis warns vigorously against the simple assumption that all the plans being made at any one time do in fact interlock perfectly. Such perfection serves as a definition only of the state of equilibrium... "(Kirzner 1966, p. 29). Equilibrium, in this sense, is never attained. It is simply a theoretical definition. Real decisions are taken in disequilibrium, that is, in the process of revising earlier plans or forming new ones. "[W]hereas we were assuming Crusoe's stock of resources (resulting from earlier steps taken in fulfillment of his multi-period plans) to be the interim outcome of a *single* integrated plan, the stock of produced things in a market represents the heritage of numberless *separate* past plans... [that] can by no means be assumed to have been perfectly interlocking plans. Taken individually each piece of tangible produced good still represents the past plans of its producers, and their expectations as to its further employments" (Kirzner 1966, p. 33). And now Kirzner alerts the reader to the limits of the Crusoe metaphor saying, "there is not much more that can be said to preserve the parallelism between a Crusoe economy and the market economy" (Kirzner 1966, p. 33). But still, "despite these very real differences between the market economy and the Crusoe economy, it must be admitted that for some rough and ready purposes these differences can be quite usefully ignored. When one observes two Crusoes, one of whom possesses tractors while the second has only a wooden plow, one knows immediately something about the likely respective future outputs of the pair and when one compares two countries and finds one well stocked with roads, buildings, machines, and unfinished goods inventories, while the other is relatively poor in these tangible things, one *does* feel that one knows which country will enjoy the greater volume of output" (Kirzner 1966, pp. 23-24). In every judgment as to the size and significance of the economy's capital there is thus an unconscious Crusoe type construct lurking in the background.

III. METAPHOR AND MEASUREMENT

Kirzner's discussion of the nature of capital in terms of Robinson Crusoe economies and the visualizing of an economy's capital structure in terms of unfinished plans is used in the remaining chapters of *An Essay* to explore common issues in capital theory. Specifically he examines the question of stocks and flows, the concept of "waiting" as an aspect of capital and, in the final chapter, the question of the measurement of capital. Each of these topics involves fascinating and related issues. We shall focus here on the last mentioned.

Kirzner surveys and analyzes the various approaches to the measurement of capital. The problem is of course that the capital of an economy is made up of a multitude of diverse, heterogeneous items, "tangible things" as Kirzner calls them. In order to reduce this collection of things to a single number, a common dimension must be found. The most obvious one is *value*. Though the capital stock of an economy may be made up of many physically different items they all have a value. The value of the capital stock thus implies adding up the individual values of its components. One must start therefore at the individual level. However, considering the discussion earlier of capital as unfinished plans, one encounters insuperable difficulties in this approach. We saw there that only in the case where no unexpected events occurred would a forward looking and a backward looking perspective yield the same valuation of a production plan and of the individual items of which it is composed. We also saw that an outside observer would generally place a different valuation on the plan than would Crusoe. Kirzner extends this general approach to the problem of measuring capital and shows that as long as the passage of time brings with it unexpected change there is no way to objectively measure the capital stock.

Trying to obtain a measure by looking backward one is forced to estimate the value of the resources in the plan in terms of the sacrifices that their employment entailed. The difficulty involved with this is that in general past sacrifices will have been heterogeneous. In the first place, the alternative outputs foregone in the past would have been of different kinds. This implies the usual index number problem. But secondly, different resources will generally have been employed at different times in the past and so Crusoe will have to estimate his valuation of the sacrifice entailed at different dates. This, Kirzner argues is an impossibility. "[S]ince an individual is at no time able to choose between two alternatives the adoption of which requires decisions to be made at *different* dates, it follows that sacrifices undertaken at different dates cannot be compared" (pp. 111-112). This applies just as much to an individual in a market economy as to Crusoe. Using historical market prices does not yield a valid measure.[11] "We conclude that the attempt to measure the 'quantity of capital' in an individual's stock of capital goods, by measuring the past sacrifices involved, must be pronounced as failure" (p. 112). And what applies to a single individual applies *a fortiori* to the market composed of numerous individuals without even the need to appeal to the impossibility of interpersonal comparisons of utility.

It follows that if there is a valid way to measure the capital stock it will be in terms of a *forward* looking measure. This, at least, has the merit of standardizing with respect to time—any forward looking measure must be as of a particular date. Kirzner identifies two types of problems. First there is the problem that the contributions to output that the stock of capital is expected to make may be of different types and occur at different future dates and must be reduced to a single quantity. Second there may be many alternative ways in which the stock of capital can be used in future production. The first problem can be solved by finding the present market value of the contribution by adding together the prospective market values of each bit of the future output flow and discounting to the present date at the appropriate discount rates. There still remain questions of allowing for risk and the problem of differences across individuals with respect to risk and expectations. However, the method of using discounted market values is at least coherent and consistent and represents some sort of "market" assessment. The second problem poses more difficult hurdles:

> First, since capital goods may be used in the production of more than one kind of output, we are required to specify the particular product towards the output of which the stock of capital is, for our purposes, considered able to make contribution. Second, since in the production of many products there exists the possibility of using either relatively more capital with other inputs, or relatively less capital, and since future output depends sensitively on the particular ratio between inputs that is employed, it is necessary to specify the degree of capital intensity that we have in mind when we talk of 'the productive contribution' of our capital goods (p. 114).

In fact further thought on the matter shows that:

> the attempt to measure a stock of capital goods in terms of their potential contribution to future output must assume that all the decisions with respect to the utilization of the capital goods have already been made in the light of current conditions. This means, in

> addition, that the forward-looking measure of the capital stock is able to provide a measure of capital only against the background of given anticipated prices for other inputs and for products... To measure the potential productive contribution that a stock of capital goods can render, in isolation from the consideration of other factors of production, appears to be an impossible task.

We conclude therefore, that:

> an individual's forward-looking measure of a given stock of capital goods is... highly individualistic, depending crucially on his own subjective expectations concerning the future. The market price of a capital good expresses the quantity of capital that it represents to other individuals in the market (the marginal buyers and sellers), based on their expectations... for an outside observer wishing to see how much capital the market ascribes to a particular capital good, the market price certainly gives him the information he wants provided he remembers that those who do not trade at the going price clearly disagree with the rest of the market as to the size of the capital good's prospective productive contribution (p. 116).

Furthermore by adding together market prices, which implies adding together measures of capital stocks possessed by different individuals, we are most probably combining valuations based on mutually inconsistent plans. The problem of evaluating diverse, heterogeneous elements of a given stock of things does not apply only to capital. It is, after all, a problem in the evaluation of output itself. But as Kirzner points out it is especially and additionally applicable to capital:

> The point of this whole discussion is that a measure of capital differs from that of output in that the former, unlike the latter, depends crucially on some definite plan of production in which capital is to play a role. Whether backward-looking or forward-looking, a measure of capital necessarily involves the consideration of some plan... [and] insofar as each individual is able to measure the capital of which his stock of machines consists, in terms of their prospective usefulness to him... it appears clear that the resulting measures are unique to each individual, do not in general permit comparisons between individuals, and yield no meaningful aggregate when added together (pp. 119-120).

What we have here is a forceful argument in favor of Kirzner's original theme that capital must be understood in terms of the individual plans (that led to their construction and employment and/or for which they are now employed). This argument, which the extensive resort to quotation above hopefully illustrates, proceeds by sustained employment of a particular metaphor. This metaphor is an individual engaged in the planning of production. Crusoe is an important special (and simple) case. What Kirzner is in effect doing is appealing to economists to apply this metaphor whenever they think about capital. Doing so reveals inconsistencies in prevailing practices that should make one feel uneasy. So, for example, contemplating the alternative methods that have been used to measure capital, one finds that they require the individual planner to possess more knowledge that is conceivably possible or that they require individuals to have consistent expectations, something we know to be contrary to the process of competition. This should persuade the user to abandon this method on the grounds that it cannot mean what he thinks it does. Bohm-Bawerk, Clark, Knight, and others are carefully subjected to this kind of treatment.[12] It can be applied to modern economics as well.

One might wonder why we should bother with the question of measuring the capital stock. After all, and after reading Kirzner, the argument can be forcefully made that an understanding of capital does not require it. Capital is composed of a bewildering variety of different things that work together in intelligible ways to produce those things that we value and on which our life styles depend. Furthermore any judgment, for example about the amount of "capital per head," upon which judgments of the economy's wealth depend should, after considering Kirzner's arguments, be considered with suspicion. Further descriptive data seem to be called for. Yet even a cursory examination reveals that it is obviously very important to modern economics that it be possible, or at least that it appear to be possible, to measure the capital stock. This is certainly true for statistical inquiries that require a measure of the capital stock. But it is also true for theoretical inquiry and the way in which economists see themselves proceeding. What McCloskey calls Kelvin's Dictum comes to mind: "When you cannot express it in numbers, your knowledge is of a meager and unsatisfactory kind" (McCloskey 1983, p. 484). The use of the idea of a "production function" suggests that one be able to associate a measurable quantity with the K that is the capital input in a function $Q = f(K,L)$. McCloskey has analyzed a famous article by Robert Solow making use of the production function which "together with some related ones he wrote about the same time, inaugurated virtually a new field of economics" (McCloskey 1985, p. 83; Solow 1957).

The article investigated the rising income of Americans from 1909-1949. To do so he sets up the equation $Q = A(t)f(K,L)$ where the "multiplicative factor $A(t)$ measures the cumulated effect of shifts over time" (Solow 1957, p. 402). The shifts in the production function referred to imply "neutral" technical change. Solow wants to account for these technical changes in terms of "how much was caused by more machinery, buildings, and other physical 'capital' and how much other things-chiefly, perhaps the increasing ingenuity of people" (McCloskey 1985, p. 83). McCloskey expands on the (at times self-consciously) rhetorical character of this article and points out that the very use of a production function is a metaphor. "The 'aggregate production function' that Solow diffidently introduces asserts that the making of our daily bread is like a mathematical function. The jumble of responsibility, habit, conflict, ambition, intrigue, and ceremony that is our working life is supposed to be similar to a chalked curve on a blackboard" (McCloskey 1985, p. 84).[13] Most treatments of capital in the production function literature do not show the level of awareness that Solow does, but even though Solow seems to understand the limitations of his metaphor he runs a long way with it.

The production function has indeed proven to be a very resilient metaphor. This in spite of the Cambridge controversy and mathematical proofs of its impossibility. Therefore, as McCloskey correctly points out, discussions about it are not really about mathematics. They are implicitly about ideology or policy. This is apparent in Kirzner's discussion as well. Kirzner explicitly discusses the concept of the production function:

> A production function can be looked at 'positively.' As such it represents simply a set of technological relationships. On the other hand, a production function can be looked at as representing *opportunities*, from among which a human being is able to make a choice. Clearly an economics in which market events are seen as the results of deliberately planned actions, ought to view production possibilities, in this second way, as alternatives from among which planned courses of action may be constructed (Kirzner 1966, p. 45).

And in a footnote to this:

> Current practice generally (and, as it seems to us, unfortunately) follows the 'technological' view. This is especially the case with respect to aggregate models... this practice is especially unfortunate in the capital theory context (Kirzner 1966, p. 45).

Kirzner is objecting not so much to the use of the production function as to its interpretation as a permanently available, technological relationship as opposed to a menu of choices. He is concerned to keep the volitional aspect in it and the automaticity out of it. Production, though governed by technological considerations, depends on choices made in given institutional environments. To abstract from the human and institutional aspects is to provide a misleading picture (presumably misleading for policy as well).

> It follows then... that to treat capital goods as if they were permanent goods, when in fact they have been constructed as part of a plan in which they are ultimately to be used up, is a distortion that ought not to win acceptance... What may be acceptable as a *technological* description of what goes on in a selected short period of time, is grossly unsatisfactory as an *economic* description of the course of events in terms of relevant human decisions that have been made (Kirzner 1966, p. 46).

The view of the production function as a set of technological relationships is very close in spirit to Knight's treatment of capital as permanently available source of output. For Knight capital "is measured by the perpetual service income which *it can be counted upon to yield.* In other words, plant itself in its quantitative aspect, is perpetual (regardless of changes in physical form), except for a possible net disinvestment in society as a whole... " (Knight 1956, p. 47 italics added; quoted in Kirzner 1966, p. 56). Interestingly, Kirzner's critique of Knight contains an explicit recognition that he (Knight) is talking metaphorically and that "the purpose of employing this figure of speech is clearly that of being able to focus attention on the source-flow dichotomy..." (Kirzner 1966, p. 60). Evidently, however, Kirzner does not consider this justification sufficient. The main reason again is that in the Knightian view "there is a temptation to ignore the *planned* character of capital goods maintenance...[and to assume that] the future course of production is completely determined by the present state of affairs" (Kirzner 1966, p. 63) irrespective of the current (policy or other) environment. There is more at stake than simply a manner of speaking.

IV. PLANS, KNOWLEDGE, AND HUMAN CAPITAL

Placing the plan at the center of an understanding of capital, in a world in which unexpected events play a dominant role (as would be the case in a period of rapid technological changes), provides some very interesting implications. As Kirzner shows, the individual tangible items that we classify as capital goods derive their meaning, and their value, from the plans of which they are a part. Any assessment of the significance of the existence of these capital goods in an economy (including any assessment of the size of the capital stock) must, either consciously or unconsciously, refer to particular modes of use, that is to say to production plans. Once we realize the importance of plans in understanding capital, however, we must also realize the importance of *shared knowledge* in that understanding. Only the ability to empathize with the imagined plans of potential producers provides us with an understanding of the significance of a steel mill or a lumber yard. To a person totally without the knowledge to which these things are usually put they would be physical items devoid of economic significance. Every plan assumes the existence of particular knowledge. Understanding the plan (in part or in whole) requires sharing that knowledge.

This suggests that there is an aspect of Kirzner's focus on individual plans that has hitherto escaped examination, namely that all plans are *human* plans and exist only in human minds. They are part of an individual's "knowledge" broadly conceived. In an important sense all capital is *human*. To see this we should draw a distinction between knowledge and information. It is knowledge that makes information valuable. Isolated information in the form of bits and bytes is valueless. Information without cognition is valueless. By the same token, what knowledge does for information it also does for capital goods as they are usually conceived. From this perspective, capital is resources (information and other resources) plus "meaning." Disembodied pieces of equipment or raw materials or blueprints of operation have no value until they are considered within a production plan conceived by someone in a position to implement that plan. But the reverse is also true. Knowledge derives its value from the purposes to which it is put. Knowledge in its many forms is thus inextricably bound up with production plans.

The statement that knowledge is valuable, that it derives its value from its combination in production with physical resources (of which information is a part) resonates with the work of Gary Becker on *human capital.* Work done by Becker and his collaborators, building on the original insights of T.W. Shultz has generated the "human capital" revolution of the past two decades. The term "human capital" is a metaphor within a metaphor that "illustrates how two sets of ideas, in this case both drawn from inside economics, can thus mutually illuminate each other by exchanging connotations" (McCloskey 1985, p. 77). McCloskey explains this further as follows:

> In the phrase 'human capital' the field in economics treating human skills was at a stroke unified with the field treating investment in machines. Thought in both fields was improved—labor economics by recognizing that skills, for all their intangibility, arise from abstention from consumption; capital theory by recognizing that skills, for all their lack of capitalization, compete with other investments for a claim to abstention (McCloskey 1985, p. 77).

McCloskey correctly explains here that Becker's understanding of human capital is an extension of the neoclassical approach to capital in general, where the idea of "abstention" is key. The impact of the concept on the profession derives from its ability to make economists think of the act of acquiring valuable knowledge in terms of capital type investments. It is possible to feel, however, that there is much more to the human aspects of capital and the capital aspects of human knowledge and that in this sense Becker's work does not go far enough.

From Kirzner's perspective "abstention" is neither a necessary nor a sufficient condition for something to qualify as a capital good. Its ability to contribute toward the fulfillment of a production plan is both necessary and sufficient. A capital item is an item that is expected to yield value over time. Knowledge fits into that category. In a sense human capital refers to the value of the knowledge possessed by individuals in a production plan (which could be in the workplace or in the household). Human capital is thus an indispensable complement to physical capital. Becker's work is valuable precisely because he has taught economists to think in terms of extended, multi-period plans when considering education, training, experience, childbearing, general household activities, and so on, in a way analogous to the way they think about capital in general. This could be valuably incorporated into Kirzner's framework. All economic activity involves multi-period planning and this includes what Becker calls "household production." Thus human capital is involved in all economic activity. It should be obvious that the same impediments that attach to the general evaluation and measurement of physical capital items apply also to human capital. Robin Crusoe's knowledge, his human capital, is as much a part of his plan as anything else.

> To the [outside] observer a plan that has not yet been fully carried out may present any of numerous possible spectacles. Everything will depend on the particular plan originally selected, and on the initial steps already taken in its fulfillment. It may be that the observer will find difficulty in discovering tangible evidence of any progress at all by Crusoe toward fulfillment of the original plan. This may be the case for example if the initial steps of the plan called merely for *the acquisition by Crusoe of a particular skill.* Or perhaps the observer will find stocks of raw materials and supplies prepared for subsequent use. Or perhaps he will find tools and equipment that Crusoe has constructed for subsequent use. Perhaps he will find preliminary operations have already been performed upon raw materials...Or, he may find that Crusoe...merely laid up a stock of consumption goods in preparation...(Kirzner 1966, p. 15, italics added).

This statement underlines the equal importance of various types of capital cooperating in any production plan, including human capital in the form of skills. The evaluation of an economy's potential owes as much to the evaluation of the skills, dedication, training, and general expertise of its citizens than it does to an evaluation of its physical items. In fact this is probably an understatement. *Capital*ist production arguably depends more on the types and qualities of human capital that exist in an economy than on the physical items it possesses. The latter can be easily obtained in a world market economy when the requisite human capital is in place.

Becker's formal presentation is in terms of equilibrium constructs. He uses neoclassical maximization ideas which rely on measurable, homogeneous quantities of physical and human capital. His message, however, transcends his method (and some would say his needlessly provocative style). In a nutshell, he shows that the profound social changes that have occurred in this century in the workplace and in the household (extending to the very meaning of "work" and of "family") can be understood in terms of *the changing nature of human capital.* Consider, for example, the following changes:

> [Looking at the period from 1950-1977 we find that] the birth rate within marriage declined by about one third, the divorce rate more than doubled, the labor force participation of married women with young children more than tripled, and the percent of households headed by women with dependent children also almost tripled (Becker 1993b, p. 350).

In a chapter devoted to "the evolution of the family" Becker states, "In modern societies markets facilitate trade and production, and dynamic environments rapidly change technologies, incomes and opportunities" (Becker 1993b, p. 337). This in turn can be related to changes in the nature of human capital. In traditional societies knowledge was passed down the generations largely through kinship connections. Human capital that was valuable was of a specific but unchanging kind. In modern societies this is no longer true. The rate at which certain kinds of human capital become obsolete has increased dramatically and human capital in general is less gender or kin specific. The rise in the earning power of women is surely related to this. The knowledge of how to acquire, use, store, and transmit useful information is a major ingredient in most aspects of modern human capital. Biological differences and social backgrounds have become much less important. As a result the gender based division of labor in the workforce and within the household has dramatically diminished. The changing nature and rising value of market based human capital has reduced the desire for large families. Child rearing is a very time intensive activity and the market value of time has risen dramatically. So people's "production plans" tend to include less children. However, with fewer children parents spend more on each child. The perceived gain from marriage has declined for a number of reasons. One is the increased mobility and earning power of women. Another is the greater uncertainty of our work environment. People marry later in life and divorce more often. These phenomena are interrelated in complex ways. "For example, fertility is reduced when divorce becomes more likely, because children are more difficult to rear and may provide less pleasure after a marriage dissolves" (Becker 1993b, p. 355). When divorce is more likely women invest more in market oriented human capital and this tends to raise their earnings and so on.

V. CONCLUSION

The choice of how to characterize capital surely depends on the kind of world in which one lives. It could be argued that in a world in which unexpected changes occur relatively rarely and in which methods of production, distribution, and interaction are very stable, it makes sense to characterize capital as an equilibrium stock, a fund of more or less agreed upon value indicated by daily market values without much attention to individual plans. In a world in which change is rapid and unpredictable, a characterization of capital as a structure of heterogeneous items resulting from individual plans becomes more compelling. In particular, with regard to the effect of change on incomes, employment and life styles changing, evolving capital structure seems to give insights that are not available from an equilibrium approach and this is as true for human capital as it is for physical capital.

ACKNOWLEDGMENT

I am grateful to Peter Boettke for helpful suggestions.

NOTES

1. The assault on Modernism has touched economics as well even if it has been less noticible than in other fields (McCloskey 1983, 1985, chapter 1, 1990, pp. 1-9). In economics the criticism is mainly directed toward the use of the metaphor of mechanism (Mirowski 1988; also see Hodgson 1993, chapter 2 and the references therein). Economists, conciously or unconciously, probably ever since Ricardo, have been building conceptual schema based on the idea of physical, mechanical forces. The most obvious element of this approach is the idea of "equilibrium" implying a determinite "balance of forces." Though there have always been reservations about the appropriateness of this methodology, for example by Austrian economists and institutionalist economists, the majority of economists have been unaware of and unconcerned with these. Gradually, however, doubts have begun to creep in.

2. "Self-conciousness about metaphor in economics would be an improvement on many counts. Most obviously, unexamined metaphor is a substitute for thinking—which is a recommendation to examine the metaphors, not to attempt the impossible by banishing them" (McCloskey 1985, p. 81).

3. "In 1989 the problem of 'transition dynamics' forced itself on economists and statesmen... In Eastern Europe... people are confronted with unprecedented opportunities, new and ill-defined rules, and a daily struggle to determine the 'mechanism' [sic] that will eventually govern trade and production. Economists who dispense advice about governmental strategies to enable transitions to a market economy can do so with ample help from 'equilibrium theories' describing how to expect a system to operate after it has fully adjusted to a new and coherent set of rules and expectations, but with virtually no theories about the transition itself" (Sargent 1993, p. 2).

4. Waldrop's book is a facinating popular account of how a group of researchers, including economists (most notably Brian Arthur, Keneth Arrow, Frank Hahn, and Tom Sargent), over an extended period of time during the 1980s examined some of the implications of "complexity" for economics. In particular, questions relating to nondeterminstic systems that are nevertheless self organizing were addressed. The book makes somewhat frustrating reading for modern Austrian economists who have been working from a market process perspective since the early 1970s. They find in it a belated recognition of many of their insights without so much as a grudging footnote. This same lack of acknowledgment permeates the literature with which Waldrop deals.

5. One important aspect of these new perspectives is that explanation and prediction can no longer be taken as methodologically equivalent categories. Because of the arrow of time, it is now increasingly held that prediction is not possible. Interactive systems, especially social systems, contain irreducible novelty. History matters. Technologies get "locked in" and influence subsequent developments in unpredictable ways (Arthur 1989). The primary goal, it can now be admitted, is explanation and understanding. The important questions become: what is it we are trying to explain and what constitutes a good explanation?

6. "The multiplicity of different formulations of the capital concept attest, not only to the elusive nature of the concept itself, but even more importantly, to the innate complexity of the economic relationships hoped to be elucidated with the aid of this concept, or rather these concepts" (Kirzner 1966, p. 36).

7. See also Lachmann 1956; Skousen 1990. The latter surveys much of the historical literature on Austrian capital theory and tries to provide a new aggregate capital concept for the economy based on the Austrian tradition.

8. In our discussion of the reemergent significance of capital theory we shall refer in some detail to this work. The reader should be made aware, however, that it is impossible to do justice to the original and that only a full and careful reading of the latter will reveal all of the many gems available to be mined.

9. "I interpret a proposal to build models with 'boundedly rational' agents as a call to retreat from the second piece of rational expectations [mutual consistency of perceptions] by expelling rational agents from our model environments..." (Sargent 1993, p. 3). Of course, many will question the rather restricted use of the term "rational," but this is a different matter.

10. In this Kirzner was, of course, applying the basic insights of Carl Menger (1871).

11. "A person may pay *x* dollars in the summer to enjoy a cold shower, this shows he prefers the latter to the former; he may pay *y* dollars in the winter to enjoy a warm bath, this shows he prefers the bath to the *y* dollars. But even if $y>x$ this does not prove that the winter bath is preferred to the summer shower. Even though we know that in the winter her prefers *y* dollars to *x* dollars, and so also in the summer, we have no decision possibility permitting him to choose simultaneously between summer and winter enjoyments. He may use the loan market to express his *present* preferences between *x* dollars in the winter and *y* dollars in the summer, but this, of course, is something different" (p. 112).

12. As indicated earlier, these theorists have their own, different metaphors for thinking about capital. For example, Bohm-Bawerk's approach to measuring capital implies that the production process is like one that matures at a given point of time after the application of certain homogeneous inputs. This would allow measuring the capital in that process in terms of the average time for which the average input is applied. Similarly, Knight's (and Clark's) approach implies that the production process of the economy as a whole is like one in which no unexpected events occur that would cause traders to revalue the physical assets at their disposal. For them capital is representative of a continuous process in which time is not directly relevant. Kirzner's argument is that the real world is too different from these metaphors for us to consider them as valid guides.

13. Earlier McClosky says, "the very idea of a 'production function' involves the astonishing analogy of the subject (the fabrication of things, about which it is appropriate to think in terms of ingenuity, discipline, and planning) with the modifier (a mathematical function, about which it is appropriate to think in terms of height, shape, and single-valuedness" (1985, p. 79). Solow himself notes at the beginning of the article, "Before going on, let me be explicit that I would not try to justify what follows by calling on fancy theorems on aggregation and index numbers. Either this kind of aggregate economics appeals or it doesn't." In a footnote to this he says, "Mrs Robinson in particlular has explored many of *the profound difficulties that stand in the way of giving any precise meaning to the quantity of capital* and I have thrown up still further obstacles... One can at least hope that the aggregate analysis gives some notion of the way detailed analysis would lead" (Solow 1957, p. 401, italics added). Concerning the meaning of K McClosky notes, "The K reduces the material inheritance of the workplace to a pile of smoos" (1985, p. 84).

REFERENCES

Arthur, W.B. 1989. "Competing Technologies, Increasing Returns, and Lock-in by Historical Small Events." *Economic Journal*, 99: 116-31.

Becker, G.S. 1993a. *Human Capital*. Chicago: University of Chicago Press.

———. 1993b. *A Treatise on the Family*. Cambridge: Harvard University Press.

Coveney, P., and R. Highfield. 1990. *The Arrow of Time*. New York: Ballentine Books.

Day, R. H., and P. Chen. 1993. *Nonlinear Dynamics and Evolutionary Economics*. Oxford: Oxford University Press.

Hodgson, G. M. 1993. *Economics and Evolution: Bringing Life Back Into Economics*. Ann Arbor: The University of Michigan Press.

Kirzner, I. M. 1966. *An Essay on Capital*. New York: Augustus M. Kelly.

Knight, F. H. 1956. *On the History and Method of Economics*. Chicago: University of Chicago Press.

Lachmann, L. M. 1956/1976. *Capital and Its Structure.* Kansas City: Sheed, Andrews and McMeel.

McCloskey, D. N. 1983. "The Rhetoric of Economics." *Journal of Economic Literature*, XXI(2): 481-516.

________ . 1985. *The Rhetoric of Economics.* Madison: University of Wisconsin Press.

________ . 1990. *If You're So Smart: The Narrative of Economic Experience.* Chicago: University of Chicago Press.

Menger, C. 1871/1976. *Principles of Economics.* Translated by J. Dingwill and B. Hoselitz. New York: New York University Press.

Mirowski, P. 1988. *Against Mechanism.* Totawa, NJ: Rowman and Littlefield.

Sargent, T. J. 1993. *Bounded Rationality in Macroeconomics.* Oxford: Clarendon Press.

Skousen, M. 1990. *The Structure of Production.* New York: New York University Press.

Solow, R. M. 1957. "Technical Change and the Aggregate Production Function." *Review of Economics and Statistics*, 39: 312-20, as reprinted in A. Sen. 1970. *Growth Economics.* Baltimore: Penguin Books.

Waldrop, M. M. 1992. *Complexity.* New York: Simon and Schuster.

LUDWIG VON MISES ON INFLATION AND EXPECTATIONS

Joseph T. Salerno

I. INTRODUCTION

Among his most important contributions to monetary theory, Ludwig von Mises originated sophisticated analyses of the social consequences of inflation and of the formation and evolution of inflationary expectations.[1] What characterizes Mises' explanation of the inflationary process, and at the same time accounts for its neglect by modern proponents of the quantity theory of money, is an emphasis on the kind of relative price effects that is inconsistent with the long-run neutrality of money usually inferred from this theory. And although modern quantity theorists (Edwards 1985; Humphrey 1984) recently have begun to address Mises' analysis, they have for the most part, misconceived his view of the nature and durability of these effects.

With respect to his theory of inflationary expectations, it is generally ignored by modern Austrian writers themselves, while some have explicitly denied either that Mises essayed to formulate such a theory or that he succeeded in integrating it with his overall vision of the economic process. For example, the late Ludwig Lachmann strongly implied that Mises offered no theory of

Advances in Austrian Economics, Volume 2B, pages 297-325.

ISBN: 1-55938-531-6

expectations.[2] And even such a careful Mises scholar as Richard M. Ebeling (1988, p. 12), while admitting that Mises "*did* attempt to formulate a constructive theory of expectations and their formation in the market process," concluded that Mises failed to fully integrate his theory of expectations formation with his theories of money and of entrepreneurship.[3] However, at least one sympathetic neoclassical monetary theorist (Edwards 1985, p. 104) has taken note of Mises' analysis of the development of expectations about the future purchasing power of money during historical episodes of inflation, criticizing it as an inconsistent amalgam of elements of the rational and adaptive expectations theories.

In the following section of this paper, I review Mises' distinctive "step-by-step" or sequential method of analyzing changes in the relationship between the supply of and demand for money, and demonstrate how this analysis yields the conclusion that money is nonneutral in the long run as well as in the short run. In the third section I take up the responses of modern quantity theorists to Mises' description of the social consequences of unanticipated monetary inflation, arguing that their responses embody a failure to adequately appreciate the subtleties of Mises' analysis. I also show how Mises' analytical method led him to an explanation of the positive employment effect typical of initially unanticipated inflation that differs markedly from the explanation derived from the Friedman-Phelps natural rate hypothesis. The fourth section of the paper addresses the attempt to interpret Mises' writings on inflationary expectations in terms of neoclassical expectations-formation mechanisms. In this section I present, I believe for the first time, a comprehensive account of Mises' theory of expectations, showing how it is integrated with his praxeological approach to economic theory and elucidating the crucial role it plays in his analysis of the effects of an ongoing monetary inflation.[4]

II. MISES' ANALYTICAL METHOD AND THE LONG—RUN NONNEUTRALITY OF MONEY

In his autobiographical *Notes and Recollections,* (1978a, pp. 57-59) written in 1940 but not published until 1978, Mises gives the following description of the "step-by-step" method he originated for analyzing monetary phenomena in his 1912 work on *The Theory of Money and Credit*:

> The step-by-step analysis must consider the lapse of time. In such an analysis the time-lag between cause and effect becomes a multitude of time differences between single successive consequences. Reflection on these time-lags leads to a precise theory of the social consequences of changes in the purchasing power of money.

As Mises (1978a, p. 59) proceeds to point out, and as I shall explain later, such an analysis yields a "theory of the inevitable nonneutrality of money," implying "... that changes in purchasing power of money causes prices of different commodities and services to change neither simultaneously nor evenly, and that it is incorrect to maintain that changes in the quantity of money bring about simultaneous and proportional changes in the 'level' of prices."

In his book-length study of Mises' monetary thought, James Rolph Edwards (1985, pp. 52-56) perceptively defends Mises' method of deriving the demand for money from the marginal utility of cash balances against objections raised by "real balance" theorists such as Howard S. Ellis, Don Patinkin, and Laurence S. Moss. In particular, Edwards successfully counters the criticism advanced both by Ellis (1934, p. 164) and Moss (1976, p. 32) that Mises' theory of the demand for money yields a demand curve that is drawn as a rectangular hyperbola in nominal cash balance space. A demand curve of this shape, they note, is logically inconsistent with Mises' repeated and vigorous denials that an addition to the stock of money—even when this increment is distributed so as to equiproportionally increase all individual cash balances—causes an equiproportional increase of all prices. Edwards (1985, p. 55) demonstrates that this criticism rests on a clearly erroneous interpretation of Mises' theory "... as saying that the individual values units of money only with a view to maintaining a predecided and given level of purchasing power, and that utility calculation is not applied to the level of real balances. From this perspective they find his nonproportionality argument contradictory. It does not occur to them that his nonproportionality argument is evidence *against* their interpretation of his theory of the demand for money."

Nonetheless, Edwards (1985, p. 56) himself falls into error when he charges Mises with "a failure to step from a non-rectangularly-hyperbolic demand for nominal balances to the rectangularly-hyperbolic market equilibrium curve." Edwards initiates his criticism by concurring with Mises that an equiproportional addition to cash balances, let us say a doubling, will not lead *initially,* that is, immediately prior to the first round of spending of the excess balances, to an inversely proportional variation or halving of marginal utilities of money on individual value scales. Thus, as Edwards recognizes, the overall elasticity of Mises' "instantaneous" demand curve for nominal balances, which is derived from instantaneously existing marginal utility schedules for goods and money, may properly take on (absolute) values less than, greater than, or equal to unity. Or, in other words, the instantaneous demand curve for money only fortuitously traces out a rectangular hyperbola.[5]

Edwards (1985, p. 56) proceeds to argue, however, that Mises erred "... in assuming that it followed that prices would not rise proportionately with M. This would occur because, as prices increased, real balances would decline, reversing all of the initial wealth effects, until equilibrium was attained at the initial level of real balances, *ceteris paribus.*" Edwards is here contending, a la Patinkin, that, notwithstanding the non-unitary elasticity of the "instantaneous" demand curve for money, real balance effects generated by an increase of money will initiate a dynamic adjustment process that culminates in an equiproportional increase in all prices. But Patinkin's demonstration that an increase in money accomplished via an equiproportional increase in everyone's cash balance brings forth an increase of all prices in the same proportion rests either on his arbitrary assumption of the constancy of the real data, that is, relative prices and real wealth, during the transition from one Walrasian equilibrium position to the next, or on his equivalent simplifying assumption that "prices rise during the *tâttonement* in an equiproportionate manner" (Patinkin 1965, p. 44).[6]

As I shall argue, however, the step-by-step method Mises consistently applies in analyzing monetary variations leads inevitably to the conclusion that the real data of the system could never, under any conceivable initial set of circumstances, remain unaltered during a dynamic adjustment process. For Mises (1966, p. 414), "The process is always uneven and by steps, disproportionate and asymetrical." In fact, Mises ([1952] 1971, pp. 141-142) rigorously demonstrates the long-run nonneutrality of money even under the most stringent assumption that new money is injected into the economic system in a manner that does not disturb the preexisting relative distribution among individuals of total, and not just monetary, wealth. As long as individual value scales are differentiated from one another and either all goods are not available in infinitely divisible units or their marginal utilities with respect to money do not decline at uniform rates throughout each and every person's value scale, then a change in the quantity of money must effect a permanent alteration in the structure of market demands for commodities and services and, therefore, a permanent change in relative prices.

Writing in *Human Action,* Mises (1966, pp. 412-413) concludes that

> Changes in the supply of money must necessarily alter the disposition of vendible goods as owned by various individuals and firms.... We may, if we like, assume that every member gets a share of the additional money right at the moment of its inflow into the system, or shares in the reduction of the quantity of money. But whether we assume this or not, the final result of our demonstration will remain the same. This result will be that changes in the structure of prices brought about by changes in the supply of money available in the economic system never affect the prices of the various commodities and services to the same extent and at the same time....
>
> The main fault of the old quantity theory as well as the mathematical economists' equation of exchange is that they have ignored this fundamental issue. Changes in the supply of money must bring about changes in other data too. The market system before and after the inflow or outflow of a quantity of money is not merely changed in that cash holdings of the individuals and prices have increased or decreased. There have been affected also changes in the reciprocal exchange ratios between the various commodities and services which, if one wants to resort to metaphors, are more adequately described by the image of price revolution than by the misleading figure of an elevation or a sinking of a 'price level.'

Thus for Mises, "real balance effects are inextricably bound together with "distribution effects." The sequential process by which the market adjusts (positive or negative) excess demands for money necessarily "revolutionizes" income and wealth positions and the price structure. And this is the case even if these (nonzero) individual excess demands sum to zero in the aggregate. Explains Mises (1966):

> Every change in the money relation alters—apart from the effects on deferred payments—the conditions of the individual members of society. Some become richer, some poorer.... Each change in the money relation takes its own course and produces its own particular effects. If an inflationary movement and a deflationary one occur at the same time or if an inflation is temporally followed by a deflation in such a way that prices finally are not very much changed the social consequences of each of the two movements do not cancel each other. To the social consequences of an inflation those of a deflation are added. There is no reason to assume that all or even most of those favored by one movement will be hurt by the second one, or vice versa (pp. 417-418).

III. THE INFLATIONARY PROCESS

Edwards (1985, pp. 91-92) recognizes that Mises conceives inflation as a time-spanning process in which an increase in the stock of money invariably results in a sequential adjustment of prices which necessarily alters relative prices and brings about a reallocation of productive resources and a redistribution of real income and wealth. The specific sequence in which prices are adjusted, and thus the identity of those market participants experiencing gains or losses, is not deducible from economic theory but depends concretely on the specific point at which the new money is injected into the economy and on the marginal utility schedules of those who constitute the links in the chain of receipt and expenditure of the new money. As Edwards (1985, pp. 92-93) points out, "This description of the inflationary process is more complex and realistic than the sort of 'airplane spreading analysis' (involving miraculous equiproportional additions to cash balances) that economists all too frequently indulge in."

Unfortunately, Edwards' earlier failure to fully grasp Mises' analytical procedure leads him to the erroneous conclusion that Mises imagined this "lagged price adjustment process" as reaching completion "only when the original price relations were restored." As I demonstrated earlier, however, Mises took great pains to deny that either the instantaneous demand curve or the Patinkinite market equilibrium curve for nominal cash balances can ever take on the shape of a rectangular hyperbola under dynamic, that is, real-world, conditions. Moreover, Edwards (1985, p. 92) commits a fundamental blunder in elementary price theory when he insists that the relative position of the group of sellers whose receipt of the new money occurs late in the inflationary process is restored at the end of the process, although their "losses suffered in the interim go uncompensated." Logically, it is just such uncompensated losses (and gains) that *permanently* alter the pattern of individual wealth holdings, market demands, and relative prices, and therefore result in a revolution and not a restoration of the relative positions of various groups of sellers in the new long-run equilibrium or "final state of rest."

Thus, as Mises (1987b, p. 96) states. "Precisely because the price increases have not affected all commodities at one time, shifts in the relationships of wealth and income are effected which affect the supply and demand of individual goods and services differently. Thus, these shifts must lead to a new orientation of the market and of market prices." Indeed, as Mises insightfully points out in his critique of Irving Fisher's statement of the quantity theory, Fisher was led to contrive his artificial bifurcation between monetary theory and value theory as a makeshift defense against just such a charge of elementary logical error. Writes Mises ([1952] 1971):

> One thing only can explain how Fisher is able to maintain his mechanical Quantity Theory. To him the Quantity Theory seems a doctrine peculiar to the value of money; in fact he contrasts it outright with the laws of value of other economic goods.... With as much justification as that of Fisher and Brown for their mechanical formula for the value of money, a similar formula could be set out for the value of any commodity, and similar conclusions drawn from it (pp. 144-145).

In fact the postwar efforts by neoclassical monetary theorists following Patinkin to "integrate monetary and value theory" seem to be beside the point, because they attempt to repair the Fisherian disjunction without forthrightly coming to terms with the value-theoretic error embodied in the neutral-money doctrine.

In discussing Mises' analysis of the social consequences of inflation, Edwards (1985, pp. 95-96) observes that Mises recognized the effect of unanticipated inflation in modifying the relative wealth positions of creditors and debtors, while also adopting Fisher's original analysis of the adjustment of the nominal interest rate to an anticipated fall in the purchasing power of money. In fact, Mises (1978b, p. 93) considers the emphasis on the link between fluctuations in the value of money and the formation of the interest rate to be "Fisher's most important contribution to monetary theory." Edwards (1985, p. 96) also notes that, in a book initially published in 1919, Mises originated (1983, pp. 160-163) the argument that inflation causes a falsification of capital accounting that leads to an overstatement of profits and brings about unintended consumption of the social stock of capital. This occurs because depreciation quotas for capital goods during inflation continue to be computed on the basis of their historical rather than their (necessarily higher) replacement costs. The entrepreneurs may dispose of these "accounting" profits by increasing their own consumption, by cutting prices to consumers, or by bidding up the wage rates of laborers. In the latter two cases, a one-time redistribution of wealth from one group to another accompanies the consumption of capital.

Because Edwards persists in imputing to Mises the view that money is neutral in the long run, he neglects to identify what Mises clearly considers the most important social consequence of inflation: the permanent redistribution of income and wealth that results from the sequential and uneven adjustment of prices to an addition to the stock of money. For Mises (1978b, p. 95), "... the social consequences of changes in the value of money are not limited to altering the content of future monetary obligations." In fact, as Mises (1978b, p. 94) argues, in a continuing inflation which comes to be more or less correctly anticipated by the public, the effects on short-term credit transactions are mitigated by the Fisherian inflation premium that comes to be incorporated into loan contracts. In the case of long-term credit, where it is much more difficult to forecast the precise degree of depreciation of the monetary unit, a commodity with a relatively stable value, such as gold or—especially in today's world—foreign currency, is substituted for the depreciating money as the "standard of deferred payments." Mises (1966, pp. 425-426) also suggests that adjusting accounting procedures for durable equipment to reflect replacement rather than historical costs would be a practicable method for greatly reducing or eliminating the unintended consumption of capital and the associated redistribution of income from capitalist-entrepreneurs to other groups in society that occurs during inflation.

In sharp contrast to Edwards and most modern quantity theorists, then, this leaves as the most significant social consequence of the variation in the purchasing power of money what Mises (1978b, p. 97) calls the "uncompensatable changes" in income and wealth that occur "... because of the uneven timing of the price changes of the various goods and services." Thus does every change in the quantity of money leave indelible imprints on the relative-price structure and therefore on the social structure.

Recently, it has been argued by Thomas J. Humphrey (1984, p. 13) that "the Austrian School's contention that monetarists invariably ignore relative price and real output effects in the monetary mechanism" is based on a misconception. Humphrey then goes on to impressively demonstrate that both monetarists such as Milton Friedman as well as protomonetarists, including Fisher and Clark Warburton, do indeed take into account "the *temporary* nonneutral real-sector effects of monetary changes" (emphasis added). But, of course, recognition only of short-term relative price and real output effects that are inexplicably and exactly reversed in the course of the monetary adjustment process to yield the long-run neutrality of money does not constitute the resolution but the very crux of the problem that Austrian monetary theorists identify with the Fisherian quantity theory. Indeed, Humphrey shows that he misunderstands the basis of the Misesian proposition that any explanation of the monetary adjustment process must proceed in terms consistent with general value theory and with the inescapable reality of the sequential adjustment of prices. Thus Humphrey (1984, p. 15) touts Fisher's allusions to "contractual restraints, legal prohibitions, and the inertia of custom [which] render individual prices sticky" as a complete and convincing explanation of the "real" effects that invariably accompany monetary changes.

Humphrey (1984, p. 18) proceeds further to claim that Austrians ignore the effect of increased employment caused by inflation's temporary distortion of the relative price between labor and output, that is, the real wage rate, an effect which has been particularly stressed by Friedman. This, at best, uninformed charge is refuted by Edwards (1985, p. 100), who shows that, in an article published in 1958 (Mises [1958] 1980, pp. 150-161), the same year A. W. Phillips' famous article (Phillips 1958) was published and a full decade before Friedman unveiled his "natural rate" hypothesis in his Presidential address to the American Economic Association, Mises set forth "... virtually all of the essential arguments Friedman later made on the subject in his Presidential address. The existence of a natural rate of unemployment conditioned by the state of real wages is clearly implicit.... The existence of a short-run tradeoff between inflation and unemployment and the nonexistence of a long-run tradeoff due to some sort of expectations adjustment are both explicit elements of the argument." Referring to an even earlier essay by Mises ([1950] 1980, pp. 83-93), Edwards (1985, p. 100) states that "Mises even more clearly anticipated Phelps and the accelerationists."

What Edwards fails to make clear, however, is that for Mises, in contrast to Friedman and the natural-rate theorists, the "real wage/employment effect" attributable to inflation is not dependent on the conjecture that "selling prices of products typically respond to an unanticipated rise in nominal demand faster than prices of factors of production" (Friedman [1968] 1987, p. 395),[7] combined with an ad hoc assumption regarding the relatively slow rate at which laborers adapt their expectations about money's future purchasing power to their experience of its depreciation. In fact, in Mises' step-by-step exposition of the inflation-adjustment process, an industry may find the real wage rates it must pay decreasing or increasing, depending on the specific point at which the additional quantity of money first impinges on individual value scales and the exact sequence of individual cash balance adjustments that is then set in train. Thus, for example, an inflation precipitated by an expansion of bank loans for purposes of business investment entails *rising,* not falling, real wage rates and, therefore, a negative employment effect for lower-order capital and consumer goods' industries, that is, those industries that are late in the chain of spending of the newly-created fiduciary media.

As Mises (1987b, pp. 120-121) argues "... in the regular course of banking operations the banks issue fiduciary media only as loans to producers and merchants.... [T]hese fiduciary media are used first of all for production, that is to buy factors of production and pay wages. The first prices to rise, therefore, as a result of an increase of the quantity of money ... caused by the issue of such fiduciary media, are those of raw materials, semimanufactured products, other goods of higher orders, and wage rates. Only later do the prices of goods of the first order [i.e., of consumers' goods] follow." In this case, which still regularly recurs in modern economies, because the rise in wage rates precedes the rise in consumer goods' prices, unanticipated inflation does not produce the paradigmatic Friedmanite real wage/employment effect.

Mises (1978b, pp. 121-122) does appreciate, moreover, that the issue of fresh fiduciary media via the expansion of bank credit to business ignites a process of monetary depreciation that will typically "follow a different path and have different accompanying social side effects from those produced by a new discovery of precious metals or by the issue of paper money." In the case of the latter two sources of new money, the ensuing process of depreciation *may* feature the phenomenon of wage rates generally lagging behind the rise in commodity prices, resulting in a general decline in real wage rates and the phenomenon of "forced saving," that is, the redistribution of wealth and income from wage earners to entrepreneurs. Mises (1978b, p. 121) even allows that such an effect on real wage rates may occur "If monetary depreciation is brought about by an issue of fiduciary media, and if wage rates for some reason do not promptly follow the increase in commodity prices...."

Thus Mises (1966, p. 549) is adamant in his conclusion that, in an economy with unhampered labor markets:

> ... forced saving can result from inflation but need not necessarily. It depends on the particular data of each instance of inflation whether or not the rise in wage rates lags behind the rise in commodity prices. A tendency for real wages to drop is not an inescapable consequence of a decline in the monetary unit's purchasing power. It could happen that nominal wage rates rise more or sooner than commodity prices.

Mises's analysis leads him to seek in another direction for the explanation of the observed positive effect of inflation on the employment of labor. His explanation begins with initially-prevailing conditions of excess supply in labor markets hampered by minimum wage laws and by the restrictionist policies of legally-privileged unions. It is under these conditions, which have prevailed in most industrial economies since the 1920s, that unanticipated inflation via bank credit expansion is capable of generating a decline in real wage rates toward market-clearing levels and, consequently, a net increase in the employment of labor. As Mises ([1958] 1980, p. 154) explains:

> Under conditions of [the inflationary] boom, nominal wage rates which before the credit expansion were too high for the state of the market and therefore created unemployment of a part of the potential labor force are no longer too high and the unemployed can get jobs again. However, this happens only because under the changed monetary and credit conditions prices are rising or, what is the same expressed in other words, the purchasing

> power of the monetary unit drops.... Inflation can cure unemployment only by curtailing the wage earner's *real* wages.

Both Mises and Friedman recognize that, when the discovery is made by laborers that their real wage rates have been eroded by inflation, supply of labor curves in nominal wage space shift leftward driving up real wage rates toward former levels. For Friedman, inflationary monetary forces have displaced the real economy and this countermovement therefore represents its return to the quasi-general equilibrium state of the "natural rate of unemployment," according to Friedman ([1968] 1987, p. 394), "the level that would be ground out by the Walrasian system of general equilibrium equations, provided there is imbedded within them the actual structural characteristics of the labor and commodity markets." In Mises's analysis, on the other hand, the reversal of the drop in real wage rates occurs because "... the unions ask for a new increase in wages in order to keep pace with the rising cost of living and we are back where we were before, i.e., in a situation in which large scale unemployment can only be prevented by a further expansion of credit" (Mises [1958] 1980, pp. 154-155).

Now, unlike the Chicago price theorists, Mises and the Misesian wing of the modern Austrian school, do not believe that the market economy is ever at or even within sight of long-run general equilibrium.[8] Rather, the structure of realized market-clearing prices is seen by Austrians as functioning, despite its non-general equilibrium character, to continuously coordinate the uses and technical combinations of available resources in light of entrepreneurial forecasts of constantly shifting future market conditions, including consumer preferences.[9] Hence, for Mises, in direct contrast to Friedman, it is the decline in real wage rates toward their market-clearing levels brought about by unforeseen inflation that is equilibrating—albeit crudely and temporarily; the ensuing restoration of the former level of real wage rates by renewed union restrictionism, on the other hand, marks a reversion to a pervasive and chronic disequilibrium situation in which the labor market is precluded from establishing even a coordinative, momentary equilibrium of supply and demand, while the market's long-run *tendency* to generate a structure of final-equilibrium wage rates and optimal allocation of labor is permanently stifled.

In his critique of the Friedmanite-monetarist downplaying of the role of labor unions in shaping the inflationary process, Gottfried Haberler (1974, p. 105), who presents a Misesian analysis of what he identifies as a money-fueled "wage-push inflation,"[10] contends that the monetarists implicitly assume "a few islands of monopoly in a vast competitive sea; where monopolies existed wages and prices would be higher, production and consumption lower, but unemployment would be transitory and moderate because the labor and other productive resources set free in the monopolized areas would find employment, at somewhat lower wages, in the large competitive sector." While Haberler

(1974, p. 106) disputes the empirical validity of this assumption, even for conditions prevailing in the U.S. economy in the early 1970s, the significant point for our discussion is that the monetarist analysis is applicable only to those situations where the assumption in question holds true. Mises ([1957] 1985, pp. 76-81), in contrast, explicitly predicates his analysis of the modern inflation-adjustment process on the existence of "institutional" or permanent unemployment of labor created by political policies that foster labor union restrictionism.

In propounding his novel theory of union activity, Mises (1966, p. 376) argues that labor unions are unconcerned with the configuration of the demand curve for their product because they "... do not aim at monopoly wage rates." Unions are restrictionist, and not monopolistic, organizations, which "... are not concerned with what may happen to the part of supply which they bar from access to the market." While a monopolistic pricing policy is advantageous only if total revenue earned at the monopoly price equals or exceeds the total revenue earned at the competitive price (or if total cost falls more rapidly than total revenue between the competitive and monopoly prices), "Restrictive action ... is always advantageous for the privileged group and disadvantageous for those whom it excludes from the market. It always raises the price per unit and therefore the total net proceeds of the privileged group. The losses of the excluded group are not taken into account by the privileged group" (Mises 1966, pp. 376-377).[11]

An important implication of Mises' analysis is that the ability of unions to restrict supply in labor markets is much greater and less predictable than would be the case if they were merely engaged in monopolistic pricing, because, in the case of restrictionism, the desired shift to the left of the supply curve cannot be explained solely on the basis of the configuration of the total revenue and total cost curves. Thus, if we accept Mises' explanation of union activity, real wage rates may not be determinate within the context of a strictly catallactic general-equilibrium model from which the concept of a natural rate of unemployment is deduced. This means that economists would have to draw their assumptions regarding union goals and plans from outside the system of catallactic theorems, from historical or, what I refer to as, "thymological" analysis. They then must be prepared to admit that these goals are apt to shift, possibly rapidly, producing corresponding shifts in the natural rate and undercutting its practical usefulness.[12]

IV. MISES'S THEORY OF INFLATIONARY EXPECTATIONS

This brings us to the vexed question of Mises' approach to the theory of expectations formation and adjustment, and his view of the role played by expectations in the adjustment of real variables to monetary inflation. Edwards

(1985, p. 100) contends that "Mises' statements on the adjustment and effects of expectations in *The Theory of Money and Credit* seem to contain two distinct and somewhat contradictory attitudes and associated mechanisms," and he adduces evidence that Mises shifted back and forth in this work between the adaptive expectations and rational expectations approaches. In fact, at some points in his writings, Mises also appears to employ the assumption that expectations regarding movements of the future purchasing power of money are, to use Hicksian terminology, "rigidly inelastic" with respect to current changes in realized prices, and that such movements are thus anticipated to be completely reversed in the course of the agent's planning horizon.[13] At other times, Mises ([1932 1990, pp, 102-103) regards expectations as apparently "unhinged" from recent experience of objective market conditions, with a small increase in the quantity of money following upon a long interlude of price stability capable of driving the demand for money rapidly toward zero and precipitating an explosive upward spiral of prices. Also of significance is the fact that Mises characterizes the simultaneous actions of different groups of individuals and the simultaneous operations of different markets as often dominated by different kinds of inflationary expectations. Nonetheless, the "contradictions" that Edwards (1985, p. 104) detects among Mises's various expressions on inflationary expectations are superficial only and are resolved within an integrated praxeologico-historical account of the nature and formation of expectations.

According to Mises, all human action is aimed at substituting, from the point of view of the actor, a more satisfactory state of affairs for the state that would emerge without the actor's specific intervention in the course of events. Because of the lapse of time between the inception and the outcome of every action, combined with the ceaseless and scientifically unpredictable change in the natural environment and in the capacities, values, goals, and plans of the actor and his fellows, the future conditions that an action will impinge upon and transform can never be known with certainty but must be forecast by the agent. Thus human action is inherently entrepreneurial, or, as Mises (1978c, p. 51) puts it, "Every action is a speculation, i.e., guided by a definite opinion concerning the uncertain conditions of the future."

However, although praxeology can indisputably establish expectations as a logical prerequisite of every act of choice, it cannot shed light on the content or temporal evolution of these elements of the choice process. Praxeology deals with the logical structure and implications of action, and, as such, "... is not concerned with the events which within a man's soul or mind or brain produce a definite decision between an A and a B.... Its subject is not the content of these acts of choosing, but what results from them: action" (Mises [1957] 1985, p. 271). For insight into the concrete process of expectations formation, Mises ([1957]) 1985, p. 310) directs us to the method of "specific understanding"

(*Verstehen*) as it is utilized in the historical disciplines and "as it is practiced by everybody in all his interhuman relations and actions."

The specific understanding that is brought to bear by the historian in explaining past events is a mental process which "... establishes, on the one hand, the fact that, motivated by definite value judgments, people have engaged in definite actions and applied definite means to attain ends they seek. It tries, on the other hand, to evaluate the effects and intensity of the effects of an action, its bearing upon the further course of events" (Mises [1957] 1985, pp. 264-265). This method of proceeding is based on the insights of what used to be referred to derisively by experimental psychologists as "literary psychology," a discipline which Mises ([1957] 1985, p. 265) redubs "thymology." According to Mises ([1957] 1985, pp. 272, 266) thymology, which is a derivative of the classical Greek term denoting the mental faculty that was thought to be the source of thought, volition, and emotion, is itself a historical discipline, which:

> ... derives knowledge from historical experience ... [from] observation both of other people's choices and of the observer's own choosing .... It is what a man knows about the way in which people value different conditions, about their wishes and desires and their plans to realize these wishes and desires. It is the knowledge of the social environment in which a man lives and acts or, with historians, of a foreign milieu about which he has learned by studying special sources.

The thymological method allows the historian to "understand" a complex historical event, in the dual sense of enumerating its causes, as far as they proceed from human values and volitions, and weighting the contribution of each of the causes to the observed outcome. The weights of the various causal factors, of course, cannot be quantitatively and mechanically determined, but are a matter of the historian's necessarily subjective "judgments of relevance" (Mises 1966, pp. 56-57). Just as thymological experience serves as the basis for the historian's interpretive understanding of past events (so far as they depend on social and not natural causes), it also conditions the actor's "specific understanding of future events" or, in current terminology, his formation of expectations about the future.

Like the historian, the acting individual must base his forecast of future conditions on an understanding both of the factors operating or likely to operate in producing the future outcome and of the degree of influence exercised by each of these factors in the emergence of the final result. But these two problems, that is, of "enumeration" and of "weighting," are precisely the problems that must be solved by the historian who seeks to explain the emergence of the same situation in retrospect. Moreover, as Mises ([1957] 1985, p. 314) points out, "The precariousness of forecasting is mainly due to the intricacy of this second problem [of weighting]. It is not only a rather puzzling question in forecasting future events. It is no less puzzling in retrospect for the historian." It is to emphasize the fact that the historian and the acting individual both must use the thymological method in solving the same type of problems that Mises ([1957] 1985, p. 320) refers to them, respectively, as "the historian of the past" and "the historian of the future."

As noted earlier, concerning expectations, all that can be logically inferred from the action axiom, that is, that individuals behave purposefully by using means to achieve ends, is that they are a universal category of action, because all actions necessarily are future-oriented and take place under uncertainty. Logical deduction from the action axiom yields no information to the economist about the content and adjustment of expectations; nor is it permissible, from Mises' point of view, for the economist to simply "assume" an expectations adjustment mechanism for the purposes of generating testable hypotheses about observed economic variables. Assumptions about expectations that are to be used to supplement the action axiom in deducing catallactic theorems, like many of the other subsidiary assumptions of praxeological reasoning, must be drawn from the general thymological experience of the theorist or from more formal historical research. Mises (1966, pp. 65-66) stresses that the incorporation of such experience-based assumptions into the chains of praxeological deduction does not alter the rigidly formal and aprioristic character of economic theory, but serves to render it useful for the comprehension of specific phenomena of real human life and action. Without such a strict delimitation of its assumptions, praxeology—and, therefore, economics also—would lose its function as a science and become merely "mental gymnastics or a logical pastime."

Thus, for example, an account of the inflation-adjustment process that is based on the rational expectations hypothesis that "the unobservable subjective expectations of individuals are exactly the true mathematical conditional expectations implied by the [simultaneous equation macroeconomic] model itself" (Begg 1982, p. 30) may offer an interesting, if idle, praxeological exercise, but it offers no scientific truths about real-world inflation processes. Such a hypothesis contradicts one of the most general and important conclusions of thymology that must be accepted as a datum of economic theorizing, namely, that there exists a broad and unpredictably varying range of differences between human beings in their abilities to anticipate and adjust to change (Mises 1966, p. 255). The rational expectations approach also rejects the thymological insight that false economic doctrines may powerfully condition the public's, including especially bankers' and entrepreneurs', forecasts of the future. The influence of these doctrines on economic activity are particularly potent when they are fostered by popular political ideologies, as was and still remains the case with the "cheap money fallacy" and the "balance-of-payments theory" of exchange rates. Similarly, misleading economic doctrines also may be promoted by a layman's superficial reading of long catallactic experience. For example, the doctrine that variations in the purchasing power of money are caused solely by extraordinary events emanating from the commodity side of the economy—which dominated economic writings until the mid-sixteenth century and lay opinion up until the inflations following the First World War and which, until the inflations of the 1970s, continued to underlie conventional accounting procedures—this doctrine is a precipitate of age-old experience with commodity money standards.

Because the very function of thymology is to provide the anticipating individual with information about the social factors that are or will be operating to promote or obstruct the achievement of his goals, it is also inconsistent with the assumption of adaptive expectations, which envisages economic agents as eschewing all causal investigation and attempting to forecast future values of an economic variable by mechanically extrapolating from their past errors in forecasting the same variable. For Mises (1978c, p. 49), a being becomes "thymologically human" as soon as it begins to cast around for specific means to apply to attaining definite goals, and thus begins to investigate the causal relationships between the various elements in its social and physical environment. As a result, all market participants, when formulating the specific understanding of the future that guides their catallactic activities, are, to some degree, depending on their entrepreneurial abilities, alive to the causal factors that determine prospective economic quantities. In the marketplace, as in every department of social intercourse, therefore, "All are eager to get information about other people's valuations and plans and to appraise them correctly" (Mises [1957] 1985, p. 265).

The thymological method of dealing with expectations also stands in opposition to the position proclaimed by Lachmann (1976b, p. 129), the late exponent of Shacklian "radical subjectivism," that expectations are "autonomous" in the same sense as human preferences, and that, therefore, the economist is "unable to postulate any particular mode of change." In such a world of divergent and unpredictably changing expectations and the speculative shifts of supply and demand curves they continually evoke, according to Lachmann (1976b, p. 130), the fact that realized prices continually clear markets "has little meaning." Such a radically nihilistic view of the price-coordinating feature of the market economy, proceeding from ignorance of the derivation of expectations from thymological and catallactic experience, was long ago rebutted by Arthur W. Marget ([1938-42] 1966, pp. 228-230, 238 fn. 34, 456) in the following terms:

> For unless we are to make of the so-called 'method of expectations' the kind of *deus ex machina* which ... would lead to 'the complete liquidation of economics as a science,' we must proceed upon the assumption [which is supported by thymology] that expectations are what they are largely as the result of the experience of economic processes as they have been actually realized in the past and as they are being currently realized in the present.
>
> Thus, 'expectations' help to determine 'realized' prices. But the prices thus 'realized' *help to determine expectations with respect to the future course of prices....* When, therefore,

> it is said that 'equilibrium' is 'indeterminate' whenever 'the final position is dependent upon the route followed' all that this can mean is that no account of the actual functioning of the economic process can be regarded as complete until it undertakes, *upon the basis of a study of the successive, actually realized steps in any economic process actually unfolding itself in time*, to establish the nature of the considerations likely to determine the nature of entrepreneurial responses to changes in the market situation, *including the possible changing nature of the goals whose attainment these responses are designed to aid*.... [W]e have insisted throughout upon the necessity for accompanying any use of an emphasis upon 'expectation' by a tracing of *realized processes* in all possible detail, in order that these realized processes may be related with all possible precision to the expectations which condition them and to which they give rise. (All emphases in this passage are Marget's.)

Contrary to Lachmann, then, the moment-to-moment structure of realized prices can be explained as a coordinative outcome of past and always fallible speculative anticipations, while yet remaining a meaningful factor in the explanation of the current entrepreneurial forecasts and price appraisements that shape the future course of the market process. Expectations are thus not "autonomous"; they are rigidly circumscribed by the actor's chosen goals, the experience of success and failure he has acquired in pursuing these and earlier goals, and his entrepreneurial ability, that is, his aptitude for culling information and deducing implications from his experience that are relevant to his future actions. Nor is it "impossible to derive a group's state of expectations from its state of knowledge" (Lachmann 1986, p. 29); as an integral element of the human choice process expectations are discoverable by the methods of thymology regularly deployed in everyday life and in historical research and thus accessible to the economist as well. Accordingly, in the final sentence of the preceding quotation, Marget perceptively argues that information about the expectations-formation process can only be derived from thymological experience or historical investigation of "realized" market processes.

Ironically, Lachmann (1986, p.29), despite his strongly avowed antipositivism and radical subjectivism, declares that an actor's thymological knowledge "... must always remain problematical in the sense in which [the actor's] knowledge of molecules, machines or the human body is not."[14] But as Mises stresses, while experience-based thymological knowledge is "categorically different" from the experimentally-established "facts" of the natural sciences, it is still real knowledge nonetheless and is just as indispensable to the planning of action. "To know the future reactions of other people is the first task of acting man" (Mises [1957] 1985, p. 311).

The knowledge about future events that thymology yields is not in terms of statistical or "class" probabilities, it is true, but in terms of rankable likelihoods or "case" probabilities.[15] For example, it is through thymological experience that I "know" (as I write this in 1993) that the likelihood of each of the following events occurring in 1994 is negligible and certainly much lower than, for example, the Clinton health plan passing Congress without significant modification: my being drafted to replace Prince Charles as heir to the English throne; the United States of America being reconstituted as a monarchy; or professional football being displaced in popularity by professional soccer in the United States. I and masses of others regularly and successfully take nonstatistical but thymologically knowable likelihoods such as these into account in planning future actions.

Not only the Lachmannian position, but also the Hayekian position on expectations, elaborated so ably in the writings of Israel M. Kirzner (1973, 1979), must be rejected from a thymological standpoint. Expectations of profit gaps between future output prices and resource prices are not formed merely on the basis of "alertness" to information about past price structures; we learn nothing directly about the future by merely absorbing, passively or alertly, information about the outcomes of realized market processes.[16] Entrepreneurial appraisements of future price structures are the outcome of a specific understanding of future market conditions that must be actively produced by deliberately bringing one's thymological experiences and insights to bear on information about past prices. Such "knowledge" about future profit opportunities is, therefore, emphatically not embodied in the objective (disequilibrium) price signals of the immediate past; its source is rather internal, resting on thymological insight and impinging on external events only through the actions it motivates.

The knowledge that is yielded by thymological investigation of human activities carried out in the market or elsewhere is embodied in what Mises ([1957] 1985, pp. 315-320, 1966, pp. 59-64) refers to as "ideal types." For example, the theoretical explanation of the German hyperinflation of the early 1920s may employ the distinct ideal types "German industrial laborer," "German entrepreneur," "German foreign exchange speculator" and so forth, depending on the economic analyst's reading of the historical record that includes his own direct experience if it is relevant. Each of these ideal types differs from the others in terms of the experiences, reactions, and appraisements it postulates with respect to the depreciation of the German mark. Only understanding based on experience and careful study of the historical record can decide whether the content and number of ideal types to be introduced at different points in the praxeological chain of theoretical deductions are appropriate. For instance, it may be helpful to distinguish between the "German entrepreneur of 1919" and the "German entrepreneur of 1922" or between the "Prussian civil servant" and "the Bavarian farmer" in order to take account of the impact of different experiences and ideologies on the formation of expectations in reaction to information about a given increase in the money supply. When theorizing about the effect of a new issue of paper money on the demand for money during the final stages of hyperinflation, the economist may register his awareness of the spread of inflationary expectations to even the least entrepreneurial and most ideologically blinkered among the populace by resorting to a single ideal-typical "German income earner."

This discussion points to the solution of the continuing controversy between Misesians and Hayekians over whether economic theory can yield knowledge about human learning and interindividual knowledge-diffusion processes. As a branch of praxeology, economic theory per se cannot and need not establish a single proposition about such processes; as in the case of human goals and values, it accepts as given data for its reasoning the concrete details of what participants are capable of learning from the historical market process (as encapsulated in ideal types). The learning processes by which participants in the market acquire and interpret information are not logically deducible from universal and timeless praxeological categories; they must be "understood" or thymologically reconstructed from historical experience and then employed among the supplementary premises of aprioristic praxeological analysis to yield economic theorems that possess both logical and substantive truth.[17]

As Mises (1966, p. 66) points out, "this singular and logically somewhat strange procedure" of analyzing economic phenomena, "in which aprioristic theory and the interpretation of historical phenomena are intertwined," can lead to serious errors among its practitioners. And one of the results of the failure to appreciate and come to grips with the indispensable role of thymology and history in establishing the subsidiary assumptions of economic reasoning is precisely the unsatisfactory and seemingly irreconcilable approaches to expectations that dominate mainstream monetary theory.

The proper, thymological approach to expectations is clearly illustrated in Mises' analysis of historical episodes of inflation. For example, at the very outset of war inflation in Germany in 1914, the ideal-typical German mark-holder, which included workers, entrepreneurs, and bankers, confronted the general rise in prices with deep-seated inelastic expectations, grounded on their long experience of the gold standard era and reinforced by general acceptance of the etatist doctrine of Knapp that State power was the source of money's value. According to Mises ([1932] 1990):

> When the war inflation came nobody understood what a change in the value of the money unit meant. The business-man and the worker both believed that a rising income in Marks was a real rise of income. They continued to reckon in marks without any regard to its falling value. The rise of commodity prices they attributed to the scarcity of goods due to the blockade (pp. 101-102).

Expectations eventually began to adjust, but "it took years" even for German entrepreneurs to recognize and adapt their expectations to the true cause of price inflation, while workers were slower still to adjust (Mises [1932] 1990, p. 100). Even on the loan market, expectations adjusted very slowly. In the early stages of the inflation, after people had disentangled themselves from the grip of their long pre-inflationary experience with commodity money, what may be loosely characterized as adaptive expectations replaced inelastic expectations. During this period, the inflation premium of the nominal interest rate lagged behind the inflation rate "... because what generates it is not the change in the supply of money ... but the—necessarily later occurring—effects of these changes upon the price structure (Mises 1966, p. 545).

As the inflation progressed, it started to become clear to those possessing the greatest degree of entrepreneurial foresight that it was likely to persist and even accelerate in the future and that there were pecuniary gains to be reaped from such an occurrence. What may be termed, again very loosely, "rational expectations" began to develop first on the foreign exchange market and then later on the stock and commodity markets. Speculators on the foreign exchange market began to anticipate the effects of current and then future increases in the money supply on domestic prices and therefore on exchange rates, and there came into existence a substantial "reverse" lag between the rise of domestic commodity prices and the rise in prices of foreign exchange. Meanwhile, the high profits being earned by speculators on the foreign exchange market drew into this market speculators who previously operated on stock and bond markets. Unfortunately the experience, knowledge, and techniques that served these latter speculators well on other markets were ill-suited to the foreign exchange market. According to Mises (1978b, p. 20), the ideal-typical stock market speculator of this period was ignorant of "the principles underlying the formation of monetary value" and "He look[ed] on the monetary unit as if it were a share of stock in the government." As a result, he was apt to buy the mark after sharp declines, believing that it was due to appreciate just as sharply because the government remained stable and the economy just as productive. Thus, until they had learned from experience, the actions of the transplanted stock speculators retarded and may even have temporarily arrested the decline on foreign exchange markets of the domestically depreciating currency.

However, as long as most earners of monetary incomes failed to shake loose their ideological blinders and to recognize the irrelevance of their past experience with a commodity money, they were unable to draw the correct conclusions from their current experiences, and domestic price inflation continued to lag behind the growth of the money supply and the external depreciation of the monetary unit. Eventually, however, after years of experience with inflation, the masses of wage earners and farmers learned the lesson that rising prices were directly linked to increases in the supply of paper money, and their faith in the long-run stability of the purchasing power of money was shaken to the core. Once the masses developed "rational expectations" based on their hard won insight into the link between money and prices and indicating that monetary inflation is a deliberate policy of government unlikely to be soon reversed, hyperinflation was at hand.

Mises (1966, pp. 427-428) describes this experience-driven evolution of inflationary expectations and abrupt transition from inelastic to rational expectations on the part of the public in dramatic terms:

> The first stage of the inflationary process may last for many years. While it lasts, the prices of many goods and services are not yet adjusted to the altered money relation [i.e., the supply of and demand for money]. There are still people in the country who have not yet become aware of the fact that they are confronted with a price revolution which will finally result in a considerable rise in all prices, although the extent of this rise will not be the same in the various commodities and services. These people still believe that prices one day will drop. Waiting for this day they restrict their purchases and concomitantly increase their cash holdings....
>
> But then finally the masses wake up. They become suddenly aware of the fact that inflation is a deliberate policy and will go on endlessly. A breakdown occurs. The crack-up boom appears.... Within a very short time, within a few weeks or even days, the things which were used as money are no longer used as media of exchange. They become scrap paper....

Once people have experienced firsthand a hyperinflationary currency collapse, their knowledge and expectations are permanently altered. Even the slightest increase in the money supply will now lead all strata of the populace to forecast that the political authorities are once again embarking on a policy of deliberate inflation that will culminate in another catastrophic monetary breakdown. The public's panic-striken attempts to reduce cash holdings, on the basis of expectations that have come "unhinged" from any reasonable appraisement of the objectively evolving economic situation, would quickly catapult the economy into runaway price inflation. As Mises ([1932] 1990, p. 102) writes:

> A nation which has experienced inflation till its final breakdown will not submit to a second experiment of this type until the memory of the previous one has faded.... Made overcautious by what they suffered, at the very outset of the inflation they [i.e., victims and witnesses of the 1923 inflation] would start a panic. The rise of prices would be out of all proportion to the increase in the quantity of paper money....

There remains for us to reconcile Mises' discussion of the evolution of expectations in the course of a hyperinflation with the pivotal role he attributes to expectations in the context of his theory of the business cycle. Mises (1978b, pp. 132-136) himself realizes that there is an important problem that must be resolved. Why is it, he asks, that while the public learns the lessons taught by their experience with hyperinflation sufficiently well to undertake actions that prevent the regular recurence of this fiat-money phenomenon, "people are incorrigible" when it comes to learning how to avoid the cyclical ups and downs associated with bank credit expansion (Mises 1966, p. 578). In Mises' words, "What calls for special explanation is why attempts are made again and again to improve general economic conditions by the expansion of circulation credit in spite of the spectacular failure of such efforts in the past" (1978b, p. 136).

The answer to this question, Mises suggests, is twofold. First, there is the ideological factor: deeply ingrained in the minds of bankers and entrepreneurs is the view, which has been long reinforced by erroneous economic doctrines, that rising prices and low interest rates are a prerequisite of favorable business conditions and economic prosperity and therefore should be a goal of economic policy (Mises 1978b, pp. 138, 146). Second, this ideological factor makes it even more difficult for entrepreneurs, untrained in technical economics, to perceive the links between interest rates lowered by bank credit expansion, the capital malinvestments of the boom, and the ensuing crisis and depression that are the consequence of the sudden revelation and liquidation of the previous malinvestments. As Mises (1943, pp. 251-252) points out, moreover, comprehending these links requires much more recondite knowledge and a more rigorous intellectual effort than that required for grasping the connection between the running of the printing presses and rising prices. This is especially true when it is considered that, after the initial phase of the credit expansion, interest rates do not appear unusually low and may even appear high to the entrepreneur because of the rising inflation premium that progressively drives up the nominal rate. So, even if the entrepreneur learned the basic lesson of avoiding an expansion of his operation when interest rates initially dropped to uncommonly low levels, he would still be enticed into malinvestments as the inflationary boom progressed.

Mises (1943, p. 252) concludes that "Nothing but a perfect familiarity with economic theory and a careful scrutiny of monetary and credit phenomena can save a man from being deceived and lured into malinvestments." Certainly, thymological analysis reveals to the economist that the assumption that entrepreneurs in the contemporary world possess this prerequisite of rational expectations, that is, a grasp of the Austrian theory of the business cycle, is patently false and would lead to erroneous theoretical deductions. On the other hand, Mises chides the many economists who do not recognize that, in dealing with historical instances of credit expansion, the theorist must adjust his assumptions regarding expectations to correspond to the concrete data of the case. Thus, Mises (1966, p. 797) argues, "It may be that businessmen will in the future react to credit expansion in a manner other than they have in the past. It may be that they will avoid using for an expansion of their operations the easy money available because they will keep in mind the inevitable end of the boom. Some signs forebode such a change."

Interestingly, in the paragraph that immediately succeeds the one from which the foregoing quotation by Mises is drawn and which appears in the third (1966) but not the first edition (1949) of *Human Action,* Mises (1966, p. 798) suggests that the public as well as the financial press has learned the main lessons of the Austrian theory of the trade cycle, that is, that the boom causes the ensuing depression and that the boom itself is engendered by the preceding expansion of bank credit. The formation of expectations on the basis of this knowledge has compelled the monetary authorities to restrict credit whenever the first signs of the boom have appeared. And it is to these factors that Mises attributes the marked reduction in the observed duration and severity of cyclical fluctuations during the decade of the 1950s.

Mises's thymological approach to expectations appears to be well suited to guide applied research into developments in the U.S. economy in the 1980s and 1990s. For example, the apparently high real long-term interest rates during the so-called "Reagan recovery" may be partially or even mainly explicable as a high inflation premium on the real interest rate, which reflects persistent inflationary expectations carried over from the public's, and especially the bond market's, experience with the double-digit inflation rates of the Carter years rather than as the direct result of a "loose fiscal, tight monetary" policy that has been alleged by Keynesian and other critics. Also, the continued slow recovery from the 1990-1991 recession even in the face of substantial declines in short-term interest rates and of increasingly rapid money supply growth might be explained by reference to the reluctance of entrepreneurs and investors to employ the additional bank credit to finance long-term capital projects, because they expect the rate of return on investment ("the natural rate of interest") to be eroded by Clinton's tax increases, increased regulations, and the costs of impending health care legislation.

From the standpoint of pure theory, moreover, the thymological approach to expectations, when taken in conjunction with the Austrian theory of the business cycle, provides an account of cyclical fluctuations which, in contrast to the rational expectations-based Real Business Cycle theory, rigorously maintains the assumption of instantaneously clearing markets without having to invoke improbably large regressive technology shocks and intertemporal labor substitution models that rely on improbably elastic responses of the labor supply to transitory fluctuations in the real wage rate.

V. CONCLUSION

Mises's theory of the inflationary process has been either neglected or misunderstood by mainstream monetary theorists, because it is grounded in Austrian price theory. This theory, which owes much more to the works of Bohm-Bawerk and Wicksteed than to those of Marshall and Walras, seeks to explain the determination and the function of the prices that are actually realized in the real world of constant change and disequilibrium. In this setting, money is not merely a numeraire but is a causal factor in the market's pricing process, and Mises' step-by-step method of analysis is the only method adjusted to the requirements of elucidating such a disequilibrium economy.

Despite its disequilibrium character, however, the market-clearing process has an important function to perform in the pricing and allocation of scarce resources, a function that Hutt (1979, p. 285) felicitously describes in terms of "the dynamic coordinative consequences of price adjustment." From Mises' point of view, the coordinative social appraisement process of the market insures that the current price of every scarce resource is equal to its expected marginal revenue product (discounted by the interest rate) and thus that all existing productive resources are always fully employed in those uses that entrepreneurs consider to be most valuable in light of their knowledge of the technological possibilities and their forecasts of future market conditions, including their appraisements of prospective output prices. As I have argued elsewhere (Salerno 1991), a Misesian conceives this coordinative process as extremely hardy and no more liable to disruption by market-produced changes in the money-spending stream, for example, hoarding or dishoarding and changes in the production costs of mining gold, than by changes in the "real" data of the economic system. As Mises argues, however, the process is capable of being hampered and distorted by external intervention that undermines or nullifies its market-clearing property in resource markets, a property that may be crudely and temporarily restored by an episode of unanticipated inflation which lowers the real prices of labor and other resources toward equilibrium levels. Thus Mises' analysis explains the observed employment/output effect of inflation in a manner that is fully consistent with the microfoundations of Austrian monetary theory and without recourse to ad hoc and unrealistic assumptions about the behavior of market participants.

Regarding the second main topic of the paper, Mises developed a theory of inflationary expectations and of expectations in general that has been largely ignored by contemporary Austrians mainly because of their tendency to conflate the views of Mises and Hayek. In the case of Hayek, his assumption of "proximal equilibrium," or a state approximating perfect ex ante coordination of individual plans in which prices are normally near their long-run equilibrium values, renders expectations a trivial epiphenomenon of the knowledge culled from past prices and in no need of independent explanation. And Kirzner, who follows Hayek in some important respects, posits alertness to the knowledge conveyed by the price system as a propensity inherent in human action. In his view, entrepreneurs able to discover gaps between resource and output prices of the immediate past are fully armed to make the correct production decisions. Kirzner's procedure, which effectively transforms entrepreneur-producers into arbitrageurs alertly scanning their present environment for profit opportunities and unconcerned with the future, obviates any discussion of the entrepreneurial process of formulating expectations of the uncertain future on the basis of their thymological experience and knowledge.[18]

Perhaps, the most valuable lesson to be learned by economists from Mises' approach to theorizing about expectations is the crucial importance of realistic subsidiary assumptions for correctly deducing and applying the laws of praxeological economics to the analysis of real-world economic events and policies. Thus Mises' theory of expectations opens up an avenue to the understanding of the proper role for historical and thymological/psychological research in the elaboration of economic theory.

ACKNOWLEDGMENT

The author wishes to gratefully knowledge the comments of an anonymous referee for helping to improve this article.

NOTES

1. Mises's pathbreaking analysis of inflation developed out of his integration of Austrian marginal utility theory with Carl Menger's cash-balance approach to the demand for money and the monetary process analysis originated by eighteenth- and nineteenth-century economists such as Richard Cantillon, David Hume, and J. E. Cairnes. On Mises' contributions and doctrinal influences in the area of monetary theory, see Rothbard 1976, Rothbard 1980, pp. 14-23; Salerno 1991, pp. 367-375; Edwards 1985; Robbins [1952] 1971. In contrast to his analysis of the inflation-adjustment process, which has gained substantial recognition, Mises' innovative approach to expectations has garnered little if any attention, even from Austrian-oriented economists.

2. Lachmann (1976a, p. 58) declares that "Mises hardly ever mentions expectations, though entrepreneurs and speculators often enough turn up in his pages. Thus from 1939 onward Schackle had to take on expectations more or less single-handedly, without much benefit of support from the Austrian side."

3. According to Ebeling (1988, p. 16), "Mises's writings on monetary theory ... [are] not integrated into his theory of expectations formation, not even in *Human Action.* His theory is incompletely developed and applied within his own system." This misinterpretation aside, Ebeling's article is a valuable overview of Mises' influences and method in developing his theory of expectations.

4. It should be pointed out here that Murray N. Rothbard follows an implicitly Misesian approach to expectations in his own work. Thus the fact that Rothbard does not provide a formal explication of Mises's approach to expectations does not mean he does not "take the problem of expectations formation seriously," as Ebeling (1988, p. 12) implies. Ebeling's implication is logically unwarranted as well as uncharacteristically unperceptive and is easily shown to be in error, if we consider only a few of the most notable doctrines expounded by Rothbard in *Man, Economy and State* ([1962] 1970). In his analysis of the pricing process, Rothbard, like the great Austrian price theorists Bohm-Bawerk and Wicksteed, focuses on the determination of actual, moment-to-moment prices, whose determinants include the speculative reservation or inventory demands of sellers. Rothbard also provides explicit and extended treatments of the influence of speculative anticipations on the conformation of market supply and demand curves, of the inherently speculative cash-balance demand for money, and of the determination of the purchasing-power component of the nominal interest rate. Finally, Rothbard recognizes the key role of the promoting, uncertainty-bearing, price-appraising capitalist-entrepreneur in driving the market

process, while emphasizing the expectational element in the market's social appraisement of the capital values of natural resources and of durable capital goods.

5. Rothbard's analysis of the demand for money implies that it tends to be basically inelastic due to the high inelasticity of what he calls the "exchange" or "pre-income" component of monetary demand, which he distinguishes from the "reservation," "cash-balance," or "post-income" component. The former is expressed by the exchange for money of the services of the original productive factors, land and labor, and of existing inventories of capital and consumer goods, for which the reservation demands of their owners or producers are usually highly inelastic. On the demand for money, see Rothbard [1962] 1970, Volume 1, pp. 662-667, Vol. 2, pp. 350-356. The inelasticity of the exchange demand for money is similarly accounted for by Herbert J. Davenport ([1913] 1968, pp. 267-273). Davenport ([1913] 1968, pp. 301-303, 316-321) also provides a surprisingly modern account of the reservation demand for money as a short-run, speculative phenomenon, but he ultimately fails to integrate the two components into a satisfactory overall theory of the demand for money.

6. On the key role played by the assumption of the constancy of relative prices for deriving the neutrality of money in Patinkin's system, see Rousseas 1972, pp. 53, 72.

7. For a demonstration that the available historical evidence does not support the hypothesis that wages generally lag behind prices during inflation, see Alchian and Kessel [1960] 1977.

8. As I have argued elsewhere (Salerno 1993), contemporary Misesians differ sharply from contemporary Hayekians on this issue.

9. Thus, Mises (1990c, p. 65) describes the market as "the essence of coordination of all elements of supply and demand." For a treatment of this concept of moment-to-moment "price coordination" as the foundation of Austrian macro theorizing, see Salerno 1991. Also see the pathbreaking discussions by William H. Hutt ([1954] 1975; 1979, pp. 137-177), who christened and formalized the concept, which long had been an essential part of classical and Austrian microeconomics, and first elaborated its relevance to macroeconomic themes. Salerno (1995a) provides a survey of Hutt's contributions to economic theory.

10. For Haberler (1974, pp. 101-102) both "demand-pull" and "cost-push" inflation "... are monetary in the important sense that they require monetary expansion.... [T]here has never, literally never as far as I know, been a case of sustained inflation without a rise in M." For the continuing Austrian influences on and orientation of Haberler's later work as an American academic, see Salerno 1995b. A similar explanation of the relationship between unions, unemployment, and inflation is offered by Hayek (1972, pp. 53-97). The point of view that ascribes an important role to unions in promoting and conditioning the inflationary process has been described as "Haberlerian" by Friedman and "Pigovian/ Hayekian/ Haberlerian" by Lord Robbins (Robbins et al. 1974, p. 44). However both of these labels obscure Misess's contributions referred to above and the fact that Mises (1978b, pp. 173-203) outlined the argument as early as 1931 in a German-language publication addressing the causes of the unprecedented depth and persistence of the Great Depression. For evidence supporting the Austrian as opposed to the Friedmanite view of the influence of unions on unemployment, see Vedder and Gallaway 1993.

11. An illuminating discussion of the "restrictionist pricing of labor" can be found in Rothbard ([1962] 1970, Vol. 2: pp. 620-629).

12. While Dan E. Birch, Alan A. Rabin, and Leland B. Yeager (1982) also reject Friedman's explanation of the positive effect of inflation on the employment of labor and real output, they nonetheless do not accept the explanation of the phenomenon offered by W. H. Hutt, which is essentially the Mises-Haberler view presented above. Indeed, they dismiss it out of hand because it dares to suggest that "villainy," that is, the restrictionist pricing of labor by unions and governments, is afoot in the pricing process (Birch, Rabin, and Yeager 1982, pp. 213-214). Hutt's analysis of the phenomenon of cost- or wage-push inflation can be found in Hutt 1973, pp. 252-270. Hutt appears to have developed his own position on this issue independently of the direct influence of Mises and the Austrians, having been heavily influenced during his formative years

as an economist in the 1920s and 1930s by his teacher Edwin Cannan and other economists at the London School of Economics. The LSE economists stressed the coordinative functioning of the market process as the solution to the persistence of depressionary levels of resource unemployment and aggregate real output (Salerno 1994). In rebutting an earlier article by Yeager that argued that the shrinkage of real output below its potential level is generally attributable to unanticipated changes in aggregate monetary expenditure, which generate disequilibrium "income constraints" of the Clower-Leijonhufvud type, Hutt (1975, p. 64) countered that "... the crucial continuity [of the market-clearing process] is *always* dependent upon valuing and pricing, whether or not monetary policy is flexible, rigid, inflationary or deflationary—that is, independently of the factors which determine the purchasing power of the monetary unit." Elsewhere, Hutt (1979, p. 284) counters a similar argument by Leijonhufvud by pointing out that, "... at wage rates equal to the 'marginal *prospective* product,' all labor is immediately employable."

13. For Hick's analysis of the concept of elasticity of expectations, see Hicks [1946] 1968, pp. 240-206.

14. Hans-Hermann Hoppe (1988, p. 48 n. 37) uncovers the logical error in Lachmann's oft-repeated asseveration that the "future is unknowable," particularly future states of knowledge and actions.

15. In this particular respect, Mises' theory of risk and uncertainty resembles Keynes'. For a discussion of this aspect of Keynes' theory, see Salerno 1992, pp. 9-10, 46-47.

16. Various aspects of this controversy are critically reviewed in Salerno 1990a and Salerno 1993.

17. This contrasts with Kirzner's view that "alertness" or the ability to notice or "discover" those changes in one's environment that promise to redound to one's benefit is a propensity inherent in human action and constitutes the essence of purposeful behavior (Kirzner 1979, pp. 13-33). For a critique of Krizner's view from a Misesian standpoint, see Salerno 1993. In Hayek's case, he wrote "Economics and Knowledge" (Hayek [1937] 1972) as a plea to render equilibrium analysis applicable to the real world by incorporating into it an "empirical element" consisting of "propositions about the acquisition of knowledge" that were adequate to explaining the tendency to equilibrium supposedly observable in the actual economy. Hayek ([1937] 1972, pp. 47-48) went on to argue in general terms that the solution lay in the introduction into formal economic theory of "ideal types," meaning "concrete hypotheses concerning the conditions under which people are supposed to acquire the relevant knowledge and the process by which they are supposed to acquire it." At this stage of his thinking, and before he had made much progress in selecting the empirically relevant ideal types to serve as supplementary hypotheses, Hayk's project appeared similar to Mises'. Nine years later, however, in "The Use of Knowledge in Society," Hayek ([1945] 1972) specifically identified the overarching ideal type to be used in economic analysis—if it can be called an "ideal type," since he himself refrains from using the term in this latter article—as an economy whose prices always approximate their long-run equilibrium values and therefore convey accurate knowledge about the scattered data of the economic system to decentralized decisionmakers. Hayek's assumption of what I have elsewhere dubbed "proximal equilibrium" represents a major departure from Mises's theory of expectations for a number of reasons, but the most important are: first, that it banishes genuine uncertainty and the necessity of entrepreneurial forecasting and appraisement of future prices from economic analysis, because it implies that "current prices are fairly reliable indications of what future prices will probably be" (Hayek 1978, p. 82); and, second, that Mises explicitly denied that the actual economy harbors an empirical tendency to operate close to long-run equilibrium or even to temporally progress toward such a state. On Hayek's notion of "proximal equilibrium" and its inconsistency with Mises's theory of entrepreneurship and appraisement, see Salerno (1993) and Salerno (1994).

18. For a recent attempt at a thoroughgoing dehomogenization of the Misesian and Hayekian/Kirznerian paradigms see Salerno 1993.

REFERENCES

Alchian, A. A., and R. A. Kessel. 1960/1977. "The Meaning and Validity of the Inflation-Induced Lag of Wages behind Prices." Pp. 413-450 in *Economic Forces at Work,* edited by A. A. Alchian. Indianapolis, IN: Liberty Press.

Begg, D. K. H. 1982. *The Rational Expectations Approach in Macroeconomics: Theories and Evidence.* Baltimore: The Johns Hopkins University Press.

Birch, D. E., A. A. Rabin, and L. B. Yeager. 1982. "Inflation, Output, and Employment: Some Clarifications." *Economic Inquiry,* 20 (April): 209-221.

Davenport, H. J. 1913/1968. *The Economics of Enterprise.* New York: Augustus M. Kelley Publishers.

Ebeling, R. M. 1988. "Expectations and Expectations Formation in Mises's Theory of the Market Process." *Market Process,* 6 (Spring): 12-18.

Edwards, J. R. 1985. *The Economist of the Country: Ludwig von Mises in the History of Monetary Thought.* New York: Carlton Press, Inc.

Ellis, H. S. 1934. *German Monetary Theory 1905-1933.* Cambridge, MA: Harvard University Press.

Friedman, M. 1968/1987. "The Role of Monetary Policy." Pp. 387-403. in *The Essence of Friedman,* edited by K. R. Leube. Stanford, CA: Hoover Institution Press.

Haberler, G. 1974. *Economic Growth & Stability: An Analysis of Economic Change and Policies.* Los Angeles: Nash Publishing.

Hayek, F. A. 1937/1972. "Economics and Knowledge." Pp. 33-56 in *Individualism and Economic Order.* Chicago: Henry Regnery Company.

———. 1945/1972. "The Use of Knowledge in Society." Pp. 77-91 in *Individualism and Economic Order.* Chicago: Henry Regnery Company.

———. 1972. *A Tiger by the Tail: A 40-Years' Running Commentary on Keynesianism by Hayek.* London: The Institute of Economic Affairs.

———. 1978. *Denationalisation of Money–The Argument Refined: An Analysis of the Theory and Practice of Concurrent Currencies* (2nd ed.). London: The Institute of Economic Affairs.

Hicks, J. R. 1946/1968. *Value and Capital: An Inquiry into Some Fundamental Principles of Economic Theory* (2nd ed.). New York: Oxford University Press.

Hoppe, H. 1988. *Praxeology and Economic Science.* Auburn, AL: The Ludwig von Mises Institute.

Humphrey, T. M. 1984. "On the Nonneutral Relative Price Effects in Monetarist Thought." *Economic Review* of the Federal Reserve Bank of Richmond, 70 (May/June): 13-19.

Hutt, W. H. 1973. *The Strike-Threat System: The Economic Consequences of Collective Bargaining.* New Rochelle, NY: Arlington House.

———. 1975. *A Rehabilitation of Say's Law.* Athens, OH: Ohio University Press.

———. 1979. *The Keynesian Episode: A Reassessment.* Indianapolis, IN: Liberty Press.

Kirzner, I. M. 1973. *Competition and Entrepreneurship.* Chicago: The University of Chicago Press.

———. 1979. *Perception, Opportunity, and Profit: Studies in the Theory of Entrepreneurship.* Chicago: The University of Chicago Press.

Lachmann, L. M. 1976a. "From Mises to Schackle: An Essay on Austrian Economics and the Kaleidic Society." *Journal of Economic Literature,* 14 (March): 58

———. 1976b. "On the Central Concept of Austrian Economics: Market Process." Pp. 126-132 in *The Foundations of Modern Austrian Economics,* edited by E. G. Dolan. Kansas City: Sheed & Ward, Inc.

———. 1986. *The Meaning of the Market Process.* New York: Basil Blackwell Inc.

Marget, A. W. 1938-42/1966. *The Theory of Prices: A Re-Examination of the Central Problem of Monetary Theory* (2 vols.). New York: Augustus M. Kelley Publishers.

Mises, L. von. 1943. "'Elastic Expectations' and the Austrian Theory of the Trade Cycle." *Economica,* 10 (August): 251-252.

———. 1966. *Human Action: A Treatise on Economics* (3rd ed.). Chicago: Henry Regnery Company.

———. 1952/1971. *The Theory of Money and Credit* (2nd ed.). Irvington-on-Hudson, NY: The Foundation for Economic Education.

———. 1978a. *Notes and Recollections.* South Holland, IL: Libertarian Press.

———. 1978b. *On the Manipulation of Money and Credit.* Translated by B. B. Greaves. Dobbs Ferry, NY: Free Market Books.

———. 1978c. *The Ultimate Foundation of Economic Science: An Essay on Method* (2nd ed.). Kansas City: Sheed Andrews and McMeel, Inc.

———. 1950/1980. "Economic Aspects of the Pension Problem." Pp. 83-93 in *Planning for Freedom and Sixteen Other Essays and Addresses* (4th ed.). South Holland, IL: Libertarian Press.

———. 1958/1980. "Wages, Unemployment and Inflation." Pp. 150-161 in *Planning for Freedom and Sixteen Other Essays and Addresses* (4th ed.). South Holland, IL: Libertarian Press.

———. 1983. *Nation, State, and Economy: Contributions to the Politics and History of Our Time.* Translated by L. B. Yeager. New York: New York University Press.

———. 1957/1985. *Theory and History: An Interpretation of Social and Economic Evolution.* Auburn, AL: The Ludwig von Mises Institute.

———. 1932/1990. "The Great German Inflation." Pp. 96-103 in *Money, Method, and the Market Process* edited by R. M. Ebeling. Norwell, MA: Kluwer Academic Publishers.

Moss, L. S. 1976. "The Monetary Economics of Ludwig von Mises." Pp. 13-49 in *The Economics of Ludwig von Mises: Toward a Critical Appraisal.*

Patinkin, D. 1965. *Money, Interest, and Prices: An Integration of Monetary and Value Theory* (2nd ed.). New York: Harper & Row Publishers.

Phillips, A. W. 1958/1968. "The Relation between Unemployment and the Rate of Change of Money Wage Rates in the United Kindgom, 1861-1957." Pp. 107-119 in *Macroeconomic Readings,* edited by J. Lindauer. New York: The Free Press.

Robbins, L. 1952/1971. "Introduction." Pp. 11-13 in *The Theory of Money and Credit* (2nd ed.). Irvington-on-Hudson, NY: The Foundation for Economic Education.

Robbins, L., S. Brittan, A. W. Coats, M. Friedman, P. J., and D. Laidler. 1974. *Inflation: Causes, Consequences, Cures–Discourses on the Debate between the Monetary and Trade Union Interpertations.* Levittown, NY: Transatlantic Arts, Inc.

Rothbard, M. N. 1962/1970. *Man, Economy, and State: A Treatise on Economic Principles* (2 vols.). Los Angeles: Nash Publishing.

———. 1976. "The Austrian Theory of Money." Pp. 160-184 in *The Foundations of Modern Austrian Economics,* edited by E. G. Dolan. Kansas City: Sheed & Ward, Inc.

———. 1980. *The Essential Ludwig von Mises* (2nd ed.). Auburn, AL: The Ludwig von Mises Institute.

Rousseas, S. W. 1972. *Monetary Theory.* New York: Alfred A. Knopf.

Salerno, J. T. 1990. "Ludwig von Mises as Social Rationalist." *The Review of Austrian Economics,* 4: 26-54.

———. 1991. "Commentary: The Concept of Coordination in Austrian Macroeconomics." Pp. 325-343 in *Austrian Economics: Perspectives on the Past and Prospects for the Future,* edited by R. B. Ebeling. Hillsdale, MI: Hillsdale College Press.

———. 1992. "The Development of Keynes's Economics: From Marshall to Milllennialism." *The Review of Austrian Economics,* 6 (1): 3-64.

———. 1993. "Mises and Hayek Dehomogenized." *The Review of Austrain Economics,* 6 (2): 113-146.

———. 1994. Reply to Leland Yeager on "Mises and Hayek on Calculation and Knowledge," *The Review of Austrian Economics* 7 (2): 111-125.

———. 1995a. "William H. Hutt." Entry in *Encyclopedia of the American Right,* edited by G. Wolfe. New York: Garland Publishing, Inc. (Forthcoming).

———. 1995b. "Gottfried Haberler." Entry in *Encyclopedia of the American Right,* edited by G. Wolfe. New York: Garland Publishing, Inc. (Forthcoming).

Vedder, R. K. and Gallaway, L. E. 1993. *Out of Work: Unemployment and Government in Twentieth-Century America.* New York: Holmes & Meier.

THE INFLUENCE OF FREDERIC BASTIAT

Murray N. Rothbard

Claude Frederic Bastiat (1801-1850) has suffered from a bad historical press. His sparkling writing style led to his being dismissed as a facile and superficial writer devoid of theoretical acumen, while his devotion to laissez-faire won him treatment as a mere propagandist by critics willing to overlook other economists' commitments to more fashionable policies. Schumpeter's brusque pronouncement that "I do not hold that Bastiat was a bad theorist. I hold that he was no theorist," is typical of the treatment meted out by later economists.[1]

Frederic Bastiat was indeed a prominent and highly influential champion of free trade and free markets not only in France but throughout Europe, but he was also a distinguished theorist who made important contributions in bringing economics away from the sterile Ricardian path dominant in mid-nineteenth-century Europe. In contrast to the Smith-Ricardo emphasis on "production" and "distribution," Bastiat focused on "consumption" and "exchange." In contrast to the Smith-Ricardian stress on production of material wealth, Bastiat analyzed exchange as the mutually beneficial way in which everyone participated in the market economy. Not only that, he saw that underlying the exchange of material goods was a flow of immaterial but vitally important "services" accruing to the consumer from such goods. As a corollary, whereas the British classicists dismissed consumption from their

Advances in Austrian Economics, Volume 2B, pages 327-343.

ISBN: 1-55938-531-6

analysis, Bastiat, harking back to the pre-nineteenth century Continental Scholastic and French writers, proclaimed consumption as the goal and hence the determinant of such economic activity as production and exchange. Bastiat summed up his emphasis in his oft-repeated triad: "Wants, Efforts, Satisfactions." Consumer wants are the goal of economic activity, giving rise to efforts, and eventually yielding satisfactions. Furthermore, Bastiat emphasized the "pre-Austrian" point that human wants are unlimited, and are hierarchically ordered by individuals in their scales of value (Salerno 1988, p. 127).

Bastiat's theoretical vision allowed him to see the fallacy of the classical Smithian distinction between "productive" labor (on material goods) and "unproductive" labor (producing immaterial services). *All* goods, Bastiat pointed out, are productive, and are valued precisely because they yield immaterial services to the consumers. In this approach, Bastiat built on J. B.Say's insistence that all market resources were "productive," and that income to productive factors were payments for productivity (Russell 1965, p. 20).

Frederic Bastiat was born in 1801 in Bayonne, in southwestern France, the son of a landowner and prominent merchant in the Spanish trade. Orphaned at the age of nine, Bastiat entered his uncle's business firm in 1818; when he inherited his grandfather's landed estate seven years later, Bastiat retired from the firm and became a gentleman farmer. He spent the greater part of the next three decades in quiet study and reflection on economic problems. Fluent in English, Italian, and Spanish, he steeped himself in the extant economic literature in these languages. He was most heavily influenced by the French libertarian economists and social scientists, including J. B. Say, Charles Comte and Charles Dunoyer, and Count Destutt de Tracy.

Bastiat entered the economic literature with a sparkling attack on protectionism in France and England in the laissez-faire oriented *Journal des Economistes* in late 1844, an article that created a sensational impact. Bastiat followed this up with another article in the journal in early 1845, denouncing socialism and the concept of a "right to labor." His book *Economic Sophisms* (1845), a two-volume collection, sold out quickly, going into several editions and was rapidly translated into English, Spanish, Italian, and German.

In the summer of 1845, Bastiat, in his first trip to England, met the great laissez-faire and free-trade statesman, Richard Cobden. For the remainder of Bastiat's brief life, the two men were close friends and frequent correspondents. The two influenced each other greatly, Bastiat providing Cobden with a broader theoretical basis for his devotion to free trade, and the latter inspiring Cobden to organize a movement in France similar to Cobden's Anti-Corn-Law League. In particular, Cobden absorbed from Bastiat a devotion to natural law and natural rights, an emphasis on the harmony of individuals, groups, and nations through the mutual benefits of the free market, and a staunch opposition to war and to an interventionist foreign policy.[2]

Returning to France, Bastiat published *Cobden et la Ligue* (1845), his history of the Anti-Corn-Law League, including principal speeches and articles by Cobden, John Bright, and other leaders of the League. Bastiat set up a Free Trade Association in Bordeaux the following year, and then moved to Paris, where he organized a national Association for Free Trade, becoming secretary-general of the Association, as well as editor-in-chief of its periodical, *La Libre-Echange*. Finally, though in frail health, Bastiat participated in the revolution of 1848, being elected to the Constituent and then the Legislative Assembly, where he served from 1848 until his untimely death two years later.

Bastiat's final political service has been undervalued by most historians. While voting in the minority in Assembly, Bastiat was highly influential as Vice-President of the Assembly's Finance Committee, where he fought tirelessly for lower government spending, lower taxes, sound money, and free trade. While he was ardently opposed to all socialist and communist schemes, Bastiat elected to sit on the Left, as a proponent of civil liberties, laissez-faire, and the republic, and as a opponent of protectionism, absolute monarchy, and a warlike foreign policy. Bastiat also exerted a political impact by converting the President of the Provisional Republic in 1848, the distinguished poet and orator Alphonse Lamartine, from his previous socialism to an at least quasi-laissez-faire position.[3]

Bastiat died in 1850, leaving his two-volume theoretical magnum opus, *Economic Harmonies* only partially published; the remainder was published posthumously. Two years later, the two-volume *Dictionaire d'Economie Politique*, a monument to French laissez-faire economics, was published, with an affectionate and respectful dedication to Frederic Bastiat. It was also a fitting memorial to Bastiat that his friend Michel Chevalier (1806-1879), a former Saint-Simonian Socialist whom Bastiat had converted to free trade and laissez-faire, should have been the one to conclude, with his friend Richard Cobden, the great free-trade Anglo-French treaty of 1860, one of the high watermarks of European free trade in the nineteenth century.

Bastiat's posthumous influence was scarcely confined to his own country or to the laissez-faire movement that dominated French economics until the early years of the twentieth century. There is no space here to discuss the French economic scene. Suffice it to say that it too has suffered a bad historical press, largely because, by historical accident, Charles Gide, one of the younger pro-socialist rebels against the French laissez-faire tradition, had denounced it bitterly as "dogmatic" and "doctrinaire," in a work that was widely translated and became virtually the world's only text in the history of economic thought from the 1910s until after World War II.[4]

One country heavily influenced by Bastiat in the nineteenth century was Sweden, where Bastiat became the major authority in Swedish economics and politics. A young Swede, Johan August Gripenstedt (d.1874), met Bastiat on a trip to France, and was deeply influenced for the rest of his life by the French spokesman for laissez-faire. During the 1860s and 1870s, Gripenstedt became the leader of the economic liberals in Sweden, as well as that country's most influential politician. By 1870, Gripenstedt, almost single-handedly, had managed to eliminate all import and export prohibitions, to abolish all export duties, to reduce tariffs on manufactured goods, and to bring about free trade in agricultural products.

Shortly after Gripenstedt's death, his followers and disciples formed the Stockholm Economic Society, dedicated to the principles of Bastiat and Gripenstedt. The Society included businessmen, bankers, and academics. Some of the prominent leaders included Johan Walter Arnberg, director of the Bank of Sweden, who warned of the danger of socialism stemming from businessmen's demands for government subsidies, A. O. Wallenberg, a founder of the Stockholm Euskilda Bank, and Count G. K. Hamilton, professor of economics at the University of Lund, who was so devoted that he gave his son the first name "Bastiat" in 1865. Two prominent political leaders on behalf of laissez-faire were prominent in the Stockholm Economic Society. One was Axel Gustafsson Bennich, right-hand man of Gripenstedt, and Director-General of the Customs; Bennich was an indefatigable and joyous battler for free trade and laissez-faire throughout his long life. Another was the President of the Society, Carl Friedrich Waern, a merchant who became Minister of Finance and head of the Board of Trade. Waern resigned from the latter post because he refused to sign a law mandating protection of young timber in the private forests, a measure which he denounced as an egregious invasion of the rights of private property.

By the mid-1880s, however, statism began to make a successful comeback and gradually to become dominant, in Sweden as well as in the rest of Europe. During the 1880s, protectionists began to infiltrate the Stockholm Economic Society, and the Society also began to champion social welfare and other socialistic policies. Sweden adopted a protective tariff system in 1888. In this way, Swedish economic opinion as well as policy shifted from its original French laissez-faire orientation toward the German Historical School and its *Kathedersozialist* and "monarchial socialist" policies. This fateful change was facilitated by German being made the dominant foreign language in the Swedish public schools in 1878.[5]

Bastiat's influence was also evident in the other Scandinavian countries during the 1870s. In Norway, Lehmann wrote a popular work on economics (1874), while in Denmark, Fredericksen wrote monographs on behalf of free competition (1863), on development (1863), and on the fundamentals of economics (1874), while Gad wrote a popular manual of similar views during the 1870s (Cossa 1893, pp. 444-446).

It should not be overlooked, however, that even in Prussia, later so inhospitable to laissez-faire, a free trade party was established during the late 1840s dedicated to Bastiat's principles. The Prussian free-trade movement was led by John Prince Smith (1809-1874), son of an English father and German mother, who corresponded frequently with Bastiat. In one letter Prince Smith wrote to Bastiat:

> The friends to whom I have shown your book [*Economic Harmonies*] are enthusiastic about it. I promise you that it will be read eagerly by our best thinkers.... We hope to establish a formal league among the democratic parties and the free traders...'Bring Bastiat here,' a leader of the democrats said to me, 'and I promise to lead 10,000 men in a procession to celebrate his visit to our capital' (Russell 1965, p. 91).

John Prince Smith was born in London in 1809, the son of a barrister. On the death of his father, who had written tracts in favor of natural law and free trade, he began working at the age of thirteen for a London mercantile firm. Later he turned to journalism, traveling to Germany, where he became a teacher, and began writing articles on behalf of the free market in the 1830s. Becoming a full-time journalist, Prince Smith championed not only the free market, but also a vigorous and consistent stand against war and militarism, urging the elimination of the Prussian standing army, and its replacement by a popular citizens militia. In 1843, Prince Smith launched his lifelong crusade for freedom of trade, putting it in a historical and sociological context reminiscent of the writings of Charles Comte and Dunoyer. Moreover, Prince Smith made clear that for him, as for Bastiat, "free trade" meant not simply absence of international trade barriers, but also an absolute free market at home with the State confined only to police protection (Raico, 1988, p. 349, n. 8).

In 1846, Prince Smith, joined by several associates, sent an address to Robert Peel, congratulating the British Prime Minister for his outstanding achievement in repealing the Corn Laws. Peel's gracious and highly principled reply caused a sensation in Prussia, inspiring Prince Smith to found, that December, the German Free Trade Union.

For the rest of his life, John Prince Smith led the way in agitating for free markets and free trade in Germany. In 1860, he founded the Economic Society as the broader successor to the Free Trade Union. His home in Berlin (he had married the daughter of a wealthy Berlin banker) became a salon for liberal Prussian politicians, some of whom formed the Progressive Party. In 1858, Prince Smith helped found the annual Congress of German Economists, which was dedicated to laissez-faire until its final meeting in 1885. At the Congresses, Prince Smith delivered papers attacking usury laws, criticizing patents, and denouncing irredeemable paper money. In 1863, Prince Smith helped found and co-edited the *Quarterly Journal for Economy, Politics, and Cultural History* (*Vierteljahrschrift fur Volkwirtschaft, Politik, and Kulturgeschichte*), along with his closest collaborator, the ultra-individualst and near-anarchist Julius Faucher (1820-1878). The *Quarterly Journal* soon became "the chief theoretical organ of classical liberalism in Germany" (Raico 1988; Henderson

1950; Carlson 1972). Prince Smith also helped organize, and wrote for, a *Concise Dictionary of Economics* (*Handworterbuch der Volkswirtschaftslehrel*) (1886), modeled after the French laissez-faire *Dictionnaire d'Economie Politique*.

During the 1870s and 1880s, however, the political triumph of Bismark and Prussian militarism over classical liberalism, and his unification of the bulk of the German nation under Prussian "blood and iron," fostered the swift disappearance of laissez-faire views in Prussia and Germany. They were replaced by the dominance of statism, the German Historical School centered in Prussia, and "socialism of the chair."

Of all the European countries beside France, Bastiat and his thinking probably made the biggest and longest mark in Italy. After Bastiat founded the French Free Trade Association, an association for free trade was formed in Italy. The Italian Association established the journal *Contemporaneo* in the fall of 1846, and printed a statement hailing the French Association. While the statement lauded the accomplishments of the British Anti-Corn-Law League, it also hailed the French Association of Bastiat as more all-encompassing in its free-market position: "the British Association has declared war against only one of the evils in its own country [the tariff on Corn], while the French association has adopted a more general plan that encompasses the entire human race. It wishes to induce all nations to fraternize, and to invite everyone to the banquet of production and consumption" (Russell 1965, p. 90).

A particularly important follower and admirer of Frederic Bastiat was the man who became the unquestioned leader and dominant force in economic theory and policy in nineteenth-century Italy. He was the Sicilian-born Francesco Ferrara (1810-1900), a stalwart advocate of laissez-faire, professor of political economy at the University of Turin, and the teacher and mentor of most Italian economists of the next generation. Ferrara also played an important political role in the unification of Italy and was at one time Minister of Finance of the new nation. In addition, Ferrara was an eminent historian of economic thought, to which he contributed the editorship of the first two series of the multi-volume translation, *Biblioteca dell' Economista* (1850-1869), and especially his highly influential two-volume *Esame storico-critico di economsti e dottrine economiche* (1889-1892). In addition to Bastiat, upon whom Ferrara lavished one hundred pages in his great *Esame*, Ferrara particularly hailed the works of Say, Dunoyer, and Chevalier.

Ferrara's theoretical contributions, like Bastiat's have been systematically underweighted by modern writers hostile to laissez faire. Thus, Ferrara's "cost of reproduction" theory of value, long derided as a clumsy rehash of Ricardian "cost of production," has recently been shown instead to be a partial anticipation of subjective, marginal utility theory. Thus, Piero Barucci writes that Ferrara's value theory "was meant to be a critical reply to Ricardo's labor theory of value, in which Ferrara did not see any element of subjectiveness. With his reproduction cost he intended to work out a theory of value that took into account both the element of cost and that of utility of goods. The value of a good would be, in this way, the comparison between the utility attributed by a subject to the good itself and the cost he thinks he would have to incur to reproduce the good" (Barucci 1973, p. 260; Salerno 1988, pp.121, 260; Caffe 1987).

For several decades Francesco Ferrara's exchange-oriented and laissez-faire economics held sway among Italian economists. In the 1870s, however, the interconnected trends of protectionism and the German Historical School, as well as outright socialism, began to infest Italian economics. Ferrara valiantly combatted the new trends. A formal split occurred in 1874, when the younger statists, centered in Padua, formed the Association for the Development of Economic Studies, publishing a journal that soon became the *Giornale degli Economisti.* On the other hand, the Ferraristas, centered in Florence, formed the Adam Smith Society, and published the weekly *L'Economista.* While outnumbered, the Ferrara group produced some notable younger disciples, including Domenico Berardi, who published a critique of government intervention in 1882 and a book on money thirty years later, A. Bertolini, who wrote a critique of socialism in 1889, and Fontanelli, who published a critique of unions and strikes. In particular, we might mention Tulio Martello of Bologna, known as the last of the Ferraristas, who wrote a challenging call for polymetallism, the allowing of metallic monies such as gold and silver to circulate freely and without fixed exchange rates, in his *La Moneta* (1883).[6]

Achille Loria, the leading Italian socialist and historicist of the late nineteenth century, noted that Ferrara and his school lauded "Bastiat, considered Ricardo and [John] Stuart Mill as dangerous and sophistical theorists and abhorred the German economists" as advocates of interventionism and socialist. Although a fervent opponent of everything Ferrara stood for, Loria was gracious enough to pay high tribute to Ferrara as "the greatest Italian economist of the nineteenth century," and "without doubt the greatest genius of which the economic science of our country boasts" (Salerno 1988, pp. 121-122, 144, n. 8).

While seemingly fighting a hopeless rear-guard action against overwhelming odds, however, Ferrara and the Ferraristas hung on long enough to turn the tide, by influencing a new "army of marginalist-liberalism" led by Maffeo Pantaleoni (1857-1924). This group seized control of the dominant economic journal, the *Giornale degli Economisti* in 1890, and was to remain dominant for years thereafter (Barucci 1973, p. 264).

Not only that, it has been little recognized that unquestionably the most brilliant member of the Pantaleoni school was all his life heavily influenced by Bastiat-Ferrara laissez-faire. Vilfredo Frederico Domaso Pareto (1848-1923), was born in Paris to a noble Genoan family. Pareto's father, Marchese

Raffaelle Pareto, a hydraulic engineer, had fled Italy as a Republican and supporter of Mazzini. Returning to Italy in the mid-1850s, the senior Pareto gained a high rank in the Italian civil service.

Vilfredo studied at the Turin Polytechnic, earning a graduate engineering degree in 1869; his graduate thesis was on the fundamental principle of equilibrium in solid bodies. After graduation, Pareto became a director of the Florence branch of the Rome Railway Comapny, and in a few years he became managing director of a Florence firm manufacturing iron and iron products.

Pareto soon plunged into political writing, taking a fiery and passionate stand in favor of laissez-faire and against all forms of government intervention, defending personal and economic freedom, and attacking plutocratic subsidies and privileges to business with a fervor equal to his denunciations of social legislation or proletarian socialist forms of intervention. Pareto was one of the founders of the Adam Smith Society in Italy, and also ran unsuccessfully for Parliament twice during the early 1880s.

Pareto was not only a partisan of Bastiat and laissez-faire, he was also an admirer and follower of Bastiat's most "extreme" follower in French economics, the Belgian-born Gustave de Molinari (1819-1912), the founder of what would be later called "anarcho-capitalism," the idea that any and all services should be supplied on the free market rather than by government. Molinari became the secretary of Bastiat's Association for Free Trade when it was formed in 1846, and one of the editors of its periodical, *Libre-Echange*. Molinari published widely in the free-trade *Journal des Economistes* in 1847. Molinari pressed on to anarcho-capitalism in 1849. The remainder of his long life Molinari was a prolific champion of laissez-faire, publishing many books, and becoming the editor of the *Journal des Economistes* in 1881, remaining at that post until his 90th year in 1909.

Heavily influenced by Molinari, Pareto's writings came to Molinari's attention in 1887. Molinari then invited Pareto to submit articles to the *Journal des Economistes*. Pareto met Molinari and the other French liberals, and formed a friendship with Yves Guyot (1843-1928), one of the last of the French laissez-faire school, and Molinari's successor as the editor of the *Journal des Economistes*. Significantly, Guyot was to write Molinari's obituary in 1912. Pareto was also the Italian correspondent of Benjamin R. Tucker's individualist anarchist periodical *Liberty*, published in Boston from 1881 and the center of the individualist anarchist movement in the United States.

Shortly after he got in touch with Molinari, Pareto's mother died, and he was able to use his inherited wealth to give up his manufacturing post, become a consulting engineer, get married, and retire to his villa in 1890 to devote the rest of his life to writing, scholarship, and the social sciences. Freed of his business duties, Pareto plunged into a crusade against the State and statism, and formed a close friendship with Pantaleoni, who drew Pareto into Walrasian economic history. Pareto, in fact, succeeded Leon Walras as professor of political economy at the University of Lausanne, and also taught there until 1907, when he fell ill, and retired to a villa on Lake Geneva, where he continued to study and write until his death.

Pareto's shift into technical neoclassical theory in no way abated his ardent battle for freedom and against all forms of statism, including militarism. Thus, Pareto wrote the following in his article on "Socialism and Freedom" in 1891:

> we can group socialists and protectionists under the name of restrictionists, whilst those who want to base the distribution of wealth solely on free competition can be called liberationists.... Thus restrictionists are divided into two types: socialists, who through the intervention of the state, wish to change the distribution of wealth in favour of the less rich; and the others, who...favour the rich...these are the supporters of commercial protectionism and social organization of a military type. We own to [Herbert] Spencer the demonstration of the close analogy of these two types of protectionism. This similarity between protectionism and socialism was very well understood by the English liberals of the school of Cobden and that of John Bright and was clarified in the writings of Bastiat (Bucolo 1980, p. 44).

Pareto's writings, furthermore, are studied with appreciative and often lengthy quotes from Molinari. Thus, in his article on "Socialism and Freedom," Pareto praises Molinari for advancing a unique and bold system that "proceed(s) towards the conquest of freedom, using all the knowledge that is offered by modern science." In his "Introduction to Marx's *Capital*" in a book on Marxism (*Marxism et economie pure* 1893), Pareto was clearly influenced by the French-libertarian, Comte-Dunoyer concept of the "ruling class" as being whatever group has managed to gain control of the State. He ended the chapter with a lengthy and admiring quote from Molinari, who carried through this libertarian class doctrine. Pareto ended the Molinari quote with this sentence; "Everywhere the ruling classes have one thought—their own selfish interests—and they use the government to satisfy them" (Bucolo 1980, p. 68).

Pareto's first great treatise on economics, the *Cours d'Economie Politique* (1896), was heavily influenced by Molinari and by Herbert Spencer. In every policy, he points out, there is a minority ruling class exploiting the majority who are the ruled. Tariffs Pareto treats as an example of legal spoliation, plunder, and theft. Pareto left no doubt that his objective was to eradicate all such legalized plunder. As Bucolo points out, Pareto adopted in his *Cours* not a Marxian view of class struggle but rather the pre-Marxian, French-libertarian class doctrine. Thus, Pareto says in the *Cours*:

> the class struggle assumed two forms at all times. One consists in economic competition which, when it is free, produces the greatest ophelimity [utility]...[For] every class like every individual, even if it only acts to its own advantage, is indirectly useful to the others...The other form of class struggle is the one whereby every class does its utmost to seize power and make it an instrument to despoil the other classes (Bucolo 1980, p. 144).

Laissez-faire liberals, throughout Europe, had been gloriously optimistic during much of the nineteenth century. It was obvious that liberty provided the most rational and most prosperous system, the system most attuned to human nature, the system that works for the harmony and peace of all peoples and nations. Surely, the centuries-long shift from statism to freedom, from "status to contract" and from "the military to the industrial" (in Spencer's famous phrases), that had brought about the Industrial Revolution and enormous improvement for the human race, was destined to continue and expand. Surely, freedom and the world market were bound to expand forever, and the State to gradually wither away, dissolving into the world market economy.

The return, first, of aggressive cartelist business statism in the 1870s, followed by expanding mass support for socialism in the 1890s, however, put a rude end to the ingrained optimism of the laissez-faire liberals. The perceptive laissez-faire thinkers saw that the twentieth century would bring the shades of night, and would put an end to the great civilization—the realm of progress and freedom—that had been the product of nineteenth-century liberalism. Pessimism and despair began to grip the slowly vanishing breed of laissez-faire liberals, and understandably so. They foresaw the growth everywhere of statism, tyranny, collectivism, massive wars, and social and economic decline.

Each of the aging laissez-faire liberals reacted to this fateful trend in his own way. Spencer continued to fight to the end, placing greater emphasis on what he considered the main threat of socialism as against the business statism upon which he had previously centered his attacks. Pareto's path was to change radically into a stance of bitter cynicism. The world, he concluded, as he saw the inexorable decline of libertarian ideas and movements, is governed not by reason but by irrationality, and now it became Pareto's chosen role to analyze and chronicle those irrationalities. Thus, in an article in 1901, Pareto notes that everywhere in Europe, classical liberalism was being ground down between its two great enemies: socialism and nationalism-imperialism, "all over Europe the Liberal party is disappearing...The extremists stand face to face: on one side socialism, the great rising religion of our age; on the other side, the old religions, nationalism and imperialism" (Bucolo 1980, p. 141).

Faced with the dashing of his hopes and the looming statist hell of the twentieth century, Vilfredo Pareto, in the words of his perceptive biographer S. E. Finer, decided to "retreat to Galapagos," a remote island which, in Pareto's day, served as a metaphor and as a vantage point for a totally detached analysis and critique of the folly looming up around him.[7] The final push for Pareto down the road to "Galapagos" came in 1902, when the Italian Socialist Party abandoned its long-standing opposition to the protectionist policy of the "bourgeois" statist government. The two mighty enemies of laissez-faire liberalism had, to Pareto's horror, now joined forces! From that point on,

Pareto's retreat to a detached and aristocratic Olympian bitterness was complete (Bucolo 1980, p. 166).

The first book of Pareto's in which the new pessimistic stance becomes dominant is his *Les Systemes Socialistes* (2 volumes, 1901-1902). But his new detachment did not at all mean that Pareto had abandoned his libertarian ideals or principles or his method of social analysis. Indeed, Finer writes of Pareto that Molinari was "a man whom [he] admired till his dying day" (Finer 1966, p. 18). Thus, Pareto writes bitterly of how in society, robbery through government is far easier, and hence more attractive, than hard work for the acquisition of wealth. As Pareto mordantly writes, in a passage that anticipated such twentieth-century libertarian theorists as Franz Oppenheimer and Albert Jay Nock:

> Social movements usually follow the line of least resistance. While the direct production of economic goods is often very hard, taking possession of those goods produced by others is very easy. This facility has greatly increased *from the moment when deprivation became possible through the law and not contrary to it.* [Italics Pareto's]. To save, a man must have certain control over himself. Tilling a field to produce grain is hard work. Waiting in the corner of a wood to rob a passer-by is dangerous. On the other hand, going to vote is much easier and if it means that all those who are unadaptable, incapable and idle will be able to obtain board and lodging by it, they will hurry to do so (Bucolo 1980, pp. 149-150).

It is not surprising that Britain, laboring under a Mill-Ricardo domination of economics since the late 1840s, did not prove hospitable to Bastiat and his ideas. The leading Bastiat admirer was the exuberant and prolific Scottish maverick Henry Dunning Macleod (1821-1902). Born in Edinburgh the son of a Scottish land-owner, Macleod was graduated from Cambridge in mathematics, and became an attorney and banker. The bulk of his writing was on monetary matters, but where he deeply angered the British establishment was in daring to stand squarely against the British Smith-Ricardo-Mill labor theory of value and material concept of wealth. Inspired by Anglican Archbishop Richard Whately, Macleod enthusiastically adopted the old Continental view of subjective value and analysis of exchange as the locus of economics, exuberantly hailing the Abbe de Condillac, whose treatise on economics was also published in 1776, as the genuine founder of economic science rather than Adam Smith. Condillac, Macleod noted, "places the origin and source of value in the human mind, and not in labour, which is the ruin of English Economics." Contrary to Smith and Ricardo who believed that the labor of producers confers value on products, "Value does not spring from the labor of the producer, but from the desire of the consumer."

As if he had not given enough offense to the British economic establishment of his day, Macleod went on to hail Frederic Bastiat as "the brightest genius who ever adorned the science of Economics." Bastiat, Macleod stated, "plucked up by the roots the noxious fallacies which are the Economics of Adam Smith and Ricardo... He simply cleared away the stupendous chaos and confusion and mass of contradictions of Adam Smith..."[8]

In his revolutionary work of 1871 which brought marginalism and at least a semi-Austrian doctrine to England, W. Stanley Jevons issued a cry from the heart against the "noxious influence" of Mill over economics in Britain. Ever generous in discovering neglected forerunners, Jevons hailed Bastiat and Macleod as well as others. But Jevons himself was a marginal figure in Britain, and it is not surprising that Macleod never received his hoped-for academic post.[9]

Another admirer of Bastiat who was marginalized in Britain was the Irish-Australian economist, William Edward Hearn (1826-1888). Born in County Cavan, Ireland, Hearn was one of the last students of the great Whateleyite economists at Trinity College, Dublin, who for decades in Irish isolation were stressing an economics very different from Ricardo and Mill, an economics steeped in subjective utility and a catallactic focus on exchange. Graduating from Trinity College in 1846, Heard in 1854 became professor of modern history, logic, political economy, and classics at the new University of Melbourne in Australia.

In a country devoid of economists, Hearn had little incentive to pursue economic studies; he became Dean of the Law faculty and Chancellor of the University, as well as leader of the Victoria House. He published books on government and law. He wrote only one book on economics, but it made a stir in England. *Plutology, or the Theory of the Efforts to Satisfy Human Wants*, was published in Melbourne in 1863 and in London the following year. "Plutology" was a term that Hearn adopted from the French laissez-faire economist J.G. Courcelle-Seneuil (1813-1892) to mean a pure science of economics, a scientific analysis of human action. There are, indeed, hints in Hearn that he sought a broad science of human action going even beyond catallactics, the analysis of exchange (Kirzner 1960, pp. 202, n. 7, 212, n. 2).

Hearn's *Plutology* was patterned after Bastiat. Like Bastiat, Hearn provided a *Harmonielehre*, demonstrating the "unfailing rule" that the pursuit of self-interest produces a flow of services on the market in the "order of their social importance." Like Bastiat, Hearn began with a chapter of human wants, the satisfaction of which is central to the economic system. Human wants, Hearn pointed out, are hierarchically ordered, with the most intense wants satisfied first, and with the value of each want diminishing as the supply of goods to fulfill that want increases. As the historian of economics in Australia writes:

> It was an innovation in English political economy to begin a treatise with a chapter on human wants, and to make the satisfaction of wants a central theme... But his is an innovation only in English writing. The prominence which Hearn gives to wants is simply a reflection of his reading from French literature. His chapter is in places almost a

transcription from Bastiat's *Harmonies*, and his subtitle echoes Bastiat's frequently repeated phrase, "Wants, Efforts, Satisfactions!" (LaNauze 1949, pp. 56-58).

A champion of free trade, William Hearn called for the removal of Catholic disabilities in Britain, the freeing of the Irish wool trade, the abolition of usury laws and entail, and the removal of all restrictions on transactions in land. Hearn maintained that government's only proper function is to preserve order and enforce contracts, and to leave all other matters to individual interest.

Hearn's *Plutology* was used as an economics text in Australia for six decades until 1924—indeed it was virtually the only work on economics published in Australia until the 1920s. While the book went unnoticed upon its publication in London, it soon drew high praise from Jevons and several other economists, Jevons hailing it as the best and most advanced work on economics to date. Jevons featured *Plutology* prominently in his path-breaking *Theory of Political Economy* (1871). Despite these citations, however, *Plutology* left no further mark in Britain.[10]

As might be expected, Frederic Bastiat found a far more favorable reception in the United States, a country with a strong individualist tradition and outside the intellectual dominance of John Stuart Mill. One Bastiat admirer was Francis Lieber (1800-1872), a Prussian scholar who emigrated to the United States, and taught political economy and history at the University of South Carolina. Lieber's two-volume *Manual of Political Ethics* (1838-1839) was a comprehensive defense of the absolute right of private property, as well as its corollary, the right of free exchange of that property. In 1856, Lieber acquired the chair of history and political science at Columbia University; in his inaugural address, Lieber delivered a paean to free exchange, which is fundamental to civilized life. At South Carolina, Lieber happily taught political economy from the text of the most popular economics textbook in antebellum America, J. B. Say's laissez-faire *Treatise on Political Economy*, Lieber argued that economics teaches the idea of "the natural, simple and uninterrupted state of things in which man is allowed to apply his means as best he thinks."

It is not surprising, then, that Lieber hailed Bastiat; indeed, he wrote the introduction to the first English translation of Bastiat's *Sophisms of Political Economy* in 1848. The translation had been made by Lieber's friend, Louisa Cheves McCord (1810-1879), daughter of a former head of the Second Bank of the United States, and wife of Colonel David McCord, a protege of Lieber's predecessor at his post, the Jeffersonian Thomas Cooper, and a South Carolina banker, planter, attorney, and newspaper publisher. A devoted admirer of Bastiat, Mrs. McCord also wrote numerous journal articles denouncing socialism and communism.

But the two outstanding followers of Bastiat in the United States were two economists prominent in their day: Francis Amasa Walker (1799-1875)[11], and his close friend and younger New Englander, the Rev. Arthur Latham Perry (1830-1905).

Walker was the son of a blacksmith, who soon rose to become a successful shoe manufacturer in Boston as well as a railroad promoter. Amasa Walker retired from industrial activity in 1840, and from then on devoted himself to economics and political activity. He lectured on economics at Oberlin and Amherst, and from 1853 to 1860 was examiner in political economy at Harvard. He also served in the Massachusetts legislature and as secretary of state for Massachusetts.

Walker's major interest in economics was in money and banking, where he was a staunch advocate of 100 percent gold banking. At the end of The Civil War, however, he incorporated his monetary views into a scintillating general treatise on economics. *The Science of Wealth: A Manual of Political Economy* (1866), which proved immensely popular, at home and abroad, going into eight editions in the next eight years. Walker emphasized catallactic analysis, and employed the concepts of wealth and value squarely in the Bastiat tradition. In fact, Walker heaped a great deal of praise on Bastiat's theory of value, and proceeded to include several pages of quotes and examples from Bastiat's *Harmonies.*

But unquestionably the leading disciple of Bastiat in the United States was Arthur Lathan Perry. Perry, a graduate of Williams College in 1852, almost immediately accepted the position in which he would spend the bulk of his life, teaching history, political economy, and German at his alma mater. Perry had been introduced to Bastiat's works by his friend Amasa Walker, and he reported that "I had secretly read a dozen pages in that remarkable book [*Harmonies of Political Economy*] when the Field of Science, in all its outlines and landmarks, lay before my mind just as it does today [1883]...from that time Political Economy has been to me a new science..." (Perry 1892).

In the spring of 1864, Perry wrote a series of articles on "Papers on Political Economy," for the *Springfield* (MA) *Republican*, which set forth Perry's Bastiat-derived viewpoint on political economy. The proper focus of economic theory, he declared was value, and value is determined by the mutual services exchanged in any transaction. The crucial axiom and focus of economic analysis, added Perry, is that men exert effort in order to satisfy desires, and trade is a mutual exchange of services to bring about those satisfactions. Both parties gain from any exchange, else they would not engage in the transaction.

Encouraged by Walker, Perry expanded his articles into a textbook, published the following year. *Elements of Political Economy*, later called *Political Economy*, going through no less than twenty-two editions in thirty years. In his text, Perry paid tribute not only to Bastiat, but also to Macleod and to Macleod's vision of the history of economic thought—saluting Condillac, Whately, Bastiat, and Macleod as leaders of the correct services catallactic, or what Perry called the "All Sales" school. Engaging in a detailed and sophisticated analysis of exchange and its preconditions in values and the division of labor, Perry went beyond Bastiat to purge economics totally of the vague and materialistic Smithian concept of "wealth," to focus instead completely on exchange.[12]

True to his focus on the great mutual benefits of exchange, Perry lauded free exchange and denounced all restrictions upon that process. Perry particularly attached such virulent interferences in free exchange as minimum wage laws, labor unions, usury laws, and paper money. He was particularly vehement in attacking protectionism, writing numerous articles and delivering hundreds of speeches in behalf of free trade and against protection. The protective tariff, Perry pointed out, was unsound economically; it violated property rights, and it violated the letter and spirit of the Ten Commandments. A protective tariff stole from the Western farmer to establish privileges for a few manufacturers. Perry courageously withstood the pressure of powerful Williams College alumni, led by ironmonger George H. Ely, against his free trade teachings. After the assassination of his former student, lifelong friend, and fellow-member of the Cobden Club of Great Britain, President James A. Garfield, Perry took the highly unpopular step in New England of leaving the Republican Party as the "party of privledge" and corruption, and joining the Democratic Party. Much admired by free-trade statemen, Perry was asked by President Cleveland to be his Secretary of the Treasury.

Thus, Frederic Bastiat's work, in economic theory as well as in his championing of free trade and free markets, was scarcely the mere footnote it has been held to be by twentieth-century historians of economics. Bastiat's work in both spheres was highly influential in economic thought throughout the nineteenth century, on the continent of Europe and in the United States. It is only with the hostile rejection, among intellectuals and in political life, of laissez-faire with the arrival of the twentieth century, that Bastiat became conventionally denigrated as a mere dogmatist and propagandist.

Emblematic of the change of intellectual tides, and in its way as poignant as the disillusion of Pareto, was what happened to the Rev. John Bascom (1827-1911), a friend and colleague of Perry's who taught rhetoric at Williams. During the 1850s and 1860s, Walker, Perry, and Bascom made a formidable team for Bastiat and laissez-faire in New England. Perry persuaded Bascom to write a book on economics, and Bascom's *Political Economy* (1859) extolled the forces of production and competition in seeking profit and thereby benefiting the commonwealth. Government's only role, for Bascom, was to protect the rights of private property, so that production and competition could do their work. After Perry retired from his chair at Williams in the 1890s, he was succeeded by his old friend. By the 1880s, however, Bascom had begun to abandon the cause and to write books in the new statist discipline of "sociology." Bascom now shifted to call for government privileging of labor unions, and for abolition of the "excess" of individualism. Indeed, Bascom had come to believe that the only danger posed by socialism and communism was "unreasonable resistance to [this] organic force which is pushing into our lives."

"Growth [i.e. collectivism]," Bascom smugly concluded, "must have its way." Clearly, unlike Bastiat's beleaguered followers, John Bascom was ready for whatever the twentieth century had to offer (Dorfman 1949, pp. 178-179).

NOTES

1. Exceptional in recognizing Bastiat's theoretical importance as well as influence in the nineteenth century are Kirzner 1960, pp. 82-84; Salerno 1988; Schumpeter 1954, p. 500.
2. For Cobden's tribute to Bastiat, see Russell 1965, pp. 73-74.
3. On the problems which the laissez-faire liberals had with the revolution of 1848, which generally had an unfavorable effect on the laissez-faire movement, see Hart 1981.
4. In reaction to Bastiat, whose works introduced him to economics, Charles Gide drew inspiration from Fourier and Robert Owen to become a moral critic of the capitalist system. See Gide and Rist 1909; Dehem 1987.
5. On the Swedish Economic Society, see Hackscher 1953, pp. 105-125.
6. Schumpeter characteristically sneered at Martello's "liberalist vagaries on free coinage." See Schumpeter 1954, p. 1081.
7. See the illuminating article by Finer 1968. Even more important is Finer's (1966) introduction to Vilfredo Pareto.
8. See Salerno 1988, pp. 130-32; Rothbard 1987, p. 377. For Macleod's writings, see Macleod 1857, 1863.
9. Nor is British academic opinion any more enlightened today, as witness by the sustained sneer in the treatment of Macleod in the article by Milgate and Levy 1987.
10. Hearn's work, however, gave rise to only one plutological disciple. English attorney and mine owner Wordsworth Donisthorpe published his *Priniciples of Plutology* in 1876, which was apparently mentioned by no economic work from that day until an article in *The New Palgrave* in 1987. While the book was top-heavy on methodological distinctions, it presented an admirable discussion of relative utilities and values, engaged in a sophisticated analysis of the time structure of production, and a remarkable foreshadowing of Wicksteed's concept of withheld supply as the "reservation demand" for a good. The book certainly did not deserve to sink without a trace.

Perhaps from disappointment at the reception of the book, Donisthorpe dropped economic theory and plutology, and spent the next two decades battling on behalf of libertarianism and individualism, in law and political philosophy. See also Newman 1987. On Donisthorpe as libertarian, see Greenleaf 1983, pp. 277-280.

11. Not to be confused with his son and namesake, a moderate statist who was to become first president of the American Economic Association, (Francis Amasa Walker, 1840-1897).
12. Despite his devotion to Walker for leading him to Bastiat, and despite his being one of those laissez-faire economists to whom Perry dedicated his book, Perry privately reproved Walker for "being too much in bondage to Adam Smith." See Fine 1956, p. 52, n. 16. For an appreciation of Perry's contribution, see Kirzner 1960, pp. 75-77.

REFERENCES

Barucci, P. 1973. "The Spread of Marginalism in Italy, 1871-1890." In *The Marginal Revolution in Economics: Interpretation and Evaluation*, edited by R. D. C. Black, A. W. Coats, and C. D. W. Goodwin. Durham, NC: Duke University Press.

Bucolo, P. (ed.). 1980. *The Other Pareto*. London: Scolar Press.

Caffe, F. 1987. "Ferrara, Francesco." In *The New Palgrave: A Dictionary of Economics* (volume II). London: Macmillan.
Carlson, A. R. 1972. *Anarchism in Germany* (Volume I), *The Early Movement*. Metuchen, NJ: The Scarecrow Press.
Cossa, L. 1893. *An Introduction to the Study of Political Economy*. London: Macmillan.
Dehem, R. 1987. "Gide, Charles." P. 522 in *The New Palgrave: A Dictionary of Economics* (volume II). London: Macmillan.
Dorfman, J. 1949. *The Economic Mind in American Civilization.*. New York: Viking Press.
Fine, S. 1956. *Laissez-Faire and the General Welfare State*. Ann Arbor: University of Michigan Press.
Finer, S. E. (ed.). 1966. *Sociological Writings*. London: Pall Mall Press.
———. 1968. "Pareto and Pluto-Democracy: the Retreat to Galapagos." *American Political Science Review*, 62: 440-50.
Gide, C., and C. Rist. 1909. *Histoire des doctrines economiques* (1st ed.). Paris.
Greenleaf, W. H. 1983. *The British Political Tradition* (volume II), *The Ideological Heritage*. London: Methuen.
Hart, D. M. 1981. "Gustave de Molinari and the Anti-Statist Liberal Tradition, Part I." *The Journal of Libertarian Studies*, V (Summer): 273- 76.
Heckscher, E. F. 1953. "A Summary of Economic Thought in Sweden, 1875-1950." *Scandinavian Economic History Review*, I: 105-25.
Henderson, W. O. 1950. "Prince Smith and Free Trade in Germany." *Economic History Review*, 2: 297. Reprinted in *Britain and Industrial Europe, 1750-1870*, edited by W.O. Henderson. Liverpool, 1954.
Kirzner, I. 1960. *The Economic Point of View*. Princeton, NJ: D. Van Nostrand.
LaNauze, J. A. 1949. *Political Economy in Australia*. Carlton, Australia: Melbourne University Press.
Macleod, H. D. 1857. *The Elements of Political Economy*. London: Longman, Brown.
———. 1863. *The History of Political Economy* (volume I). London.
Milgate, M., and A. Levy. 1987. "Henry Dunning Macleod." Pp. 268-269 in *The New Palgrave: A Dictionary of Economics* (volume III). London: Macmillan.
Newman, P. 1987. "Donisthorpe, Wordsworth." Pp. 916-917 in *The New Palgrave: A Dictionary of Economics* (volume III). London: Macmillan.
Perry, A. L. 1892. *Political Economy* (21st ed.). New York: Scribner.
Raico, R. 1988. "John Prince Smith and the German Free Trade Movement." P. 349 in *Man, Economy, and Liberty: Essays in Honor of Murray N. Rothbard*, edited by W. Block and L. Rockwell. Auburn, AL: Ludwig von Mises Institute.
Rothbard, M. N. 1987. "Catallactics." *The New Palgrave: A Dictionary of Economics* (volume III). London: Macmillan.
Russell, D. 1965. *Frederic Bastiat: Ideas and Influence*. Irvington-on-Hudson, NY: Foundation for Economic Education.
Salerno, J. T. 1988. "The Neglect of the French Liberal School in Anglo-American Economics: A Critique of Received Explanations." *The Review of Austrian Economics*, 2: 113-56.
Schumpeter. 1954. *History of Economic Analysis*. New York: Oxford University Press.

SCIENCES OF POLITICAL LIES, OR GOVERNMENTS AND MARKETS OF IDEAS

Reuven Brenner

Among economists today, to say that one has the courage of his convictions—maybe to excess—is to describe a very scarce resource. No matter whether or not one subscribes to all the viewpoints, methodology, and conclusions that the school of thought called "Austrian Economics" has advanced (and I subscribe partially only), Israel Kirzner's books and articles (1963, 1973, 1980) bear witness to the message that trade is a process of discovery where entrepreneurs play central roles. What people do, according to Kirzner, is not entirely determined by circumstance, but imagination, choice, and purpose. Discovery and imagination cannot be replicated either by centrally planned agencies, summarized by simple-minded production functions and aggregates, or be described in terms of the metaphors of physics and mechanics.

These viewpoints, simple and obvious as they might seem to businessmen and the public at large, have been all but absent from the works of mainstream economists and their textbooks for the last forty years. The curious nonacademic reader will be surprised to discover that with very few exceptions,

Advances in Austrian Economics, Volume 2B, pages 345-369.

ISBN: 1-55938-531-6

the mainstream economic literature has little to say about entrepreneurship, risk-taking, discovery, imagination, inventions and innovations, new ideas, or the creative spark in general. She or he will also be surprised to learn that the metaphors of economics draw on physics rather than the everyday language of markets and business (or when they rely on the latter, they distort it out of recognition). Whatever people will think of Kirzner's work and the school of thought within which he was a leader, I am sure that people, not subject to groupthink, will feel indebted to him for keeping these viewpoints and these notions in sight.

So I thank the editors of this volume for giving me the opportunity to write this paper in Israel Kirzner's honor. I'll devote it not to further comments on his work, but apply and then extend some of his views on entrepreneurship, discoveries, competition and government intervention to the trade Kirzner himself chose to practice, and the industry he himself chose to be in: the trade of ideas, in economics in particular. I believe that there is no greater compliment to one's work than to show that notions one thought useful apply to topics of which the original author might have been unaware.

I shall also try to do something more in this paper, and argue that those who share some of the Austrian school's ideas must be ready to bring their ideas *outside* either the economic publications and circles or even the academic ones—if they want to expand this school's sphere of influence. I realize that this idea seems to contradict cherished academic principles. I shall show that today this strategy is necessary in order to counteract the pernicious effects of government intervention in the business of ideas in general, in economics and the social sciences in particular. One must then be ready to make considerable effort and try and communicate the nonorthodox ideas and findings in simple language with both specialists and nonspecialists, giving clear, concrete reasons to outsiders to see the value in such work.

I. COMPETITION AND IDEAS

Consider the meaning of "competition." Its meaning in science and business corresponds to the Austrian definition of the term rather than the so-called "neoclassical" one in mainstream economics.[1]

In science, as in business, new ideas and free-ranging imagination are the essence of the competitive process. Competition either in science or business cannot be understood, and the institutions of science and of business cannot even be evaluated by assuming, as the standard economic analysis of competition does, that all the ideas have long been invented, that all demands for new ideas have long been discovered or anticipated, and that business and science have settled down to, what mainstream economics calls, a comfortable, ever-lasting, "steady state."

Scientists and intellectuals in the market of ideas do the same thing (in principle, though, as later discussed, not always in practice) as entrepreneurs are assumed to do in the Austrian view of competition. They perceive opportunities in unsolved puzzles and in unsatisfied demands and try to respond to them by coming up with new ideas. Just like businessmen, they sometimes fail and sometimes succeed. Businessmen fail when they do not succeed to commercialize their knowledge, and they succeed when they do, solving a problem and discovering the customers' latent demands. Scientists fail when they do not succeed to solve problems, and succeed when they do.

Both scientists and businessmen take risks, and occasionally they overcome them. When they make mistakes, but not repeatedly, institutional arrangements are in place that allow both businessmen and scientists to take additional chances. If they fail in some ventures, businessmen can still have access to credit (though at a higher interest), especially if they have already shown successes in the past. The same holds true about scientists. Occasional mistakes do not destroy a scientist's reputation, though repeated ones do. The mistakes and errors in judgment are and should be expected: everyone knows that businessmen and scientists learn through trials and errors, their own or others'. Learning from mistakes is part of the process of competition.

The metaphors which describe the competitive process in the Austrian tradition thus fit the market of ideas too. In contrast, the metaphors that describe competition within the mainstream, neoclassical analyses do not. What meaning can one give in the market of scientific ideas to the view that there is competition, when there are many buyers and many sellers, who all produce a homogeneous, interchangeable product at the same price, and where there is ease of entry and exit? As far as I can see the use of this view is limited, uninteresting, and trivial. These economists have adhered to their *own* view of "competition" by they themselves offering one homogeneous product, though they competed one with the other in the mathematical techniques of offering that same simple idea. Briefly, as far as the mainstream economic view of competition is concerned, method has substituted substance.

At this stage an unavoidable question arises. One must ask how can it be that the latter approach, its view of competition in particular, became dominant during the last forty years, whereas the Austrian one found few followers and thus stayed relatively frozen in time and had a marginal influence? How can a field expand if based on false premises, whereas one based on correct premises fall behind? In order to understand the answer it is not enough—no, it is even misleading—to discuss the enterprise of "science" and "knowledge" in the abstract. One must take a closer look at the institutions of the "scientific" or the "knowledge" market and their links with institutions having political powers.

II. "SCIENCE," OR IS IT?

When Copernicus came up with his startling new story of the heavens, the critics asked: Who will place the authority of Copernicus above that of the Holy Scripture? It is not surprising that, considering the power of religious institutions of those days whose authority his ideas threatened, Copernicus circulated part of his writings among his friends only and did not want to publish them during his lifetime.[2] The Holy Scripture's view of the heavens continued to play center stage, whereas Copernicus' view stayed out of sight.

In a recently translated book, Redondi (1987) reexamines events in Galileo's life and gives a far richer, and somewhat different account of his condemnation than the customarily accepted one. He suggests that what was controversial in Galileo's views was not just his rejection of the idea that the sun rotates around the earth, but his heretical physics.[3]

Galileo's condemnation took place at a time when the prestige of the science was rising, whereas that of the Jesuits declining. The Jesuits seemed ready not only to fight new ideas, if they were found inconsistent with their dogma, but even the Pope if he endorsed some unconventional viewpoints. Their objection to Galileo's *The Assayer* was that the physical theory he presented explained sensations through "subjectivism" and "atomism." This explanation contrasted with the Jesuits' view of physics, which *was* part of their dogma.

For the Jesuits, the role of "physics" was to explain how the body of Christ transformed itself into bread and wine without anything remaining of the "substance" of the bread and wine (the dogma of the Council of Trent), but at the same time taking on "the color, taste and smell" of bread and wine. According to Redondi, the only physical theory that could explain this phenomenon was the Aristotelian, and any symbolic interpretation of the Eucharist was called "nominalist" and judged a heresy. He concludes that this issue was of primary relevance to "science", as viewed by the Jesuits during the seventeenth century. The cosmological question was secondary, though Galileo's ideas threatened institutions based on both ideas. The Jesuits used all the arms in their arsenal—persuasion, deceit, diplomacy—to reach their goal. One result was that after 1650, when a rigid orthodoxy was imposed, Italian science died (and much art with it).[4] They were only resurrected in the late eighteenth century.

The inventiveness of the Chinese happened when China did not have a rigid ideological structure. Under the Ming Dynasty, and even more so under the Manchu, when rigid Confucianism was imposed by *state* power, Chinese inventiveness ceased. There were reasons to expect this outcome. Following Confucius' teaching, becoming a government official was the only avenue of social mobility open to the ambitious and talented poor. They would have been foolish to offer ideas that could have threatened their only way to success. Whether or not these socially mobile officials believed sincerely in the teachings is a marginal issue. Acts are far more important than motives. The conformist acts survive, whereas the motives die, or, as in Copernicus' case, the motives for the conformist acts are discovered when they are of historical interest only.

Here is one of the many examples Needham (1956) discusses, showing the Chinese's persistence in error:

> ...we must consider for a moment the five-element theories from the more practical point of view as a help or hindrance to the advance of the natural sciences. They may seem odd to the modern scientific mind approaching them without reflecting on the history of science in Europe. In the hands of the adepts they attained absurdities but these were no worse than medieval European theorizing on elements, stars and humours. Looking back on all the foregoing, the five-element and Yin-Yang system is seen to have been not altogether unscientific. Anyone who is tempted to mock at the persistence of it should remember that the founding fathers of the Royal Society spent much of the valuable time in deadly combat with the stout upholders of the four-element theory of Aristotle, and other 'peripatetick fancies.'...The only trouble about the Chinese five element theories was that they went on too long. What was quite advanced for the 1st century, was tolerable in the 11th, and did not become scandalous until the 18th (pp. 293-294).

Francis Bacon (1605) commented on the persistence in error of the European schoolmen, to which Needham (1956) alludes in the previous quote. Bacon's statement too is worth quoting because it reflects accurately much of what is happening in the academic market of ideas today:

> This kind of degenerate learning did chiefly reign among the schoolmen; who, having sharp and strong wits, and abundance of leisure, and small variety of reading (their wits being shut up in the cells of a few authors, chiefly Aristotle their Dictator, as their persons were shut up in the cells of monasteries and colleges), and knowing little history, either of nature or Time, did, out of no great quantity of matter, and infinite agitation of wit, spin unto us those laborious webs of learning, which are extant in their books. For the wit and mind of man, if it work upon matter, which is the contemplation of the creatures of God, worketh according to the stuff, and is limited thereby; but if it work upon itself, as the spider worketh his web, then it is endless, and brings forth indeed cobwebs of learning, admirable for the fineness of thread and work, but of neither substance nor profit (pp. 95-95).

From these observations Bacon reached the conclusion that science should be made accessible to outsiders, should influence people in a general way, but not be used to build up research schools. This did not happen. The history of false social knowledge that passes for science, the lasting effect being due to interventions by institutions holding monopoly powers, continues to be written.

Yet the considerable evidence also shows that "fanatic" innovators could pursue their ventures and prevent a society's persistence in error *if* there were outside, nonacademic, nongovernment markets for the nondogmatic ideas. Indeed, Needham (1956) concludes his detailed history of the lack of inventiveness of scientists in China by noting that sticking to the cherished principles of science does not provide insurance against persistence in error. Access to commercial interests—outsiders, entrepreneurs who cannot afford being dogmatic—does.

He notes that for the Chinese: "Interest in Nature was not enough, controlled experimentation was not enough, empirical induction was not enough, eclipse prediction and calendar calculation were not enough—all of these the Chinese had. Apparently a mercantile culture alone was able to do what agrarian bureaucratic civilization could not—bring to fusion point the formerly separated disciplines of mathematics and nature—knowledge" (p. 44). Looked upon from this angle, these famous examples from the past show that once science and politics intermingle, erroneous ideas in science can persist for longer periods of time, and the checking procedures of "science," about which more will be said later, fail even in the natural sciences.

The relationship between government interventions providing various degrees of monopoly power and persistence in error on one side, and more commerce (that is, greater access to "outside markets") and more innovations in science on the other, also comes to the fore when one looks at the next sequence of events.

"If anyone had asked during the quarter-century of wars that followed the French Revolution of 1789, where true science was to be found," wrote Knight (1986)," the answer would have been 'in France'" (p. 25). In chemistry, astronomy, and mathematics, the French were then the undisputed leaders. But science became centralized more quickly in France than in England. Once this happened, "it was difficult to stand out against this orthodoxy; the very efficiency and centralization of things meant that a small group exercised a great deal of power and patronage in Paris, which was the center of action. Newtonian heresies had more chance to develop in Britain, where patronage in the early years of the century was not yet much in the hands of men of science and there was no strong centre."[5]

Ben-David and Zloczower (1972) describe in detail the centralization of science in Germany. The German universities, during the nineteenth century and the beginning of the twentieth century, served as models of academic institutions, but by the end of the nineteenth century their vitality diminished. The initial rise was due to the fact that the German cultural area extended over the major part of Central Europe, exceeding the limits of any German state. Thus, central national universities, like Paris in France or Oxford-Cambridge in England, did not arise. Innovations were thus more easily introduced since the universities were in perpetual rivalry and had access to funding from various sources.

The eventual decline of the universities took place because of political changes. The universities came to depend on the whimsical support of a few members of the ruling, military-aristocratic class rather than the diversified business, middle class. Because of this reason the situation of the universities became precarious, and when demands for both increasing the number of chairs and granting academic standing to new, practical, subjects were rejected, the scientific enterprise's decline in Germany started (Ben-David and Zloczower 1972, pp. 48, 56-58).

Now consider two examples from medicine. While the use of mesmerism as therapy in the early ninteenth century was just promising, its use as anesthetic was startling. Parssinen remarks that before the introduction of ether in 1847 in Britain, "British surgeons either drugged their patients with alcohol or opium, or gave them nothing at all. Especially after 1842, mesmerists began to report large number of cases in which their patients underwent major surgery—for example, the removal of a tumour or a limb—completely insensible to pain while in a mesmeric trance" (Parssinen 1979, p. 107). Yet, in spite of enjoying the support of one of the leading medical men of the day, Dr. John Elliotson (1791-1868), a professor of medicine at the young University of London, and the obvious evidence, the medical establishment denounced the practice as quackery, as fraud. It forced Elliotson to resign from his position at the university and ridiculed his followers. The practice was eventually ignored. Parssinen shows how the medical establishment used their power outside the scientific establishment to discard mesmerism, since it threatened their social and professional status and aspirations.[6] A similar sequence of events is documented by Webster (1979), who shows how institutions linked with traditional medical occupations, to whom governments gave monopoly powers, have succeeded to restrict the practice of acupuncture in the West, in spite of its proven benefits.[7]

In France, and to varying extents in all Europe, there is still today much control from the top, politicians and bureaucrats deciding who gets the grants for scientific work (Coutu 1983). The money then goes to the "Grand Chef" (Big Professor), who then decides what to do with it. The outcome has been best captured by Gleick (1987) when he described what has happened in France in the field of applied mathematics:

> Bourbaki [a school of thought in mathematics] succeeded as his founders could not have imagined. Its precepts, style, and notation became mandatory. It achieved the unassailable rightness that comes from controlling all the best students and producing a steady flow of successful mathematics. Its dominance over the Ecole Normale was total and to Mandelbrot [a father of fractals, chaos theory and much of today's applied mathematics], unbearable. He fled Normale because of Bourbaki, and a decade later he fled France for the same reason, taking up residence in the United States. Within a few decades, the relentless abstraction of Bourbaki would begin to die of shock brought on to by the computer... But that was too late for Mandelbrot, unable to live with Bourbaki's formalism and unwilling to abandon his geometrical intuition (pp.89-90).

Similar arrangements and consequences characterize Japanese universities too. An article in *The Economist* in 1988 titled "No Ideas, Thanks, We're Academics," describes them in these words:

> Japanese universities are one of the strictest members-only parts of clubbish Japan. An academic career is organized around a *koza*, a chair. The chair is really a team consisting of a full professor, an associate professor and a few assistants. Its job is to carry out the full professor's research. Young academics are expected to do the legwork and help out with teaching undergraduates; they do not carry out research of their own... professors pick the best undergraduates to join their *koza*.... They get lifetime appointments within a couple of years, and are thereafter promoted by strict seniority. (Hence the outrage over Mr. Nichibe's [a professor at Tokyo University, Japan's Oxford] attempt to bring in an assistant professor who had not worked his way up through the professor's *koza*). Ten years at each level is common, with a professorship hovering in the mid-40s. That brings with it a place on the most powerful institution in any Japanese university, the board of professors, which alone can appoint new professors and so re-start the dismal promotional cycle.

As Rauch (1993) notes, though he does not link the groupthink with the government-sustained institutional arrangements, the consequence has been that Japanese universities "are, by international standards, backwaters; [Japan's] record on intellectual innovation is bleak. From 1901 to 1985 Japan won five Nobel Prizes in science." One of them, Professor Susumu Tonegawa, who was trained at Kyoto University, won the Nobel prize in medicine for work done in Europe and America. He said that he could not have done this work if he had stayed inside the stifling Japanese university system.[8] Although the aforementioned article notes that Kyoto University at least tries to circumvent the *koza* system by creating university research institutes.[9]

This brief summary of evidence—and I did not even refer to the well-known ones from the once communist countries—shows that abstract scientific principles cannot prevent persistence in error even in the natural sciences when, one way or another, governments intervene giving access to monopoly powers. Scientists appear to adhere to the cherished, abstract principles of science. In fact they circumvent them. People's thinking, those of scientists in particular, is not independent either from institutional arrangements at universities or broader considerations in society at large.[10] Let us now turn and show where such sequence of events lead in the social sciences, economics in particular.

> *I do not wish to hide the fact that I can only look with repugnance... upon the puffed-up pretentiousness of all these volumes filled with wisdom, such as are fashionable nowadays. For I am fully satisfied that... the accepted methods must endlessly increase these follies and blunders, and that even the complete annihilation of all these fanciful achievements could not possibly be as harmful as this fictitious science with its accursed fertility.*
>
> *Kant*

III. PERSISTENCE IN ERROR IN THE SOCIAL SCIENCES

Hegel's obscurity is well known. Scientists of the time, uncorrupted by politics, did not take him seriously. Schopenhauer, quoting Shakespeare, described his philosophy as "such stuff as madmen tongue and brain not."

What was then the source of Hegel's initial power and his lasting reputation? His philosophy about the advantages of concentrating power in the hands of the state, and that all learning should be subordinated to state interest—an idea drawing on Plato—fitted his employer, Frederick William III. It was he who, in Schopenhauer's words:

> ...installed [Hegel] from above...as the certified Great Philosopher. [But Hegel] was a flat-headed, insipid, nauseating, illiterate charlatan, who reached the pinnacle of audacity in scribbling together and dishing up the craziest mystifying nonsense. This nonsense has been noisily proclaimed as immortal wisdom by mercenary followers and readily accepted as such by all fools, who thus joined into as perfect a chorus of admiration as had ever been heard before....Governments make of philosophy a means of serving their state interests, and scholars make of it a trade...(Popper 1950, pp. 228-229).

Popper, who brought attention to this sequence of events, also notes that Schwegler, an admiring disciple of Hegel, does not dispute the facts surrounding the source of his teacher's influence, even if he disagrees with Schopenhauer's views of Hegel's philosophy. Schwegler recognized that "The fullness of [Hegel's] fame and activity...properly dates only from his call to Berlin in 1818. Here there rose up around him a numerous, widely extended, and...exceedingly active school; here too, he acquired, from his connections with the Prussian bureaucracy, political influence for himself as well as recognition of his system as the official philosophy; not always to the advantage of the inner freedom of his philosophy, or of its moral worth" (Popper 1950, p. 229).

Now consider features in the establishment of macroeconomics as a field of science. Initially, many prominent economists agreed with Keynes that in the particular circumstances of the 1930s, spending on public works, even for digging "holes in the ground" (as Keynes put it), was a proper, temporary solution. The critics did not disagree with Keynes' idea about the occasional usefulness of public works, but with the novelties: both the obscure definitions and the theories Keynes put forward to justify government expenditures on such works and, mainly, with his elitist suggestion that depressions can occur regularly in decentralized economies unless politicians' wisdom, based on economists' theories, prevented them. The latter was the theory's controversial feature, and not Keynes' idea of the occasional usefulness of public works, which had ancient roots and for which one didn't need to come up with new theories.[11]

The idea appealed both to politicians, who could expand their powers by relying on economists' theories, and to economists seeking power. Since there were strong monetary and other incentives to become Keynesian, I just do not find it particularly surprising that many economists became Keynesians. By saying this I do not want to imply what Schopenhauer says about Hegel and his followers that Keynesians were charlatans, but merely say that economists, like anyone else, respond to incentives. Once they do, delusions can be powerful, especially when they serve one's interests, and I have no doubt that, as a result, many economists became sincere Keynesians.

People in general, academics in particular, invent and manipulate symbols when responding to incentives. Later, they shape their behavior in response to the ideas and symbols they have invented. Looked upon from this angle, the market of ideas works like any other market within which people respond to incentives. When monarchs believed in astrology, and had for almost two centuries councils of astrological advisers, there were many astrologers who wrote mathematical treatises on the subject and checked predictions of their models. Some also believed, sincerely or not sincerely, that what they did was scientific. A few confided in their private correspondence that they were in this business for the money, though they did not believe a word of their astrological forecasting. The great Kepler belonged to the later group, and confessed that he made predictions based on astrology to make a living. Maybe someone will discover in the future how many Keynesians, or economists for that matter, really believed in what they were doing during the last fifty years.

It also becomes clear from the evidence already presented why economists' ideas, be they Keynesian, Monetarist, Austrian, or fit the "supply-side" school, can be overturned and discredited through political manipulations, no matter which school has been scientifically closer to the "facts." For, "facts" and "science" become mercurial when governments manufacture the "facts," and when "scientists" expect governments to use their "contributions" and bestow on them honors and an aura of "science." That is the reason why the cherished principles of "positivism" sometime fail for decades and even centuries, and why "facts" and "science" did not and cannot provide lasting remedies against erroneous government policies.

To make this point concrete, let us continue the brief summary of the history of macroeconomics, and show how Keynes' political idea was transformed into a neutrally-sounding "scientific" theory.[12] In 1932 the U.S. Senate decided that information about national income should be prepared for the years 1929-1931, and nominated Simon Kuznets for the task. In 1942 he published the National Income and its Composition, 1919-1938. However, by 1947, and in his later writings, he became critical of the thoughtless repetition of his calculations. Meanwhile, Milton Gilbert, Head of the National Income Division of the Department of Commerce in the U.S. Government, a man influenced by Keynes' ideas, advocated the use of national income measures for examining relationships between defense expenditures and total output. Neither Kuznets's criticism during the 1950s nor that of Oscar Morgenstern during the 1960s about the unreliability of the numbers, because of both conceptual and practical reasons, had any impact.

The use of aggregate statistics gained much legitimacy with the publication of *A System of National Accounts and Supporting Tables* in 1953 by the Statistical Office of the United Nations. In spite of the fact that Kuznets warned explicitly against both the use of uniform methods of calculation for all countries and the difficulties of interpreting such aggregate data in developing countries, the United Nations report on its first page described their "outstanding use...in connection with public policy."[13] The illusion of macroeconomics as a science was enforced. Now there was "hard," neutral, positive-sounding, numerical evidence to support it. Statistical tests could be run on relationships concerning undefined and unreliable measures of consumption on undefined and unreliable measures of the neutral sounding terms of "national product."

Nothing could be proved or disproved since by using different statistical methods on unreliable and undefined numbers one could always come up with something—that is why "positivism" confined to this field of study doesn't lead anywhere (whereas commonsense arguments may). If issues come and disappear from sight in macroeconomics, it is not because they are checked and rechecked in attempts to falsify, but because people get bored with them. However, once topics are out of sight for a while, they can be rediscovered, especially if a change in the political arena agitates hopes of their re-use. The renewal of interest in Keynesian and Phillips-curve analyses in 1993 in the United States had little to do with science and much to do with the fact that democrats won.

The emphases on national aggregates kept the view out of sight, that in one country such products measured something that people wanted, whereas elsewhere they measured things that rulers and governments wanted; torture, prisons, hospitalization of dissenters, military and other expenditures among them. The fact that behind the aggregate counting there is a strong assumption that the relation between governments and citizens is, like in a private transaction, based on an exchange of services, was soon forgotten. The macroeconomic models, summarizing the working of the economy in a few simple-minded equations, have led to the same predictions whether "production" and "output" referred to something disastrous or something positive. Since employment by governments and the governments' "output" have been added to employment and to whatever was produced in the nongovernment sector, respectively, and since there are good reasons, though not "macroeconomic ones," for governments to intervene and be able to do constructive things at times,[14] it is no wonder that government expenditures were found to create both jobs and output from time to time. By using these numbers unquestioned, economists transformed a self-serving political idea, with the help of extensive government subsidies to bureaus of statistics and to academics, into a neutrally-sounding scientific debate about numbers and statistical methods, keeping political institutions out of sight.

Macroeconomics became thus a nonthreatening theory that could be taught at many universities around the world. The students became teachers, and macroeconomics and the illusion of comprehensible "objective," national aggregates a myth, one that governments and bureaucracies have had the incentives to sustain and promote. Students, some ambitious and others passionate to find and understand the best, living with the illusion that what they are taught at universities must have passed scientific scrutiny, drove themselves hard to understand the obscure languages of macroeconomics and the shallow, silly works. By the time some matured and noticed that emperors had no cloths, they might have faced the dilemma Kepler faced, and either do as he did and disguise beliefs, or drop out of the "scientific" enterprise. As to the mediocre followers—they stayed and sustained the enterprise unquestioned, writing most of the "scientific output," checking it, publishing it, and insisting that everyone should go through channels controlled by them.[15]

> *When...the plasticity of men, and especially their capacity for transforming themselves by their own creative activity, is omitted from the model, it becomes a caricature and, if applied to reality, leads only to errors and absurdities.*
>
> *Isaiah Berlin*

IV. ECONOMICS—IN BROADER CONTEXT

When discussing the dismalness of economics, Mencken (1959) not only noted the obscure language and dull style in which the economic treatises of his days were written (in contrast to Adam Smith's, Bentham's and Mill's works, whose styles he admired), or the ostracism of those who deviated from orthodoxy,[16] but also that when he was reading these works a troubling question bothered him: "What would happen to the learned professors if they took the other side? In other words, to what extent is political economy, as professors expound and practice it, a free science...?"[17]

Harry Johnson (1977) raised a similar point and argued that economics has no universal validity, since one cannot separate the question of wealth distribution from other questions traditionally examined by economists. He too suggested that the separation occurred because of accidental, political reasons, noticing that:

> [T]he position of economics as a 'hard' science in the United States is unparalleled, in comparison to its position in other countries, both 'Western' and 'communist'....This unique character can, in turn, be associated with more fundamental characteristics of American society...Most societies are stable enough, sufficiently static, and enough used to poverty to make sharing what there is a major political issue...By contrast, American

> society...emphasizes production and efficiency...Hence economics, which in its production aspect emphasizes minimizing inputs, becomes 'science,' whereas, when the problem is sharing what is available fairly among claimants, it remains philosophy (Johnson 1977, p. 101).

To put it differently, in a society in which people could expect to move up and down the social ladder—the case of the United States and, until recently, only few other countries—the issue of the distribution of wealth was relatively less pressing and less important than in another society, or at another time, when and where expectations of social mobility could not be held.[18]

Yet economists do not make the distinction between the two types of society either in their models, or in interpreting national statistics. Bureaus of statistics compute the macroeconomic numbers in the same fashion for all societies, and theories have used these and other numbers and did not make distinctions when interpreting them. Once this happens, the political dimension of the problems under examination disappear, and the language used to describe economic events appear to be politically neutral. I have shown before how the terms "aggregate output" or "production" have achieved this goal. Other linguistic innovations, now thoughtlessly used, give an equally misleading neutral signal.

Consider the term "input." It leaves out innovation, entrepreneurship, risk-taking, and human creativity in general.[19] By omitting them from the language, economists have also omitted them both from their models and from discussions on the broader conditions in society that give rise to such creativity.[20] The models became a caricature. When applied, they have led to bad policies. Yet, as one can infer from the previous discussion, the resulting narrowness, instead of diminishing such models' appeal, might have promoted them since politically they became nonthreatening altogether.

Indeed, Harry Johnson has also pointed out that the transition from social philosophy to social science in the American economic profession's view of itself, occurred in response to the agonies of the McCarthy period. Despite the largely successful defense of academic freedom at the time, Johnson remarks that the long-run effect was the inculcation of habits of self-censorship which directed economists toward research and toward theorizing about how the American economic system worked and away from dangerous thoughts about the possibility of revolutionizing it.[21]

Another accidental event that has shaped economics into what it is today, was the launching of the Sputnik by the Soviet Union in 1957. The apparent Soviet lead in technology seemed to many in the United States to be due to deficiencies in the educational system. A major program of federal support for education was launched in 1958, under the National Defense Education Act. The following numbers give a rough indication of the expansion that took place.

Between 1960 and 1983, undergraduate enrollments trebled, growing from 3,227,000 to 9,707,000, the proportion of young people attending college rising from 34 to 58 percent. The greatest growth occurred in state schools of the second rank and in two year colleges. Whereas in 1960, schools with two-year programs accounted for only 14 percent of all enrollments, by 1982 such institutions were handling 42 percent of the undergraduate students. In 1962, professors were relatively young, with 44 percent in their twenties or thirties. By 1981, fewer than a quarter were under forty.[22] Johnson (1977) argues that economics, more than the other social sciences, enjoyed a free ride on this federal bandwagon and the declared government interest in scientific research as a general panacea for the domestic and international problems of American society.[23]

An unexpected consequence of such sudden expansion was the hiring of people who became "scientists" only by this chance event when making a choice of career, rather than any particular interest in science in general, economics in particular (Hacker 1986; Bowen and Schuster 1986). However, Huxley (1963) predicted the ruinous effects of such sudden expansion on science:

> Let us face the facts. A large number of young people take up scientific research as a career these days, but regrettably few are impelled into it by a passionate curiosity as to the secrets of nature. For the vast majority it is a job like any other job... Moreover it is not generally realized outside of academic circles how far a mediocre research worker can get... In commerce and industry there are those who are exceptionally endowed with brilliance, ruthlessness or luck and achieve proportionate success; then come the vast majority who somehow manage to get through, and the minority who go under. The proportion of scientists who actually go under is probably much lower and the weeding process is correspondingly less effective. Indeed, the relative security and stability of the research career are probably more attractive to mediocrities than the romance of inquiry to the brilliant ones (pp. 72-73).

Such people turned out to be ideal candidates to become blind followers, leading to a slow, continuous decline in the vitality of many disciplines. The decline has been reflected in the shift that took place in the content of undergraduate courses in the social sciences in the United States during the 1960s.

Graduate school preoccupations took hold in many schools, undergraduate studies reflecting the way the disciplines were conceived at the doctoral level. Faculty members started to spend much of their time discussing the work of their fellow professors, and gave more attention to the models of their discipline than to concrete evidence. Johnson (1977) remarks that in economics this trend was on its way already in the postwar period, when large numbers of GI Bill-supported veterans started to pursue graduate studies. It had then become clear "that the least-risk way for graduate student to surmount the hurdle of the Ph.D. qualification and establish his professional reputation was to develop and apply some new mathematical or statistical technology. At the same time, testing and certifying competence of this kind was a more manageable task for the academic teachers than certifying Ph.D's by the traditional university standard of demonstrated knowledge of an extensive literature and originality of some ill-defined kind in devising and solving an intellectual problem, particularly in view of the large number of institutions and departments, often of rather pedestrian caliber, involved in processing them."[24] In other words, the subsidized, mediocre professors started to count rather than maintain responsibility and use judgment.

Thus, the obscurity, irrelevance of sterile, unfalsifiable mathematical speculations and other features that characterize social sciences today, economics in particular, do not just reflect reactions of practitioners in any academic discipline to insure themselves, but consequences of far broader considerations and of accidental events linked with government's interventions in the business of ideas, whose effects were not always foreseen.

With all this evidence in mind, let us now look more closely at the process through which "science," "political science," and "philosophy" all become mercurial when institutions with political clout interfere in the business of ideas, even if cherished principles of science seem to be fulfilled.

V. WHEN DOES SCIENCE FAIL?

To show why the usual checking procedures of science fail when governments intervene, let us contrast first the procedures in this case with the "ideal" principles of science.

When one scientist goofs, it is an individual error of judgment. What is puzzling at first sight in the abundant evidence from the history of sciences, as well as other fields of human activity, is not one or the other scientist's or innovator's error of misjudging a new theory, a new finding, a new product, but that scientists *as a group*, or people as a group, get things wrong frequently and persistently. When one encounters such evidence in the field of science, one may raise these questions:

- What can go wrong with the established checking procedures in science on which the credibility of science rests?
- How can such groupthink be established and persist in science? Why are creativity and imagination constrained to very thin domains?
- How can one fight such groupthink, once established?

"Science" is one of the products of the "knowledge" or the "information" industry, consisting of a set of statements which, to quote Rauch (1993), "have been found worthy and which we rely on" (p. 39).

But found worthy by whom? In the abstract, the answer is straightforward. Scientists have established institutions to settle disagreements: discussions in scientific seminars, conferences, anonymous peer reviews. These institutions' goal is to find "worthy" statements and prevent persistence in error. To achieve the goal scientists adhere to two rules—in principle. Rauch puts these rules in simple words:

> No one gets the final say: you may claim that a statement is established as knowledge only if it can be debunked, in principle, and only insofar as it withstands attempts to debunk it.
>
> No one has personal authority: you may claim that a statement has been established as knowledge only insofar as the method used to check it gives the same result regardless of the identity of the checker, and regardless of the source of the statement (pp. 48-49).

In other words, if one wants one's work to be recognized as "knowledge," be incorporated in textbooks and taught, one must adhere to the aforementioned rules of the scientific game. Scientists are supposed to be offended if told to teach anything as "knowledge" because it serves someone's political interests. Only claims thoroughly checked by none in particular—and certainly not just by members of one group—should be considered "knowledge" and be taught. Yet, all these principles can be circumvented once governments intervene.

At the beginning of this chapter I drew a parallel between the world of business and the world of science, and pointed out that as far as the response to incentives is concerned, the producers of knowledge are not different from anybody else. Drawing such parallel becomes once again useful and helps show how governments' intervention distorts the scientific process.

If a producer tries to sell a product but finds no buyers, he may either decide to do something else, go bankrupt if he persists, or, if he finds creditors, he may continue to try and sell. Banking and legal institutions are among those who determine the outcome. For companies traded on stock markets, the fluctuations in price give an indication of people's expectations of the viability of an enterprise. Even if a company has no revenues whatsoever, it can still secure credit if people expect that innovations in future will lead to successful commercializations. And the contrary, a company may have substantial revenues and profits today, but if it is expected to have small ones in the future, it will be unable to secure long-term credit.

This process, and the institutions within which it takes place, prevents persistence in error as far as decisions in business are concerned, and as long as governments don't interfere directly. Once they do, the picture changes. If governments subsidize an industry, for whatever reason, giving it a large advantage in price or guaranteed access to markets, businesses in this industry can persist even if innovators could have offered better substitutes and at less than the nonsubsidized price. This market can "persist in error," offer inferior products, and can even pay pliable intellectuals to come up with theories rationalizing the government's intervention. Meanwhile the innovator who wants to bring his innovations to life, can move to another country where this particular industry is not subsidized, appealing to *outsiders* for credit. If the innovator stays, he will direct his energies to other matters.

This process gives us insights into the ways in which conflicts in the sphere of ideas are being dealt with too. False ideas can have lives of their own once governments give subsidies to this business (guaranteed credit, that is). Just as for other trade, error then persists. When governments have the incentive to subsidize a particular myth and pass it for science, it becomes "science."

Professors specialize in it, write articles about it, which are then published in subsidized books and journals, passing peer reviews limited to a select group of "insiders." The books and journals are bought by subsidized libraries to stay on subsidized shelves, and are then quoted. The government subsidizes conferences in this field of study, hires the professors as consultants and bestows on them honors and prizes.[25] The signals of the game of science are all there, but being subsidized by the government, they are all false. That is why when a contrarian finds himself in these circumstances, he faces the same options as the aforementioned innovator: either turn away from pursuing a scientific career altogether if disagreeing with the orthodoxy, or appeal directly to outsiders. If one doesn't pursue either of these options, he can expect to languish in the margins of academia. Just as the entrepreneur in business could not expect credit from his competitors, an innovator in science cannot secure "credit" from his opponents, in particular if he threatens their subsidized livelihood.

Bad ideas and obscure writings thus persist and pass for deep thinking and science. Since the producers of knowledge, like the producers of anything else, respond to incentives, academics will come up with mainly minor, technical, nonthreatening elaborations of the initial ideas that fit the political interests to start with. Nevertheless trivial ideas will be—and have been—praised for their great originality and as major scientific contributions. The ideas spread, since academics teach them at universities, journalists repeat them in the media, and the government bestows money, honors, and power on all these practitioners, whereas nonorthodox views stay out of sight and mind.

Once this happens, vain, venally ambitious young idea peddlers call attention to themselves by claiming to have found depth and greatness either in the sometimes shallow, silly, obscure works or those having political-rationalizing functions. Hegel's, Marx's, and Freud's works and Keynes' *General Theory* and his followers' works are among the prominent examples. Through constant, implicit or explicit government-subsidized repetition, such works have found many mediocre followers both at universities and outside them. Though the followers have also aroused opposition, which *eventually* has led or might lead to preventing persistence in error, for many years the debate has only managed to transform discussions on obscure or self-serving political ideas to serious and "scientific" causes.

How *many* years has depended on just how far governments got involved in the business of science or what happened to established political powers. Once governments or groups having monopoly powers granted by governments become deeply involved, there is no reason to expect that debates confined to the "scientific" community would prevent persistence in error. Much will be written and nothing said. Skeptical scientists, uncorrupted by politics and willing to say something, will have to look beyond the "scientific" procedures and institutions if they want to try and defeat their rivals, who, sincerely or not sincerely, consider themselves to be "the" scientists, and keepers of "the" flame.

When a discipline arrives at this stage, all the cherished principles of science have been violated—and yet, superficially perceived, they all seem fulfilled.[26]

The skeptical reader may raise a question at this point and ask: Well, and what about those whose ideas advocate no government intervention, or, like me, advocate that the type and extent of government intervention should be decided by citizens in sequences of referenda and initiatives, a political system that helps voters learn through trial and error? (Brenner 1991b, 1994, chapter 6). Isn't this group pliable too, trying to satisfy "business" interests? The answer is no. Intellectuals cannot establish dogmatic schools of thought by shaping their ideas to anticipate handouts from business interests. Businesses cannot afford either being dogmatic or paying for dogmatic academic schools—as long as they do not have monopoly powers granted by governments. Once they do, then of course they can. Yet when the latter is the case, then we are back to square one: the cause for persisting pollution in the business of ideas, resulting in dogmas, is government, not business.

VI. MONOPOLY POWERS AND THE MYTH OF THE FRAMEWORK: WHY POPPER IS RIGHT AND KUHN WRONG?

How are all these arguments and evidence about science in general, of the effect of degrees of monopoly power in particular, linked with the ongoing much-discussed debate between Kuhn and Popper about the nature of the scientific enterprise? Let me show, based on the evidence and arguments presented here, that although Popper is right, Kuhn's arguments are at times close to the facts. However, the occasional correspondence is not because his view—which does not make reference to links between scientific enterprises and those having monopoly powers—is correct. The occasional fit is due to interventions of enterprises having monopoly powers on the scientists' views, effects that Kuhn (1970, 1977) forgot to take into account.

Sir Karl Popper argued that science "grows" when scientists explore the limitations of accepted theory, or subject a current theory to maximum strain, (Kuhn 1979, p. 5) and he gave detailed examples of many such events (Popper 1963). In contrast, Kuhn argued that one cannot characterize the scientific enterprise by such occurrences. Moreover, he argued that without what he called "normal science," the revolutionary one that Popper demands could not take place. For, he pointed out, "it is normal science that discloses both the points to test and the manner of testing.... No puzzle-solving enterprise can exist unless its practitioners share criteria which, for that group and for that time, determine when a particular puzzle has been solved" (Kuhn 1979, pp. 6-7).

Kuhn's is a logical thesis, but, as Popper has pointed out, it is mistaken, and he called it "The Myth of the Framework." Popper admits that "we are prisoners caught in the framework of our theories; our expectations; our past experiences; our language." However, he concludes that we are prisoners in a Pickwickian sense: if we try, we can break out of our framework at any time: the Myth of the Framework only "exaggerates a difficulty into an impossibility" (Popper 1979, pp. 56-57).

Popper also linked Kuhn's view of "normal science" to teaching in general and not only in the social sciences. He noted that:

> [N]ormal science... is the activity of the non-revolutionary, or more precisely, the not-too-critical professional: of the science student who accepts the ruling dogma of the day; who does not wish to challenge it; and who accepts a new revolutionary theory only if almost everybody else is ready to accept it—if it becomes fashionable by a kind of bandwagon effect. To resist a new fashion needs perhaps as much courage as was needed to bring it about... The 'normal' scientist... has been taught badly.... He has been taught in a dogmatic spirit: he is a victim of indoctrination. He has learned a technique which can be applied without asking for the reason why (p. 53).

Thus adherence to framework is due to a mediocrity's interests, which, if subsidized, becomes stronger. However, the stronger adherence is not a necessary feature of science.[27]

Popper suggests that there is no reason why people could not change their minds, or why two or more lines of research could not be pursued simultaneously in a field of scientific inquiry and be taught: on one side, to continue to examine implications of a traditional approach and, on the other, be in doubt and speculate that such an approach may be inaccurate and explore other ideas. If many scientists had doubts and told their students about them, it would be easier to break traditional, mainstream, ways of thought, and thus be in a permanent state of innovations in science. Who is right, Kuhn or Popper?

Popper's suggestion is sensible: many businessmen pursue *exactly* the strategy he advocates—*when* fearing competition. They continue with their traditional line of business and, at the same time, they are both constantly on guard about what their competitors might come up with, and they think about innovations and inventions and make investments so as to facilitate their appearance.[28]

Now there is little doubt that scientists also do what Popper is advocating—but only during what he calls the "revolutionary periods." Then, although scientists still continue to work within the traditional framework, they are also open to conversion. The question is whether this observation—of the scientists being of two minds so rarely—is due to a particular, *necessary* feature of the scientific enterprise, as Kuhn suggests, or is it due to the use of degrees of monopoly power which slow down innovations, lead to persistence in error, and thus insure some scientists' reputations, status, wealth, and peace of mind.

Popper is far closer than Kuhn to the truth. In science, as in business, the degree of innovation varied with the degree of monopoly power. When scientists had less protection and less security of one form or another, departures from conventions occurred more frequently. This means that more people deviated from the established framework, nonorthodox thinkers being able to expect to have a scientific career. Persistence in error could be prevented. If Kuhn was right, one should *not* observe such variations across countries and time for the same disciplines. After all the "purely scientific crises," that in his view are at the root of "scientific revolutions," are the same in a specific field, whether the scientists live in a country where they have greater monopoly power or in one where they have less. Geography and national boundaries play no role in Kuhn's abstract view of the scientific enterprise.

However, such variations, according to national borders, should be expected if in some societies, but not in others, scientists had access not only to the usual tools of their enterprise—peer reviews, publications, decisions on grants and others, control of publications in their field—but could also expect to rely on institutions outside this enterprise, guaranteeing varying degrees of power. "The Myth of the Framework" should be much stronger in the latter societies than in the former. This has been the case.[29]

Kuhn's description is accurate *when* scientists succeeded to get some monopoly power. Once a school of thought obtained monopoly power on "truth," the scientific revolutions Kuhn describes will indeed be viewed as "irrational," a matter of "mob psychology" (Lakatos 1979, p. 178). Where Kuhn is mistaken, is in his view that such sequence of events should *necessarily* characterize the scientific enterprise in general, rather than being linked with institutional features providing degrees of monopoly power which created "the mobs" to start with. Kuhn ignores this possibility, as well as the lapse of "normal science" into "scientism," the latter meaning the appearance of adherence to the abstract principles of science of publication, peer reviews, falsifiability, while in essence violating them.

In contrast, Popper's arguments are based on the perception that whenever one does not observe "revolutionary science" one must be suspicious that we are indeed in the stage and age of "scientism." Lakatos (1979) shares Popper's point of view, and uses the language of "competition" when referring to the scientific enterprise, concluding that: "The history of science has been and should be a history of competing research programmes (or, if you wish, 'paradigms'), but it has not been and must not become a succession of periods of normal science: the sooner competition starts, the better for progress" (p. 155). However, he neither examines why it isn't, or how the persistence in error is linked with the exercise of degrees of monopoly powers.

Briefly, Kuhn's idea of the importance of the paradigm and its enormous popularity in academia must be taken with a grain of salt. It is a very convenient idea and serves the interests of today's subsidized scientists admirably.[30] Whether they really believe in the "paradigm," in the shared framework (as Kuhn would like to think), or they just pretend to is secondary. As I emphasized before, deeds are far more important than motives.

VII. CONCLUSIONS

By all this, and with all the respect, I do not intend to absolve completely the School of Austrian economics from blame of their present marginalized condition. I hope they will admit it: there is no dishonor in admitting mistakes, on the contrary.

The main fault of its practitioners has been that in their debate with mainstream economists they put undue emphases on clarifying the meaning of all terms and finding flaws in mainstream economists' definition. Instead they should have examined facts about innovations, risk-taking, government intervention and entrepreneurs—and not only the deeds of those to whom they have given positive connotations. Pirates, once on high seas and now on super-highways, Robin Hoods, smugglers, drug dealers, and intellectual charlatans seeking political rents are entrepreneurs too.[31] Some, though not all of these notions, justifiably played crucial roles within this school of thought's departure point. Those who believed in it should have examined their concrete implications.

They also should have contrasted their view of prosperity within which the commercialization of knowledge played the central role with the silly macroeconomic and Solow-type growth models, in which there was neither commerce nor knowledge. If they pursued these lines of inquiry, and brought their findings in clear language to the attention of a wide audience, contrasting the facts examined from this angle with the frivolous game-playing of much of macro- and mainstream economics, I have little doubt that the situation in economics would be different today.

It is unfortunate that those sharing some of the Austrian School of thought's departure point did not pay attention to Popper's observation that "philosophy, which for twenty centuries has worried about the meaning of its terms, is not only full of verbalism but also appallingly vague and ambiguous, while a science like physics which worries hardly at all about terms and their meaning but about facts instead, has achieved great precision" (Popper 1950, pp. 215-216). By just affirming principles and eschewing *concrete* evidence (though shunning aggregate national statistics was a good idea), the Austrian School was marginalized. Maybe those believing partially or completely in this school's teachings should have also remembered that facts and ridicule kill more effectively than serious philosophizing and fault finding.

But I don't know and do not want to speculate how much more effective the School of Austrian economics would have been if its members pursued these strategies. One must take into account the fact that during this time economists sharing some of its tenets would have had to fight the powerful, ruinous effects of government-subsidized trends on pliable economists around the world. Maybe they could never have fought successfully the comfortable, technical, politically nonthreatening economic models from which commerce, entrepreneurship, and innovations were all absent, and within which governments played so many benevolent roles. The latter served political interests, whereas emphases on innovations, entrepreneurship, risk-taking would have raised uncomfortable political questions and numerous doubts. Anyway, sunk costs are sunk costs. The only interesting question about them is whether or not one derived lessons from such past investments.

The most important lesson is to get out of today's mindset which requires a "serious" economist to try and respond to unintelligible, pedantic, and pompous texts in economics and the social sciences, published in subsidized academic publications, by writing in a similar vein for other subsidized academic publications. There are times when one has to discard the attitude that there is something unscientific in wanting to attract the attention of a wide-reading nonacademic audience *directly* to some findings, without going through the now-customary, academic channels and writing in the dreary style required by typical academic publications.

Let me repeat what is at stake here. The public distrusts today not only economists, but universities too, and with some excellent reasons. They realize that much of the dull, obscure writing gives academics insurance. The public cannot attack what academics write either because they cannot get through the thickets of jargon, or because academics say nothing of interest, even if they write a lot. These circumstances can provide the perfect timing for going directly to the nonacademic audience and try to put an end to subsidized scholarly publications in economics, and for that matter in all the social sciences and humanities as well.

All these disciplines deal with human behavior. If academics have something new to say about it, why shouldn't they say it in plain language? Why shut out all but specialist academics? The larger the market, the more information would be brought to it, and the faster inferior products—pollution of minds in this case—would be eliminated. Checking each other's claims through public criticism in the market of ideas seems to me the only legitimate way to decide who is right, in matters dealing with human behavior in particular (maybe by establishing a futures market where one could bet on ideas?) (Hanson 1994). Anyone who believes in markets, as practitioners of the Austrian School of thought do, must have reached by now this conclusion.

True, such attitude requires that somebody *has* something concrete to say, and *is* willing to make strong, clear statements. I hope that more economists in the future, not subject to groupthink, will do so, finding inspiration in Israel Kirzner's views on the links between competition and free-ranging imagination.

REFERENCES

Bacon, F. 1605. *Advancement in Learning* [*Philosophical Works*].

Ben-David, J., and A. Zloczower. 1972. "The Growth of Institutionalized Science in Germany." Pp. 45-60 in *Sociology of Science*, edited by B. Barnes. Middlesex: Penguin.

Bercuson, D. J., R. Bothwell, and J. L. Granatstein. 1984. *The Great Brain Robbery: Canada's Universities on the Road to Ruin.* Toronto: McClelland and Stewart.

Brenner, R. 1983. *History–The Human Gamble.* Chicago: University of Chicago Press.

———. 1985. *Betting on Ideas.* Chicago: University of Chicago Press.

———. 1987. *Rivalry.* Cambridge: Cambridge University Press.

———. 1990. "Innovations and Antitrust." Pp. 235-257 in *Perspectives in Industrial Organization*, edited by B. Dankbaar et al. Boston: Kluwer.

———. 1991a. "Extracting Sunbeams Out of Cucumbers: Or, What Is Bad Social Science and Why is It Practised?" *Queen's Quarterly*, 98 (3): 519-553.

———. 1991b. "Canadian Choices." Pp. 117-148 in *Economic Dimensions of Constitutional Change*, edited by R. Boadway, T. Courchene and D. Purvis. Kingston: John Deutsch Institute.

———. 1994. *Labyrinths of Prosperity.* Ann Arbor: University of Michigan Press.

Colander, D., and R. Brenner. 1992. *Educating Economists.* Ann Arbor: Michigan University Press.

Coutu, D. L. 1983. "European nations Fret Over Mounting Losses of Scientists to the U.S." *The Wall Street Journal*, October 21.

Friedman, M. 1972. *Capitalism and Freedom, 1962.* Chicago: University of Chicago Press.

Gleick, J. 1987. *Chaos.* New York: Penguin Books.

Hacker, A. 1986. "The Decline of Higher Education." *The New York Review of Books*, February 13.

Hanson, R. 1994. "Could Gambling Save Science? Encouraging an Honest Consensus." *Social Epistemology*, forthcoming.

Hayek, F. A. 1948a. "Economics and Knowledge." *Economica* (Feb. 1937). Reprinted in *Individualism and Economic Order.* Chicago University of Chicago Press.

———. 1948b. "The Use of Knowledge in Society." *American Economic Review* (Sept. 1945). Reprinted in *Individualism and Economic Order.* Chicago: University of Chicago Press.

———. 1979. *The Counter-Revolution of Science, 1952*. Indianapolis: Liberty Press.

Huxley, A. 1963. *Science and Literature*. New Haven: Leefe's Island Books.

Johnson, H. G. 1977. "Economics and the Radical Challenge: The Hard Social Science and the Soft Social Reality." In *Culture and Its Creators*, edited by J. Ben-David and N. Clark. Chicago: University of Chicago Press.

Keynes, J. M. 1936. *The General Theory of Employment, Interest and Money*. London: Macmillan.

Kirzner, I. M. 1963. *Market Theory and the Price System*. Princeton: D. Van Nostrand Co.

———. 1980. "The Primacy of Entrepreneurial Discovery." Pp. 3-30 in *The Prime Mover of Progress*. London: The Institute of Economic Affairs.

———. 1973. *Competition and Entrepreneurship*. Chicago: University of Chicago Press.

Koopmans, T. 1957. *Three Essays on the State of Economic Science*. New York: McGraw-Hill.

Knight, D. 1986. *The Age of Science*. Oxford: Basil Blackwell.

Kuhn, T. S. 1970. *The Structure of Scientific Revolutions*. Chicago: University of Chicago Press.

———. 1977. *The Essential Tension*. Chicago: University of Chicago Press.

———. 1979. "The Logic of Discovery or Psychology of Research?" Pp. 1-25 in *Criticism and the Growth of Knowledge, 1970*, edited by I. Lakatos and A. E. Musgrave. Cambridge: Cambridge University Press.

Kuznets, S. 1942. "National Income and Its Composition." *National Bureau of Economic Research*, 2.

Lakatos, I., and A. E. Musgrave (eds.). 1979. *Criticism and the Growth of Knowledge, 1970*. Cambridge: Cambridge University Press.

Lakatos, I. 1979. "Falsification and the Methodology of Scientific Research Programmes." Pp. 91-196 in *Criticism and the Growth of Knowledge, 1970*, edited by I. Lakatos and A. E. Musgrave. Cambridge: Cambridge University Press.

Mencken, H. L. 1959. *Prejudices*. New York: Vintage Books.

Mendelsohn, E. 1977. "The Social Construction of Scientific Knowledge." Pp. 3-26 in *The Social Production of Scientific Knowledge*, edited by E. Mendelsohn, P. Weingart, and R. Whitley. Dodrecht: D. Reidel.

Morgenstern, O. 1963. *On the Accuracy of Economic Observations*. Princeton: Princeton University Press.

Mulkay, M. 1972. "Cultural Growth in Science." Pp. 126-142 in *Sociology of Knowledge*, edited by B. Barnes. Middlesex: Penguin.

Needham, J. 1956. *Science and Civilization in China* (volume 2) *History of Scientific Thought*. Cambridge University Press.

Parsinen, T. M. 1979. "Professional Deviants and the History of Medicine: Medical Mesmerists in Victorian Britain." Pp. 103-120 in *On the Margins of Science*, edited by R. Wallis. Keele: University of Keele.

Popper, K. 1950. *The Open Society and His Enemies*. Princeton: Princeton University Press.

———. 1979. "Normal Science and Its Dangers." Pp. 51-59 in *Criticism and the Growth of Knowledge, 1970*, edited by I. Lakatos and A. E. Musgrave. Cambridge: Cambridge University Press.

Rauch, J. 1933. *Kindly Inquisitors*. Chicago: University of Chicago Press.

Redondi, P. 1987. *Galileo: Heretic*. Princeton: Princeton University Press.

Shapin, S. 1979. "The Politics of Observation: Cerebral Anatomy and Social Interests in the Edinburgh Phrenology Disputes." Pp. 139-178 in *On the Margins of Science*, edited by R. Wallis. Keele: University of Keele.

Tintner, G. 1968. "Methodology of mathematical Economics and Econometrics." In *International Encyclopedia of Unified Science*. Chicago: University of Chicago Press.

United Nations. 1953. *A System of National Accounts and Supporting Tables. Studies in Methods, no. 2*. New York: Department of Economic Affairs, Statistical Office.

Wallis, R. (ed.). 1979. *On the Margins of Science*. Keele: University of Keele.

Webster, A. J. 1979. "Scientific Controversy and Socio-Cognitive Metonymy: The Case of Acupuncture." Pp. 121-137 in *On the Margins of Science*, edited by R. Wallis. Keele: University of Keele.

Whitley, R. 1974. *Social Processes and Scientific Development*. London: Routledge and Kegan Paul.

THE "OBJECTIVITY" OF SCHOLARSHIP AND THE IDEAL OF THE UNIVERSITY

Don Lavoie

I. INTRODUCTION

> In order to justify universities and research institutes, and what they can and should be, besides responding to the dominant interest in the economy, one has used, for decades, a differentiation which does not exist. I mean the difference between applied research and basic research. In truth there can be no other research except basic research. That means there is no other type of research except research which in its own activity is not concerned about the practical and pragmatic purposes which may be related to it. The freedom of the will to know consists exactly in pursuing to the end all possible doubts and one's own possible self-critique. So it is already indicated that the situation of the university in modern society is necessarily a critical one. It must seek to discover a balance between the duty to prepare students for a profession and the duty to educate which lies in the essence and activity of research. Not without reason has the characteristic word for industrial work, namely the word 'industry' [Betrieb], been extended into the research sector. We speak unreservedly of the research industry and regard our place of work as an industrial institution. In fact, all the professions we know are dependent upon the research industry and teaching industry—the doctor, the lawyer, the economist, the minister, and not to forget all the teachers who through their profession indirectly have the broadest area of influence in the modern state. We need to think through the continual opposition between the educational task of the university and the practical utility which society and the state expect from it (Gadamer 1986, p. 49).

Advances in Austrian Economics, Volume 2B, pages 371-403.

ISBN: 1-55938-531-6

What is scholarly "objectivity?" It is both a false hope and a legitimate value.

The legitimate value the word "objectivity" names is that of making a serious effort to honestly disclose the truth, regardless of the temptations the world may place before us to do otherwise. It refers not only to a seriousness about the pursuit of truth, but a passionate, unswerving, incorruptible doggedness about following the research wherever it goes, a patience to keep trying when easy answers don't readily appear, a willingness to risk one's deepest beliefs against the claims of others, and a commitment to listen to others in order to learn. It is a demanding moral criterion, involving, as Gadamer puts it, "pursuing to the end all possible doubts and one's own possible self-critique." When it is achieved it embodies the fundamental ideal of higher education. The university, when it is what it aspires to be, is a haven for those who adhere to these values, and who enhance one anothers' capabilities by engaging in unrestrained discourse in terms of them. The main thing students can get from a college education is to learn the virtue of these values, and to make them their own. I will call this idea of objectivity "openness."

The false hope the word objectivity also names is that of achieving this legitimate value by means of an institutional or intellectual separation from the world. Institutionally, the hope is couched in terms of (somehow) insulating the scholar from the temptations of market rewards or of political power. Intellectually, the hope is couched in terms of (somehow) attaining a stance of value-freedom, of either unprejudiced theoretical contemplation or direct empirical observation, which manages to forget or suppress the situated moral context from which the pursuit of truth always proceeds.

I'll call this false ideal of objectivity "detachment," and will criticize it in sections II and III. My critique suggests that "historicism" is the culprit. Historicism may be defined as the point of view that seeks to dispense with theory in the human sciences. It pursues this goal by trying to completely sever theory from any involvement with the empirical world from which theoretical questions arise, and to which they are directed. It demands of the empirical investigator a detachment from her own presuppositions, and an immersion in the details of the historical process under study. Pointing to the critiques of historicism provided by the economist Ludwig von Mises and the philosopher Hans-Georg Gadamer, I argue that scholarship needs to recognize its connectedness to the institutions and intellectual values which it serves.

I contend that the intellectual and institutional ideals associated with detachment are both impossible and undesirable. The institutional dangers of market and political "contamination" are misleadingly put, and exaggerated as compared with other sorts of dangers. And the intellectual ideal of detachment encourages the belief that moral values do not belong inside the scholarly world, a belief that does little to promote the inculcation of the moral virtues which in fact objectivity as openness demands. The two notions of detachment together have been positively harmful, making the noble ideals of scholarship an easy target of derision, and leading to a real crisis of higher education, in which the value to society of scholarly objectivity in the legitimate sense of the term is now widely unappreciated.

Universities have often been attacked from the ideological left for "prostituting" themselves to market and political forces instead of serving their own ideals. The notion of prostitution is suggestive of the prevailing attitude. Scholars, it is feared, are selling their souls to outside clients in order to eke out an existence. The danger to "objectivity" comes from external influences, from the temptations of private sector consulting money, or lucrative government contracts, which lure the scholar toward projects that pay the rent, and away from the sorts of genuine research that would be called for by the current state of knowledge. To improve, that is, to become more objective, universities need to restore their own sources of funding, so that their scholars will not be shopping around for monetarily attractive but intellectually dubious projects. For these critics, detachment, either institutional or intellectual is the ideal, but poverty and human imperfections prevent many scholars from attaining it.

Recently the academy has come under fierce attack by critics from the other end of the ideological spectrum, conservatives such as Anderson (1992), Bartley (1990), Bloom (1987), D'Souza (1991), Sowell (1993), and others.[1] The extraordinary venom of the language with which some of these writers condemn higher education is a sign of the extent to which the university's basic legitimacy in contemporary society is at issue. In a well known diatribe against higher education, *ProfScam*, Sykes (1988, p. 7) calls American universities "vast factories of junkthink." A book review in the catalogue of the classical liberal bookstore, Laissez Faire Books, asks whether higher education can be "revived from its cesspool of mediocrity and corruption."[2]

For the conservative critics detachment is still the relevant consideration, but instead of idealizing it, they demonize it. They contend that higher education is comfortably insulated from market forces, and identify this insulation as the cause of its increasing irrelevance. Arrogant professors, it is said, do research on whatever interests them, regardless of what their "customers," the students, want. Professional advancement in the academic community is gauged by standards that are formed internally to that community, and in complete disregard for the question of how the results of academic efforts can help anybody outside of academia. The claim by the critics is that were academics to view themselves more as entrepreneurs in the intellectual marketplace, instead of privileged aristocrats in the ivory towers, the university would be better able to serve society. The solution lies in forcing the academics to show more deference to the outside world upon which they are dependent, stop judging themselves by their own self-serving criteria, and start obeying their customers. "Consumer sovereignty" should dictate their activities.

Many scholars respond to this in horror, offended at the implication that universities ought to abandon responsibility for maintaining their own standards of scholarly quality, that they should succumb to the crass discipline of impersonal and amoral market forces. They insist that their sublime activities in the pursuit of scholarly values ought to maintain a protective distance from the grubby world of commodities, that what higher education aspires to has nothing to do with the peddling of wares to customers.

Some of the attacks, from either side, on the irrelevance of modern university research are certainly deserved. There is much "research" going on in academia which it would be difficult to defend as worth anything to anybody. Much of it, as the leftists contend, is the research paid for by outside contracts and grants, which often promises little intellectual fruit. And also much of it is generated by internal priorities, which, as the conservatives argue, are frequently too isolated from real world relevance. But the preoccupation with the issue of detachment distracts us from the real problems of contemporary scholarship.

I will attempt to defend universities from both of these kinds of critiques. I will contend that both the right- and left-wing critics of universities exhibit a basic misunderstanding of markets when they take consumer sovereignty to mean that producers meekly substitute the consumers' standards of quality for their own. Israel Kirzner's important contributions to economics show, on the contrary, that entrepreneurs in the market are often active inventors of solutions that no consumer has yet imagined, and that they are not passively obedient to the consumer's unilateral dictates.

Like the conservative critics, I support the idea that scholarly production should be responsive to competitive market forces. But like the leftists I respect the ideal of a certain autonomy for scholars to be free to pose the questions they consider worth posing, and to follow internally-generated criteria of what makes for quality research. But this relative autonomy is not contrary to consumer sovereignty, but consists precisely in a profound responsiveness to the consumers and investors of higher education.

The last section uses Kirzner's work on entrepreneurship to challenge the interpretation of consumer sovereignty as passive obedience to the market, but it challenges it not only for scholarly production but for all production processes. The kind of connectedness scholarship ought to have to the outside world is not different in kind from that which any other kind of production has to its outside world. In effect I will argue that scholars are more like business entrepreneurs (and vice versa) than either seems to like to admit. The ideal university offers an appropriate home for relatively autonomous scholarly activity, and yet is integrated with, and offers enormous benefits to, the market in which it is situated.

The problem with academia today, I think, is that the legitimate value named by the word "objectivity" is commonly misunderstood. The cure for the ailment is neither to patch up the leakage of influence across the alleged walls of the ivory tower, nor to simply make academics meekly subservient to their customers. The cure may lie in replacing the notions of institutional and intellectual detachment with the fundamental moral value of openness in the search for truth.

II. OBJECTIVITY AS INSTITUTIONAL DETACHMENT

> Economic calculation cannot comprehend things which are not sold and bought against money.
>
> There are things which are not for sale and for whose acquisition sacrifices other than money and money's worth must be expended. He who wants to train himself for great achievements must employ many means, some of which may require expenditure of money. But the essential things to be devoted to such an endeavor are not purchasable. Honor, virtue, glory, and likewise vigor, health, and life itself play a role in action both as means and as ends, but they do not enter into economic calculation....
>
> Loquacious sermonizers disparage Western civilization as a mean system of mongering and peddling.... In the eyes of these babblers money and calculation are the source of the most serious evils. However, the fact that men have developed a method of ascertaining as far as possible the expediency of their actions and of removing uneasiness in the most practical and economic way does not prevent anybody from arranging his conduct according to the principle he considers right. The 'materialism' of the stock exchange and of business accountancy does not hinder anybody from living up to the standards of Thomas à Kempis or from dying for a noble cause.... It is not true that honesty does not 'pay.' It pays for those who prefer fidelity to what they consider to be right to the advantages which they could derive from a different attitude (Mises 1966, pp. 214-216).

If scholarly "objectivity" in the legitimate sense is to be protected from contamination by the allure of money and power, one might imagine two alternative strategies: an institutional isolation by which the temptations are avoided in the first place, or a straight-forwardly moral culture in which the virtues of strict adherence to the standards are so thoroughly inculcated that the rules are rarely broken. The first, taken up in this section, might be called the monastic approach, the second, taken up in the next, could be called the moral suasion approach.

A. Are Universities Insulated from Market Forces? Should They Be?

Higher education bears the marks of many years of trying to protect the objectivity of scholarship by taking the monastic approach, trying to make universities into intellectual monasteries where its inhabitants would be shielded from the seductions of money and power. Many features of contemporary universities confirm that they have been attempting to turn themselves into civilized islands of purity, buffered from the seas of barbaric unscholarliness that surround them. There is the whole physical separation of campuses from the outside world, the tortured distinction academic administrators try to make between inside and outside funds, the limitations put on consulting activities, the separate accounting systems in terms of FTE (full time equivalents) that state universities put in place to control teaching activities, the disconnect between revenue from enrollments and rewards to employees, and so forth. A common rationale for using taxes to support universities has been premised on the notion that this would protect them from "strings attached," strings that are somehow thought to be uniquely attached to private sector support. In so many ways universities clearly have been seeing themselves as, for better or worse, in a world apart.

This sense of being utterly different is reflected in the resistance one meets to any suggestion that the principle of consumer sovereignty, which is widely thought to be a good thing in many other contexts, ought to apply to scholarly production.[3] Indeed one finds resistance even to calling what is going on in academic institutions a "production process," or what is being created a "product," or the audience of the work a "market." Academic workers do not merely have a wage-paying job, they have a higher calling. The services and products of this calling, the teaching of students, the scholarly articles, are not mere commodities, and the recipients of the efforts are not best seen as customers. The whole economic way of talking about production for a market clashes with the self-image of most college professors.

The conservative critics of universities leap at this resistance and argue that this is exactly what is wrong with higher education. Were consumer sovereignty to reign in this industry, they suggest, much of what goes on in the universities would be forced by market pressures to stop. The conservative critics agree with the leftist defenders that the world of academia is set apart from the rest of the market. They will also cite in this regard the substantial government funds most colleges receive, which many business-persons envy, and the attractive employment contracts, including long summers "off" and tenure, which many workers in other industries envy. Thus there is certainly an appearance of detachment, and of special privilege, and there is much in the rhetoric of the place, whether that of the critics or the proponents, which implicitly assumes the separation.

But how seriously should we take all this? There is something here that doesn't quite ring true. To be sure, there certainly are individual scholars who manage to sequester themselves away from the concerns of anybody outside of their own specialized field, and there are even whole fields of research residing within the protection of universities that seem to have lost most of their contact with the rest of the world. But it seems hard to describe any university, whatever its aspirations, as effectively isolated from the market. This "monastery" is thoroughly infested with the mundane world at every turn. It keeps budgets in the coin of the external realm. It bids against other colleges when it seeks grants and bequests, when it purchases materials, hires services, and recruits talent, competing intensely for its students and for its faculty and staff.

Higher education is, as one of its severest critics, Martin Anderson, points out, one of America's big industries, and judging by its continuing growth, it is a highly successful one. In 1960 the total budget of the nation's colleges and universities was about $7 billion. In 1989 it was $130 billion.[4] Anderson refers to America's colleges, the firms of this big industry, as "mini-socialist states,"[5] and attributes their difficulties to their insulation from market competition. But any college in the United States faces brisk competition from thousands of domestic and foreign rivals. A recent study by the Carnegie Foundation for the Advancement of Teaching put the number of accredited post-secondary institutions in the United States at 3,600, up by over two hundred from the count of their last study in 1987.[6] People come from all over the world, at considerable personal and financial cost, to attend American colleges. Indeed higher education is one of America's most impressive export products. People are choosing to pour an awfully large amount of money into American colleges, and if these institutions are "vast factories of junkthink" and "cesspools of mediocrity and corruption" these consumers must be dense indeed.

I think the conservative critics do make a telling point when they question the use of taxation to support higher education. The funds universities receive through the coercive powers of government represent an unfair advantage as against many other institutions which lack this source of funding, including those colleges which receive less of it. Moreover even the partial protection colleges receive from competition has negative effects. It is possible for many colleges and universities to pay less attention than they should to the interests of the voluntarily-paying customers and investors when a substantial proportion of their support comes though taxation.

Coercive interventions into the market process can perpetuate error by protecting from competition the producers who err. This represents the issue on which the conservative critics of higher education have been able to make their most effective arguments, and in my view nearly all the aspects of higher education today which tend to bother the general public come down to this. Maybe a sabbatical to study some obscure question in mathematics is a very nice idea for the professor, and maybe his hunch is right that working on it will prove one day to have advanced our society's store of mathematical knowledge, but why should we taxpayers have to pay for it?

Why indeed? I personally take a radical view on these things, and would favor relying exclusively on voluntary methods throughout the economy, but a more modest argument could be made that higher education is a particularly inappropriate industry to support by taxation. Basic research, which I contend is the fundamental business of higher education, is necessarily a matter of exploring new ideas before they could yet have become widely understood and valued. What scholars want to have in universities (and what I think the primary demanders in their market want them to have, so long as they are accountable) is a place where they are free to investigate any topic they find promising. A scholar would like to be able to do so without first having to justify to, say, a Congressional committee, why the question is worth studying. The virtue of the market is that it facilitates an astonishing diversity of funding possibilities. If a scholar happens to want to investigate something that the political system would have found too hot or too obscure to handle, say, lesbian images in early twentieth-century Chinese literature, it is not unlikely that some individual investor could be found to pay for it. But how likely is it this could get through Congress?[7]

Leftist academics routinely assume that subjecting themselves to market forces would threaten their more obscure work, and so they plead for continued government support. Right-wing critics make the same assumption, and urge the government to remove the funding. Ironically I think if the conservatives win and universities become more subject to market rather than political pressures, the rarefied research, even work in Marxism and gay studies, will be *less* vulnerable to attack. All that scholars who are convinced that they are asking important questions need to do in a free market is find some voluntary consumers or investors for their work, foundations, businesses, or individuals willing to support it. They do not need to control the political system, or sway the median voter.

So it can be argued that higher education as a whole would benefit from a continuation of the present tendency for replacing taxation as its basis of funding with tuition, grants, and contracts. Reducing government support would not destroy our institutions of higher learning. America's industry essentially depends on the professional training and liberal arts education provided by its colleges. And higher education is one of the most popular targets of generosity, so that if its subsidies and corresponding taxes were reduced one could expect a significant proportion of the loss to be replaced. Of course, we'd expect the proportion to be less than 100 percent, and that some colleges would go bankrupt, as happens now and happens in any market, but the overall health of the industry would be strengthened.

Even so, the conservatives exaggerate the extent of current governmental involvement in this industry. Whatever insulation from market forces American colleges can be said to enjoy has never been more than partial, and is diminishing. Anderson (1992, p. 197) makes the facile claim that colleges and universities are "about as close as you can get to socialism in this country." Yet by his own figures (1992, p. 29) he admits that only about 20 percent of the funding of private universities comes from taxes, and even the so-called public universities get only about 60 percent of their funding from governments. This proportion is gradually dropping, and the bureaucratic rigidities that come with the tax money are so restricting that several public universities are considering privatizing, just so they can make their decisions more flexibly. When nearly half of the funds of state universities come from the voluntary choices of paying customers and donors, it is hard to describe these institutions as comfortably insulated from the market. On the contrary, they have always been situated within market forces, and increasingly they are feeling the effects of competition. And it is good for them.

Are university professors a uniquely privileged class, enjoying working conditions that would be the envy of the rest of the society? I'm not so sure. Although professors at research universities often get paid summers off from teaching, they are expected to use that time to do research, and since that, of all the work they do, is the part which makes the biggest difference in their raises, they tend to work hard in the summer. In liberal arts teaching colleges professors typically get summers off without pay, during which they often work at their research anyway.

What about that controversial institution of academic tenure? Surely this sets college professors apart from workers in other fields, who can never expect a guaranteed job. Yet as Sowell (1993, pp. 274-277) has pointed out, a careful economic analysis of the effects of tenure does not suggest that it privileges academics over other workers in the job market, it only shifts the uncertainties of employment onto the professorial underclass, untenured, and part-time professors.[8]

If academic working conditions are attractive, it is not because people in this industry don't have to work hard. I suspect that academics tend to enjoy their work so much that they work harder and for longer hours. They may have a self image that they do all this for a higher calling, and are unconcerned about the crass economic side of it all. But so do many workers who take pride in their work. Whatever can be said about them they are not insulated from the market. They work for wages, which vary in accordance with professional accomplishments, and they respond to incentives. They may prefer to think of themselves as unconnected to the mundane world of buying and selling, and to be living instead The Life of the Mind, but let's get real. They are earning a living in the higher education industry. They are part of the economy.

The point is not that the sense many academic workers have of pursuing a higher calling is to be cynically dismissed. The point is that this sense is shared by people who like their work everywhere in the economy. Medical doctors are typically just as offended to be told that they sell services to a health care market; software engineers are just as offended to be told that their beautiful code is a "commodity" for sale to the highest bidder.

What is wrong here is the reductionistic connotations of economic language, which makes it sound as if being oriented toward markets is inherently degrading, like prostitution, while adhering to professional standards of excellence is something necessarily completely different and uplifting, like romantic love. The sense academics have of being outside of, and in a sense above, the market is not something that makes them different from other producers; in our culture, suspicious of markets as it is, this sense of being above the ordinary exchange nexus is the norm. But the real market is precisely made up of such products that are more than mere commodities, and of such producers who adhere to professional standards they consider sacred.

In short, friends and foes of "higher" education paint a picture of an isolated tower separated and protected, for good or ill, from market forces, but something is wrong with this picture. Perhaps universities have wanted to set themselves apart from the nonacademic world, but they are nevertheless deeply and inextricably connected to it.

B. Mises' Answer to Historicism

Ludwig von Mises' general theory of human action, and the way he deployed it to criticize historicism, is a useful framework from which to view the goal of institutional detachment. Historicism is the point of view that the Austrian school throughout its history has been most concerned to answer, from Menger's critique of the German historical school, to Kirzner's critique of the alleged historicist tendencies of Ludwig Lachmann and George Shackle.[9] In the nineteenth century, economics in the German-speaking world was dominated by historicism, a point of view that denies the potency of general theories of social phenomena, and thus amounts to a wholesale rejection of economic theory. It pretends to "tell it like it is," to tell the historical story directly as it happened, untainted by theory, or other presuppositions we the social scientists might bring to it.

Classical economists had been in the habit of treating economic behavior as a special type, reflecting a particular kind of business rationality. This made it easier for their historicist critics to dismiss economic theory as only relevant to a particular model of man, a rational, calculating being, and to those parts of a society to which such a being might be relevant. Economics, then, is not relevant to entities such as universities, which are populated by more well-rounded people who are above this narrow, economistic behavior, and are motivated by higher ideals.

Mises sums up the historical school's version of historicism:

> It was a fundamental mistake of the Historical School of *Wirtschaftlishe Staatswissenschaften* in Germany and of Institutionalism in America to interpret economics as the characterization of the behavior of an ideal type, the *homo oeconomicus.* According to this doctrine traditional or orthodox economics does not deal with the behavior of man as he really is and acts, but with a fictitious or hypothetical image. It pictures a being driven exclusively by 'economic' motives, i.e., solely by the intention of making the greatest possible material or monetary profit (1966, p. 62).

Mises insisted that it is a mistake to try to draw a sharp distinction between the sphere of "the economy" and the rest of social phenomena, or between rational action aimed at material goals and irrational action aimed at ideal goals. For Mises all purposeful action is rational.[10] All human action embodies the basic principles of choice, scarcity, supply and demand, and so forth. There is no difference in kind between a business person trying to satisfy her customers and, say, a university professor trying to supply educational services to his students.

As Mises wrote:

> It is usual to call an action irrational if it aims, at the expense of material and tangible advantages, at the attainment of 'ideal' or 'higher' satisfactions. In this sense people say, for instance—sometimes with approval, sometimes with disapproval—that a man who sacrifices life, health, or wealth to the attainment of 'higher' goods—like fidelity to his religious, philosophical, and political convictions or the freedom and flowering of his nation—is motivated by irrational considerations. However, the striving after these higher ends is neither more nor less rational or irrational than that after other human ends (1966, p. 19).

The market sphere cannot be understood as a realm separate from the rest of a social system, but has to be understood as an integral part of it, permeating universities as well as governments. The pursuit of higher virtues, such as the scholar's search for truth, is a fundamental part of social life, which market institutions neither guarantee, nor prevent.

> Acting man is always concerned both with 'material' and 'ideal' things. He chooses between various alternatives, no matter whether they are to be classified as material or ideal....
>
> [W]e must not overlook the fact that in reality no food is valued solely for its nutritive power and no garment or house solely for the protection it affords against cold weather and rain. It cannot be denied that the demand for goods is widely influenced by metaphysical, religious, and ethical considerations, by aesthetic value judgments, by customs, habits, prejudices, tradition, changing fashions, and many other things (1966, p. 233).

The distinction that *can* be made is between those economic choices to which money calculation applies, and those to which it doesn't. This distinction cuts across all kinds of institutions. Within businesses some choices are made which money prices do *not* help to measure; within families some choices are made which money *does* help to measure. Within universities there are budgets and there are also qualitative judgments about scholarly virtues to which no price can be attached. As Mises put it in the quote that leads off this section, a virtue, such as a belief in scholarly openness, plays a role in action both as means and as ends, but does not enter into economic calculation. At the same time, the fact that it lies outside the orbit of calculation does not at all prevent actors who value it from taking it fully into account. "Those things which do not enter into the items of accountancy and calculation are either ends or goods of the first order" (1966, p. 215), that is consumption goods, whose subjective value can be directly assessed.

From a Misesian point of view it would be nonsensical for universities to aspire to institutional detachment from the "market sphere." Universities are thoroughly ensconced in market relationships. Like all other institutions in modern societies, they benefit enormously from the information contained in prices, but at the same time they regularly make choices over goals to which no price is attached. What may protect the scholar from the temptations of money or power cannot be institutional isolation from the world, but moral adherence to professional standards.

Even though the belief, that the path toward scholarly objectivity lies in a monastic separation from the mundane world of commodities, is a self-delusion, it has undoubtedly had harmful effects. It drives a wedge between the scholar's image of her professional ideals and the larger society of which she is a part. When the honest search for truth is essentially defined in terms of insulation from the everyday world, it is hardly surprising that scholarship is increasingly uninterested in addressing everyday problems. While the university is in fact thoroughly embedded in the world, its self-understanding as being in its own world leads to an irresponsible attitude, according to which the usefulness of research to the rest of the world is not considered an important matter.

Moreover, the detachment ideal focuses attention exclusively on external temptations that might threaten the honest pursuit of truth, to the exclusion of internal ones. Today it may be argued that the most serious dangers to a scholar's objectivity come not from his being "bought off" by nonacademic influences, but from his selling his soul to narrowly defined, intra-disciplinary standards about what counts as scholarly productivity. The chief threats to the quest for truth come from complacent attitudes about what constitutes scholarly contributions, where the application of mindless formulae about how to do research takes the place of a genuine search for knowledge.

The pursuit of truth, and of other virtues, does not take place in an institutional vacuum. Scholars do not live in a monastery or an ivory tower, though many seem to wish they could. They occupy a world filled with economic and political opportunities, and circumscribed by economic and political constraints. The legitimate aim behind the ideal of scholarly objectivity, to avoid temptations of money and power, and to pursue the truth in whatever direction it is found, is achieved by inculcating a set of moral principles about these virtues. The true scholar is protected from being "bought off" by the rich and powerful, not by being locked away from market and political realities, but simply by the fact that her values are such that the offer is not seen as tempting in the first place. Honor and professional self respect are more highly valued than the money or influence that is being offered.

III. OBJECTIVITY AS INTELLECTUAL DETACHMENT

> Detachment or being liberated from tradition cannot be our first worry in our attitude towards the past in which we—who are ourselves historical beings—incessantly participate. Quite the contrary, the authentic attitude is that of looking at an inherited culture—in the literal sense of both inherited and culture, that is, as a development (a cultivation) of what we recognize as being the concrete link among us all. Obviously, what is handed down by our forebears is not appreciated when it is looked at in the objectivist spirit, that is, as the object of a scientific method, as if it were something fundamentally alien or completely foreign.
>
> Temporal distance is not... a distance to be bridged or overcome. This was the naive prejudice of historicism. It believed it could reach the solid terrain of historical objectivity by striving to place itself within the vantage point of a past age and think with the concepts and representations particular to that epoch (Gadamer 1963/1987, pp. 114, 136).

If one doesn't try to attain protection from the temptations of money and power via the monastic option, one is really left with no other option but that of moral suasion. One needs to inculcate values that prevent the scholar from seeing the offers as tempting in the first place. In fact I think this is the position that Mises, following Max Weber, actually holds, but the label they and many scholars of their day attached to this moral suasion option was paradoxically "value freedom." It describes itself as a position of intellectual detachment, a position that avoids the temptations by detaching the scholar from all moral points of view. The idea that economic (and other) science protects its objectivity by attaining a kind of detachment which refuses to endorse any ethical point of view has been an unquestioned article of faith in the Austrian school. But within the scholarly literature of which Weber was a part, the so-called *verstehen* (understanding) tradition, this way of expressing the aims of science has come under serious challenge. Indeed there are analogies between these challenges to intellectual detachment and the challenges a Misesian position raises against institutional detachment.

A. Can Scholars Attain a Value-free Point of View? Should They Try?

Value-freedom is unobjectionable if all that is meant by it is that, for example, one should refrain from using the classroom as a pulpit, that one respect the differing views of students and fellow scholars, and concentrate on the discovery and clarification of truths, rather than the propagation of opinions. But the phrase suggests something more. It suggests that one can and should suppress or forget ones' own values when one takes on the role of the scholar, that in some sense one should deny that one sees the world from a definite moral perspective.

Max Weber pointed out that "All knowledge of cultural reality... is always knowledge from *particular points of view*" (1904/1977, p. 31). His notion of value-freedom in the cultural sciences was a moral exhortation to scholars to take care in how they worked with what was invariably value-laden, perspectival knowledge. As such, he did not seem to be adhering to the strict ideal of intellectual detachment.[11] He certainly did not pretend to reach some kind of perspectiveless perspective, an objective, Archimedean point from which reality can be seen "as it is in itself," as philosophers like to say. He admitted that the perspective from which the social scientist *ought to* see cultural reality, is itself a particular moral standpoint, which in principle demands an ethical defense.

But the *verstehen* tradition seemed to be conceding this kind of amoral status to the natural sciences. The physical sciences need take no moral position but simply describe, in a neutral way, the laws governing the natural world. The Weberian view of value-freedom held that while the natural sciences are able to provide objective explanations of phenomena, the human sciences are obliged to come to terms with intentionality, to comprehend human purposes. The model for understanding human purposes with which Weber was working is called empathy, and is generally associated with the work of Wilhelm Dilthey.[12] Empathy can be described as the idea of, in some sense, "getting into the head" of the individual person one is trying to understand in order to grasp his or her purposes. Moreover, the *verstehen* tradition (though not Weber himself) sometimes seemed to be willing to abandon the goal of providing causal explanations at all, as was suggested in Dilthey's notorious phrase that the natural sciences explain, but the human sciences understand.[13] For some proponents of the *verstehen* tradition, objective explanations of what actually caused what are only available to the physical sciences, and the historian can only provide interpretive narratives from distinct, value-laden perspectives. Thus the human or historical sciences seemed to be put into a second-class status relative to the natural sciences in regard to the all-important value of scholarly objectivity.

Mises was significantly influenced by Weber's notion of value-freedom, and by the *verstehen* tradition's notion of understanding, but he did not think they did justice to the status of economic theory. He considered the logic of the general theory of human action to be no less "objective" than that of geometry or the natural sciences, and he was certain that economics was as capable of explanation as it was of understanding. He was willing to agree with Weber's and Dilthey's account of historical knowledge, and saw historical research as objective in only the limited sense, that it obeyed rules of scholarship, and was not a matter of personal opinion. Historical knowledge was objective in a non-detached sense.

But Mises insisted that the *theoretical* knowledge achieved by the science of human action was similar in this regard to the knowledge achieved by the natural sciences. It was not tainted, as historical understanding necessarily was, by the moral perspective of the historically situated observer. It took no point of view of its own, but neutrally analyzed the implications of the subjective points of view that prevailed in the social circumstances under study. In fact, he saw this as the very principle upon which the objectivity of the science of human action was based:

> In this sense we speak of the subjectivism of the general science of human action. It takes the ultimate ends chosen by acting man as data, it is entirely neutral with regard to them, and it refrains from passing any value judgments. The only standard which it applies is whether or not the means chosen are fit for the attainment of the ends aimed at.... [I]t is in this subjectivism that the objectivity of our science lies. Because it is subjectivistic and takes the value judgements of acting man as ultimate data not open to any further critical examination, it is itself above all strife of parties and factions... (1966, pp. 21-22).

In other words subjectivism, the position of taking as ones' point of departure the perspectives of consumers, rather than that of the scientific observer, is itself the observer's guarantee of objectivity. The economist detaches his or her personal preferences from the research, and asks only whether the preferences of the consumers are being met.

But again there is something wrong with this picture. The fact that subjectivists decline to debate with the subjects about their preferences only pushes the question of values back one level. The reluctance to debate over preferences is surely understandable, given the purposes of economic theory, and indeed reflects adherence to a definite scholarly value, that one not make pronouncements on matters outside of one's expertise. There is still the issue of why this and other moral values are operative. It may be granted that it has been an advantageous strategy for economics to avoid debating the issue of what consumers value, and concentrate on the logical implications of their valuations, and that this has helped economists to focus on the issues about which they have special competence. But it does not necessarily follow that this stance of taking the consumers' evaluations as given is itself an objective, value-free point of view. Is it not, on the contrary a specific and value-laden stance in itself? Is it not in fact open to moral argument about whether this is the proper attitude of the economist?

And in fact this stance *has* been disputed, for example by the Marxian economist Maurice Dobb during the socialist calculation debate.[14] From his point of view it was not so obvious that respecting consumers' evaluations, which he thought were systematically distorted by the exploitative and alienating institutions of capitalism, constituted taking a position of detached objectivity. He asks why subjectivist economists privilege the perspectives of the consumers, as they happen to exist under capitalistic conditions.

Now I happen to agree that the standpoint which prefers to ask what the consumers themselves want, rather than what the economist might think they ought to have, is a superior moral standpoint. But it is a moral standpoint. To answer Dobb involves one in a moral argument about why respecting the voluntarily choices of consumers under capitalism is a good way to conduct oneself as a scholar. It demands that we expose a dubious moral paternalism on Dobb's part, which cannot stand up to counter-argument. But I don't think one disposes of his challenge by claiming that the subjectivist position puts one "above all strife of parties and factions."

Subjectivism is not so much the renunciation of the scholar's own perspective in favor of those of the consumers, as it is the endorsement of that moral perspective which regards those of consumers as of primary importance. The subjectivist too sees the phenomena of markets from her own particular theoretical, historical, and moral perspective, and deliberately chooses to respect the (perhaps very different) points of view of the consumers. This constitutes a moral position that can stand up well to its rivals, but to do so it needs to admit that it is in fact a moral position.

The scholar is necessarily caught up in social strife, and cannot avoid it, either by hiding in a temptation-free monastery, or by claiming to stand apart from all moral controversy. On the contrary, what scholars need is precisely moral principles to defend their "objectivity."

B. Gadamer's Answer to Historicism

The stance of value-freedom, and its implied intellectual detachment, was deployed by the Austrians to fend off the danger of historicism, to make sure that the potency of the theory of human action was appreciated, and that economic theory was considered to be as solid as physics. Mises granted that while the historian must necessarily work from a particular, value-laden point of view, this does not imply that history is arbitrary. Yet he wanted to secure what he thought was a more profound kind of objectivity for the social theorist, a kind he believed was achieved by the natural sciences. It was generally conceded in his day that mathematics and the natural sciences really could achieve a morally detached objectivity, and he properly saw no less a degree of objectivity in, say, the law of supply and demand than could be claimed for the law of gravity. So he sought an intellectual detachment for economic theory that set it apart from the moral situatedness that necessarily accompanies historiography.

But perhaps this approach is getting things backward. Maybe what was wrong with historicism was not that it made the social sciences insufficiently detached, compared with the natural sciences, but that it was striving to attain an ideal of detachment which is impossible for either the social or natural sciences. In historicism's case the separation is sought not so much through a celebration of detached theorizing as through a theory-denying *immersion* in the historical detail, but the effect is the same: avoiding the direct engagement of theory with history. Just as Mises sought to detach theory from the value-embeddedness of history, so historicism sought to detach history from the value-embeddedness of theoretical presuppositions. Either strives for a separation of the scholar's own intellectual presuppositions, which may come from his historical situation or from his theoretical lenses, from research.

The challenge that has dealt historicism its most devastating blow is the one that was issued in 1960 by Gadamer in his magnum opus, *Wahrheit und Methode.* Gadamer's approach manages both to undermine the aspiration of objective detachment as something to be valued, and to substitute a different notion of objectivity, that of openness, which can better serve as a standard of scholarly virtue.[15] His critique shows that the problem with historicism is not that it leaves no room for the would-be theorist to gain a foothold for detached theorizing, but that it aspires to an illusory detachment. As Joel Weinsheimer, one of the translators of *Truth and Method,* put it, historicism can be described as "the endeavor to keep ourselves out of the past, or to separate the past from the present so as to understand it objectively, as it once was" (1985, p. 132).

Too often critics of the antitheoretical implications of historicism have tried to secure for our theories the kind of objectivity that historicism was claiming is the virtue of pure, theoretically unmediated, historical narrative. In effect such critics concede too much to the historicists. Historicists said of their own histories that they were pure narratives, untainted by the biases of theories. They took as an ideal the historian who immerses himself in the details of the historical moment of the past, and brings nothing of the systematic social sciences in there with him. To answer them we must not justify theory by claiming it lies in another, purer world, untainted by historical contexts, so that when it gets used it won't in turn contaminate the narratives. On the contrary, theory is to be restored to its place of distinction by denying the value of the historicists' notion of purity, and by recognizing and honoring the embeddedness of our theories in the historical process.

The proper standpoint of the social scientist is neither to aspire to stand utterly apart from the world she studies, nor to aspire to lose herself in it. Neither aloofness nor immersion makes sense of what really happens when we understand. And both share the goal of self-denial, of avoiding a genuine engagement by the scholar with the subjects under study.

When Mises was working out his general theory of human action the best available work on the nature of historical understanding was that of Dilthey. His empathic model came hazardously close to a position of psychologism, in which the point of understanding seems to be a matter of reading the mind of another, and even intimately experiencing his feelings. Of course if understanding requires this, it will be deemed a task lying outside the capabilities of the social scientist.

One can identify two significant steps by which the *verstehen* tradition advanced from the position held by Weber and Dilthey. The first step, taken by the founder of phenomenology, Edmund Husserl, was the move from a psychologistic notion of empathy, whereby the observer metaphorically enters into the individual mind of the agent under study, to a participatory notion, whereby the observer enters into the social group of the agents.[16] And then in the second step, on the strength of Gadamer's work, this participatory idea is replaced with a notion of understanding as translation, or mediation between the observer's and the subject's perspectives. These transformations of the theory of understanding have important implications for the issue of value-freedom and the ideal of objectivity.

Husserl exposed the questionableness of the sciences' claims to detachment. His path-breaking development of phenomenology showed that all scientific observation, even the most simple kinds of perception, gain their validity only through acknowledging the specific perspective from which they are seen. There is a value-laden *life-world* behind even the natural sciences.[17] Phenomenology began to make it possible to accept that knowledge is relative to the perspective of the observer, but is nonetheless valid knowledge.

Moreover, with Husserl the process of understanding is no longer seen in a psychologistic sense. It is not depicted as a matter of entering into the private thoughts of the agent being studied, and is not some sort of mysterious sharing of mental energies, but takes place out in the open space of discourse in the life-world. What is at issue in an attempt to read the meaning of any human expression is not a mind-reading but an inquiry into the subject matter of the discourse. The question is not what an author or speaker or actor was thinking but what was written or said or done. As Gadamer put this point:

> When we understand a text we do not put ourselves in the place of the other, and it is not a matter of penetrating the spiritual activities of the author; it is simply a question of grasping the meaning, significance, and aim of what is transmitted to us (1987, p. 127).

That is, the question here is not one of getting into somebody's head, is not immersion into an individual mind, but is one of coming to terms with *die Sache*, the subject matter at issue. This is not, as some contributors to the *verstehen* tradition may suggest, a preoccupation with interpretations of reality, to the exclusion of concern for reality itself. Georgia Warnke describes Gadamer's point:

> The different historical vantage points from which texts and text-analogues are viewed reveal different aspects of them; every generation of interpreters participates in different dialogues and arrive at new mediations with their objects. Still, it is crucial for Gadamer's view that these dialogues remain dialogues over *die Sache* and that the different dimensions revealed are facets of it. The important point...is not only that inquiry is always oriented by our concerns; although Gadamer makes this point, his argument is also that inquiry is always inquiry into a subject-matter and that the consensus reached about this subject-matter can reveal something 'true' about it (1987, p. 146).

With Husserlian philosophy, however, while science's claim to detachment is undermined, there is not yet the basis for a challenge to historicism. Ironically the detached standpoint phenomenology denied to science was reappropriated for the philosophy itself. It attempts to play the role of the uninvolved spectator, and to secure its own objectivity by detachment from the perspectival horizon of the scientists it describes.[18]

Dilthey's empathic understanding leaves us wondering what happens to the social scientists' own perspective when she "enters" the mind of the subject. Husserlian participation leaves us wondering what happens to the observer's own perspective when he participates in the life-world of the subjects he studies. What these models of understanding tend to neglect is the value of what the social scientist who attempts to understand leaves behind when understanding is treated as immersion into the mind or life-world of the subjects. What is left behind is the historical and theoretical knowledge we in the present have and are able to use to understand the past. As Gadamer said, historicism's error was that it thought one could achieve an objective understanding of an historical period by trying to "think with the concepts and representations particular to that epoch."

What has been missing in the efforts to secure a position of objective detachment is a clear recognition of the *productivity* of what historicism considered a contamination, the connection between the present scholar and the past historical agents under study. Historicism aspires to keep the theoretical and factual advantages of the present from polluting the otherwise clean study of the historical events. Gadamer turns this around by seeing the contribution of the observer's theories, as well as the specific knowledge of events that have unfolded since, as being the very source of our ability to understand at all.

When an anthropologist enters into a culture he does himself no good to pretend he has become a native, as if he were to suppress all the theoretical knowledge the discipline of anthropology has developed about culture. When a sociologist, fully equipped with the theories that she has gleaned from Durkheim and Weber, studies a family, she deludes herself if she thinks she becomes a member of it, and somehow stops being a well-trained sociologist. And an economist who examines a market likewise misleads himself if he thinks he attains objectivity by suppressing his own perspective, and claiming to be detached from the historical process.

Understanding for Gadamer is a process of open dialogue, modeled on a good conversation among participants who respect one another. The observer engages in a conversation with the texts being studied, whether literally if possible, as in ethnography, or metaphorically if necessary, as in exegesis or archival history. True understanding involves attaining an openness, by which the claims of the subject are given voice. The scholar tries to make sure the subject is allowed to "speak" and is truly listened to. This requires a patience where what might at first appear absurd is given a chance to elaborate itself in its own terms. At the same time openness does not mean a subservience to the claims of the subject, such that whatever is said is meekly accepted, and taken at face value. Indeed this "Whatever you say" attitude would show as much of a lack of respect as a refusal to listen. To engage in a real dialogue with subjects is to give them the benefit of the doubt, and try to hear what they are saying, yet it is also to *engage* with them over the subject matter, such that when a claim appears not to make sense it is questioned. This engagement is not only a way to challenge what is being said, but also to challenge ones' own presuppositions:

> In fact our own prejudice is properly brought into play by being put at risk. Only by being given full play is it able to experience the other's claim to truth and make it possible for him to have full play himself (Gadamer 1989, p. 299).

Weinsheimer clarifies Gadamer's view of the openness with which we should read a "text" in this way:

> We hold our own opinions open to disconfirmation and place them at risk not because we are neutral but, quite the opposite, because we too are interested....
>
> For just this reason, our openness does not mean that we present ourselves as a blank slate ready to be inscribed. Because we are concerned and interested, our receptivity implies that we are willing to integrate the meaning of the text with our previous preconceptions by making them conscious, bringing them into view, and assimilating them to what the text reveals. Only if we are not disinterested can we take—and the text give—offense, so that our prejudices emerge into the open, and we thereby become able to understand the things themselves (1985, p. 167).

Scholarly objectivity consists precisely in learning to achieve this dialogical openness in a serious effort to understand a subject matter. In many ways I think this notion of openness represents only a clarification of what many scholars have meant when they spoke of value-freedom. But the misleading aspects of objectivity as intellectual detachment may have had significant negative consequences on higher education. The main problems in academia today seem to involve the sense most disciplines have of separation from the world and from one another. If objectivity is understood as involving open engagement with other perspectives, rather than some kind of distancing from them, scholarly traditions may find themselves better integrated with one another and with the outside world. For while value-freedom suggests that to be a scholar requires one *suppress* ones' own point of view, openness makes it clear that what we are really doing is *risking* our point of view against those of others. Our perspective is never eliminated, as if it were a contaminant, but neither is it permitted to dominate the scene, as if it were already known to be valid.

The upshot of this perspective on understanding is that the scholar needs to be given freedom to pursue the question where it leads. By the dynamic of open dialogue, the researcher is led by *die Sache*, by the subject matter that is the topic of the dialogue, to a discovery of truth.

IV. CONSUMER SOVEREIGNTY AND THE RELATIVE AUTONOMY OF THE ENTREPRENEUR

> Precisely that vision in which Menger saw how the economic system transmits consumer judgements of economic significance to the arrays of goods of higher order is, we wish to suggest from the perspective of modern subjectivism, flawed in failing to recognize the entrepreneurial steps—taken imaginatively, daringly and spontaneously, in the face of the impenetrable fog of the uncertain future—through which these judgements must necessarily be transmitted. These entrepreneurial steps represent the imagination and vision of the entrepreneurs peering into the unknown. Any claim to the effect that consumers' preferences dictate the allocation of resources can have validity only to the extent that these preferences are sensed and transmitted by market entrepreneurs (Kirzner 1992, p. 76).

The conclusion I draw from Mises' answer to historicism is that scholars should view themselves as fundamentally connected to, and not detached from the institutions they serve. They should see themselves as producers within the research industry, catering to the demands of their customers, and they should submit their work to the market test.

But the conclusion I draw from Gadamer's answer to historicism seems to move in the opposite direction. Gadamer argues that scholars must follow their *own* sense of where the truth leads them. Consumers, whether they be considered the students, or the outside funders, or the citizenry, who expect good things to flow from research, may not in general know what questions most urgently need to be addressed at the current state of knowledge. Bowing to consumer demand would seem to represent a relinquishment of the scholar's professional responsibility to discover what most needs to be discovered. Scholars must not view themselves as value-free, in the sense of being detached from moral considerations, but instead must recognize the moral virtues scholarship itself demands from them. They must follow the logic of the questions they ask, they must let *die Sache*, the subject matter itself, be their guide. Far from asking them to defer to consumers' dictates, this point of view would seem to encourage scholars to follow their own sense of what the honest search for truth tells them to do.

Can the principle of "consumer sovereignty," understood as implying that consumers unilaterally dictate to producers what needs to be produced, serve as the basis of the scholarly ideal? If the scholar, following Mises' argument, abandons the hope of complete autonomy from the "outside" world, must she then be reduced to passively responding to the dictates of the customers?

So who is in charge here? Is it the consumers or the producers?

A. Are Consumers Unilaterally Sovereign Over Producers? Should They Be?

Let us first ask this question not of the specific context of scholarly production, but more generally. In the market, who is really in charge?

Maybe the proper answer is "Nobody." The market can be viewed as a spontaneous order, a process of dialogical interplay among consumers and producers, in which no one is really dictating the outcome, which emerges from the give and take of the participants.

Perhaps the contradiction between the Misesian and Gadamerian views is only apparent. The language of "consumer sovereignty" may be somewhat misleading, especially in light of the mechanistic understanding many have of the workings of the economy. Neoclassical economics tends to interpret the sovereignty of consumers as if it implied that producers do nothing but respond obediently to pre-existing customers' commands. But in Austrian economics, and especially in the form in which it has been developed by Kirzner, things are not so simple. The modern Austrians, most notably Mises and Kirzner, endorse consumer sovereignty but also stress the active and even decisive role of the entrepreneur.

As Mises (1966, p. 328) put it, "The driving force of the market process is provided neither by the consumers nor by the owners of the means of production...but by the promoting and speculating entrepreneurs." Or in another passage:

> The direction of all economic affairs is in the market society a task of the entrepreneurs. Theirs is the control of production. They are at the helm and steer the ship (1966, p. 269).

And yet Mises immediately takes back this assertion of the entrepreneur's power when he adds that the entrepreneurs "are bound to obey unconditionally the captain's orders" and that the captain of the ship is the consumer (1966, pp. 269-270). One can find many powerful statements of the principle of consumer sovereignty in the Austrian literature from Carl Menger on, and these statements declare consumers to be "in charge" of the direction of the economy. Menger's founding vision which launched the school was that of an economy which was completely shaped according to the demands of consumers. He showed that "higher order" or production goods are only valued according to their perceived ability to contribute to the production of lower order consumption goods, and thereby helped to liberate economics from an excessively physical view of production. Kirzner (1992, pp. 71, 73) sums up this vision:

> For Menger the entire economic system is seen as a complex of activities directly or indirectly inspired by the goal of satisfying consumer needs. Every single item or service bought and sold in the market is valued only in so far as it can, in the purchaser's judgment, contribute valuably, directly or indirectly, towards the satisfaction of consumer needs.
>
> ...This perspective transmutes all the phenomena of the economy from being simply physical transformations, relationships or ratios into direct or indirect expressions of human valuations, preferences, expectations and dreams.

This way of seeing all productive activity as *meaningfully* connected to consumer satisfaction constitutes the Austrians' most fundamental principle, which they call subjectivism. In short, the idea that consumers are in some sense sovereign is not only a commonly held belief of the school, it is among the school's core beliefs. It may appear, then, that for Mises and Kirzner entrepreneurs are completely subservient to their captains, the customers.

It seems to me, however, that this "captain of the ship" metaphor is misleading in at least three respects. First of all, even from within Mises' own perspective, we need to remember that Austrian economists use concepts such as "consumer" in a special analytic sense. We are all to some degree the captains of this ship. As Mises points out:

> When economics employs the... terms it speaks of catallactic categories. The entrepreneurs, capitalists, landowners, workers, and consumers of economic theory are not living men as one meets them in the reality of life and history. They are the embodiment of distinct functions in the market operations.... Moreover the functions... are very often combined in the same persons (1966, pp. 251-252).

The catallactic concept of consumer is whoever expends resources on lower order goods for their own sake, and the producer is whoever attempts to satisfy such consumers through direct or indirect means in exchange for money. Thus if a producer, say a self-employed, ice cream man, chooses to forgo possible profit he might have earned catering to a customer by indulging himself in a few scoops, he thereby to that extent becomes the consumer. The case is no different if instead of eating some of the product, he works longer at the job, not in the expectation of earning extra money but because he wants to remain his own boss. Or if a banker chooses to make a loan to this business, not because she thinks it stands much chance of making her any return on the investment, but because she would like to give the ice cream man a break, then she becomes the consumer. Thus to say consumers are sovereign is not to say everyday folks we think of as customers are exclusively in charge. Whoever is willing to expend their resources to support activities are the consumers of those activities.

Secondly, in light of the way Mises' theory has been elaborated by Kirzner, there are the issues of alertness and futurity. Unless somebody exhibits alertness about what consumers are likely to find attractive, they cannot exercise their sovereign powers. And the embeddedness of production in time means that often the people who are really important are future consumers, who may not even have been born yet. Investors in a sense are standing in for *future* consumers, who may or may not ever materialize. In effect, they too enjoy some degree of sovereignty, in that they can experiment with their capital in the directions they believe in. Enormous sums of money are spent on projects consumers never buy, so that a healthy proportion of the economy sails in directions the so-called captain never identified. Entrepreneurs stand in the middle of all this, trying to anticipate consumer desires, and trying to convince investors about where the best opportunities will be found.

And thirdly, there is the issue of the creativity of entrepreneurship. The future is not an already fixed thing that is simply anticipated, it is subject to being shaped by the persuasive efforts of human actors. The entrepreneur does not only find what is already there, or what is, regardless of her own actions, going to be there in the future, she deploys her creative imagination to bring into reality what would otherwise not be there at all. And indeed, Kirzner would have us think of the discovery of existing opportunities as itself, in an important sense, creative. A resource that lies idle because nobody has yet thought of its possible uses is, for all practical purposes, as nonexistent as the new product or technology that has not yet been invented. As Kirzner eloquently says:

> The inspired hunch which leads the discoverer to notice islands where others only see clouds, to notice opportunities for innovative products or innovative applications of technology which others fail to see, is as creative, in its own context, as the inspired vision of the sculptor who sees, in marble and chisel, not merely marble and chisel but a sublime form awaiting to be brought forth (1992, p. 222).

Kirzner's elaboration of the role of the entrepreneur helps to restore the role to its proper place in the market process. Not that Kirzner is any less adamant than other Austrian economists that the *ultimate* power in a free market is in the consumer's hands, but it might be better described as a kind of veto power, exercised after the fact, rather than that of a captain giving orders to the helmsman. By disclosing the creative aspects of entrepreneurship he has clarified the fact that there is considerable room in the market for the entrepreneur to deploy her own imagination about what might be of interest to consumers, and to experiment with new products and production methods to see what might work.

If production, scholarly or otherwise, needs to remain ultimately in the service of the preferences of consumers, it need not be seen as utterly and passively subservient to them. Economic production is not a matter of consumers handing over a list of their desires to producers, who then dutifully follow orders. What consumers demand from producers is in large part their creative judgment, whereby they are expected to figure out what consumers *would* find desirable, were it to be offered them. The producer who merely responds passively to the consumers' requests tends to lose in competition to those who creatively inquire into what might really serve the consumer better than anything he can now imagine.

What the consumer really wants from producers, and is willing to pay for, is not some kind of amoral, detached obedience, but rather their engagement, their moral commitment, their impassioned involvement, their personal dedication, to providing what will turn out to be satisfying. The economists' imagery of *homo oeconomicus* is responsible for a completely false idea of what it means to maximize profit. It is as if the producer needs to choose between what she knows is the right way to do things, and what the consumer tells her she must do to make money. This dichotomy is by no means the general situation. Money can be made, and is very often made, from honestly doing the job by the highest professional standards. The pursuit of profit is not something that takes place in a moral vacuum, any more than the pursuit of truth is something that takes place in a market vacuum.

Advocates of markets have not yet done justice to the full moral context of economic production. While it is often admitted that the morality of voluntariness, nonaggression, and the respect for property, are prerequisites for a working market, we also need to recognize that, under cicumstances where there are relatively strong beliefs in the value of critical reasoning, markets can themselves enforce an adherence to professional norms of quality. Entrepreneurs in such circumstances don't succeed by "simply maximizing profits," in the sense of passively responding to consumer demand. They can "do well by doing good," they can succeed by actively applying professional standards to production processes, and being rewarded for doing so.

Where the prevailing culture sees the professional standards as legitimate, the primary profits to be made in that profession are made by conforming to those standards. The point is not that consumers of professional services will necessarily demand only the highest quality products, as judged by the state-of-the-art of knowledge in that field.[19] The point is that in many circumstances consumers actively seek out those who can show a professional stamp of certification, that is, they want to buy from those who meet the professionals' own standards of quality. In these situations consumers are not prepared to develop their own standards for quality, but in fact see the definition and enforcement of appropriate standards as one of the central services they are paying for.

The rationale of established professions with elaborate professional certification standards is to try to certify for consumers who in that field knows what he is talking about. Of course we know that professional certification is also abused, and deployed simply to limit competition. Of course we know that even when certification represents real quality standards, some consumers will ignore the professionals' judgments and seek services from the uncertified.

But the *primary* demand for services in markets with elaborate certification requirements stems from a belief that some genuine quality standards are involved in those services. Any *secondary* demand, which consists in trying to get the stamp of certification without the rigor of the certifying process, has to be understood as parasitic on the primary demand for certification, and is premised on a widespread belief in the legitimacy of that process.

Take for example a patient going into the doctor's office with a discomfort. He may demand of the doctor "Remove my pain" to which she could merely respond by doing what she is told, and offering pain killers. She is more likely to genuinely serve him, however, if she deploys her own specialized knowledge to determine how to best solve the problem. There are cases, to be sure, where doctors don't listen to patients at all, and try to play the role of detached health experts who will unilaterally tell their customers what is good for them. That is one way in which consumer sovereignty can be violated. But is it not also a violation when the producer reneges on her professional responsibility to inform the consumer what she thinks is the best course of action? Does not the attitude of "Whatever you want" show as much disrespect for the consumer as the attitude of "Whatever I think is good for you?" In both cases the producer is failing to truly engage with the consumer.

Now there will be occasions where the consumer does not want to hear the painful truth. If the standards of critical thinking in a society are not high, then doctors will prosper by ignoring their own professional judgments, and telling patients what they want to hear, even when it is not good for them. But if critical standards sink beyond a certain point, the whole rationale for the professional certification process would dissolve, and patients would do better to get the easy answers from their friends for free, rather than from expensively certified doctors. Where the professional standards still hold some validity, the relationship between the consumer and the producer is one where the consumer demands that the producer exercise her own professional judgment about quality, and not merely give the answers that are soothing.

In other words the relationship between consumer and producer ought to be understood as a dialogical one. The producer is obliged to listen to what the consumer is asking for, and this listening requires not simply mindlessly handing over exactly what is requested, but thinking creatively about what would be most satisfying, were it available. The focus of the metaphorical conversation between the producer and consumer is not on the psychology of what is in the consumer's head, but on *die Sache*, the subject matter. What is sought is the kind of satisfaction that entrepreneurial judgment concludes would both work for the consumer, and be workable and consistent with quality standards, for the producer.

The entrepreneur is not entirely free to do whatever pleases him, nor is he a mere puppet of consumers. He enjoys what might be called a relative autonomy, such that he is free to experiment on his own initiative, yet constrained by the need to ultimately find buyers and investors. This autonomy strives to secure a certain distance for the entrepreneur from both the government and the consumer, but it does not seek insulation. It asks for relevance from production for both politics and the market, but does not demand direct or immediate relevance. Both politics and the market will be better served if such relative autonomy for entrepreneurship is preserved.

B. Entrepreneurship in the Research Industry

How then, might one apply this concept of consumer sovereignty, understood now to involve the relatively autonomous entrepreneur, to the domain of higher education? What would unfettered market forces, in a culture such as ours, which is reasonably inclined to support scholarship, lead to?

First we need to be clear about who the consumers are. In light of the fact that the word consumer means the catallactic category, the consumers of higher education are not only the students and their parents who pay tuition, but equally the corporations and foundations which offer research grants, the alumni who make bequests, and even the faculty and administrators who expend their own monetary and other resources in order to see their colleges flourish. In their capacity as producers, those who work at universities are there to pull down a salary. But as in many industries where there is a high level of professional dedication, they are also pitching in for the cause, working extra hours for the love of the goals, and not for an extra salary. To that extent they are among the consumers, and as such are among those whose choices are sovereign.

We also need to be clear about what the product of this industry is. Conservative critics of higher education such as Martin Anderson have been saying the product should not be taken to be research, but ought to be seen as teaching what is already known. It seems to me this represents a profound misunderstanding of the nature of this market.[20] There are surely cheaper ways to transmit bits of already-known knowledge than this, for example making a few trips to a good library, or navigating the internet. The reason for personal contact between students and scholars is that something else is imparted at a college that cannot be easily gotten in any other way. Students can experience first-hand what the critical process and the discovery of new knowledge are like. The main teaching services students in universities are able to get, which they could not get as well on their own or on the job, are those which come from participation in research. Fundamentally, even when they are teaching students, universities are in the research business.

What counts as research? The critics are all too eager to reject quality research merely for being "abstract" or "impractical," but society depends on, and has been willing to pay for, the advances in abstract knowledge which are being developed in scholarly research. The deepening of theoretical understanding, which scholarship excels at when it is at its best, yields enormous *practical* benefits. But even this argument falls short, for after all, what is practical? Consumers express a real demand for beautiful mathematics or music, and not only for the solution to what we might think of as practical problems.

This is not to say, however, that anything goes. Scholars need to ask themselves whether they are fulfilling their moral obligations to advance the truth of their subject matter. While there is room for a great deal of discretion by scholars about what questions are worth asking, they should also keep in mind that they are "public servants." This phrase is cheapened when it is taken to mean merely employees of government, but what I am trying to say applies equally to private and public universities. Scholars who help us to advance the truth are acting in service of society.

Let's admit that there is much research that now goes on in institutions of higher learning which amounts to nothing but intellectual gamesmanship, with no prospect of serving anybody outside of academia in any manner.[21] And let us also admit that not all of this is attributable to coercive interference into competitive market forces. But there is no way to know in general whether what I find boring and pointless is what you find interesting and provocative. The best we can do is depend on the pressures of open criticism and market competition. Although lip service is regularly paid to the notion that scholarship needs to earn its keep by surviving the intellectual market test of criticism, the division of academia into disciplines tends to serve as a protectionistic policy. Criticisms are only allowed if they issue from within the paradigm of the discipline. Fundamental challenges are considered "foreign" and excluded.

With a different understanding of objectivity, as openness instead of as detachment, scholars might be more inclined to entertain fundamental objections to their research, and perhaps we could eliminate some of the waste that now exists. And with a more forthright acknowledgment that we are embedded in the market, and ultimately must serve our consumers, we might be trying harder not just to answer the questions we find interesting but to justify why these questions are worth asking.

Now does this mean that scholars in a free market research industry should view themselves as somehow directly in the employ of their paying customers from businesses and foundations? No, but precisely because that is not what the market for higher education demands. What the consumers of this product we call research want, by and large, is the independence of judgment which the values of open-minded scholarship generates. Organizations that want to invest in scholarly research are better served when the scholars they "hire" maintain a substantial degree of autonomy from them, and from other particular interests. The *primary* demand that supports the research industry is asking scholars to exercise their own professional judgments about what is worth studying, *and also* to be accountable for their choices, to attempt to explain their judgments.

Now this is not entirely true of course, even aside from the issue of the existence of government interventions into the free market. First, there is error, that is, scholarly producers in an uncertain world will fail to serve consumers by mistake. Error is a pervasive feature of markets, as Kirzner has convincingly shown. In this particular market, where the discovery of new knowledge is the main goal, error can be very widespread indeed. It is difficult to know how to find a cure for urban poverty or for breast cancer, and one will have to expect many mistakes along the way.

Second, mistakes can take the form of responding to the wrong consumers, such that the primary consumer demand is left unmet. Although I am contending that the primary demand for higher education services is for the pursuit of truth, there is also a secondary demand. Some administrators, some faculty, and some students are always trying to get a free ride on the reputation of the institution. There are students who really only want a good grade in order to get credentials for a job, regardless of the truth about how little they have learned, and there are donors who really only want a research result that endorses their product as safe, regardless of the truth about its dangers.

But there are reasons to hope that both of these deficiencies of higher education from its ideals contain their own built-in limits. As Kirzner reminds us, errors in a competitive market will tend to get noticed. Colleges which gain a reputation for making more mistakes than their rivals, or for satisfying their parasitic secondary demands, will find their primary demands drying up.

So then it is possible to reconcile the view (from Mises) that scholars at universities are institutionally inseparable from the market, and thus need to understand their work as serving consumer demands, with the view (from Gadamer) that they are intellectually inseparable from their own moral and professional standards of scholarly production. What consumers in the market for higher education primarily want from the producers is precisely that they pursue the truth open-mindedly and in accordance with established professional standards of scholarship.

C. Conclusion: The Ideal of the University

The university ought to be a home for the kind of relatively autonomous scholar we have been discussing, scholars such as Mises and Gadamer, who courageously continued to pose the questions that they found worth asking, even when the main trends of their age went in the opposite direction. The university should be the place where the scholar can work who attempts to ask those questions which the "consumers" will find, at least after the fact, to have been worth asking. It should be the place where the virtues of scholarship can be cultivated, and where those who adhere to the exacting moral and professional standards that scholarly objectivity in the sense of openness demands, will be welcome.

Moral suasion tends to work more by example rather than by preaching. The virtues of honest and open scholarship are learned by an apprenticeship whereby students observe the behavior of exemplary scholars and absorb the attitudes proper to the conduct of scholarly activity. It is by watching a true scholar at work, somebody like Kirzner, that one discovers what it really means to be "objective" in the best sense of the word. The ideal of the university is no more and no less than to provide a safe haven where men and women of such moral excellence can provide a beacon for the rest of us.

NOTES

1. A useful collection of essays by a variety of scholars responding to some of these attacks is Edmundson (1993).

2. This is a review by the catalogue's editor, Jim Powell (1994, p. 5) of another conservative book condemning academia entitled *The Fall of the Ivory Tower: Government Funding, Corruption, and the Bankrupting of American Higher Education* by George Roche.

3. Many professionals readily concede that *other* people's work is subject to consumer sovereignty, but that their own responds to a higher, professionally-derived standard.

4. *Statistical Abstract of the United States*, U.S. Department of Commerce, 1990, Table No. 208, "School Expenditures, by Type of Control and Level of Instruction, 1960 to 1989," p. 129.

5. Indeed Anderson (1992, pp. 38-39) goes so far as to say that "Virtually all the major universities and colleges in America are mini-socialist states in which the trustees, administrators, and faculty answer only to themselves."

6. The Carnegie Foundation said that academe is "healthy and expanding," in its study on the status of American higher education in its widely used "Carnegie Classification," as reported in Evangelauf (1994, p. 17).

7. Now it might be argued that our recent experience has been that government funding has in fact supported some rather bizarre research at our universities, about which the conservative critics get endless delight in expressing their moral indignation. But of course, this is only because government has not been particularly representative of the average opinion, and has been run by elite intellectuals much like those at universities. These same elite intellectuals like to think of themselves as favoring a more democratic and more representative political system. By having universities depend on taxes, they in fact put the conservatives on the side of popular democratic opinion. If taxpayers get informed and mobilized they will, by and large, find much of what goes on in higher education incomprehensible or pointless, if not evil. If college curricula were put to the vote, how many courses in, say, Marxist literary theory, or how many advanced courses in specialized fields of any kind, would survive? Indeed I would worry as much about issues that are not so esoteric. If political processes were to decide on academic content I would expect that we'd find creationist opinion overcoming evolutionary biologists in many state universities. While it is conceivable that this outcome could happen under a regime of free market consumer sovereignty as well, I think it would be much less likely.

8. Of course an argument can still be made against it on these grounds; it is perhaps too tough on the younger scholars and too easy on the older ones. But it does not constitute a privilege this industry enjoys over other industries.

9. Although I am not sure about Shackle, I do not accept this interpretation of Lachmann as a historicist. I find his work makes more sense when taken in the spirit of the Gadamerian challenge to historicism which I summarize in section III.

10. It is often objected to this view of rationality that it is tautologous, that since it explains everything it explains nothing. But as Kirzner (1992, p. 203) has pointed out, the Misesian theory of rationality is not in fact even *trying* to explain decision making, which it considers to be a task for psychology. Instead, "the function of the microeconomic theory of the decision is *precisely* that of providing the tautologous framework required for the subsequent theory of the market process."

11. This is not to say that Weber's notion of scholarly objectivity was identical with the view being advanced here. For example, he seemed to think that it was possible to separate judgments of significance from judgments of fact, and that the personal perspective of the scholar only needed to shape the former. This is the view that Gadamer criticized in Emilio Betti's work, and which more recently has been associated with E.D. Hirsch (1967).

12. In fact Weber was more directly under the influence of another member of the *verstehen* tradition, the neo-Kantian philosopher Heinrich Rickert, but for the purposes of this overview the differences are not important.

13. The standard accounts of Dilthey's point of view always make more of this catch phrase than a careful reading of Dilthey would justify. In fact he was a subtle thinker who in many ways saw beyond this kind of simplistic dichotomy. For our purposes here, though, it is useful to focus on the oversimplified version of the theory which circulated in the early twentieth century. For a more adequate interpretation of Dilthey, see Ermarth (1978).

14. In a dispute with market socialist Abba Lerner, Dobb (1933, p. 591) mocked the idea of the "sacredness of consumer preferences."

15. Gadamer's book *Truth and Method* is extraordinarily difficult, but fortunately a number of excellent works have been published which translate it into a more accessible language. Of particular help are the books I cite by Weinsheimer and Warnke. The paper by Madison (1991) relates Gadamer's work to the Austrian school. A useful overview of Gadamer's argument that also compares and contrasts it to the later Wittgenstein is Jürgen Habermas's review (1970). Although this was a very sympathetic treatment, at the end of the review Habermas raised a criticism which touched off an important debate, highly relevant to the themes of this paper, about the nature of scholarly objectivity.

16. There is circumstantial evidence to suggest that Mises was influenced by, and perhaps even enthusiastic about, the phenomenological movement. It is said that Husserl's work was a favorite topic at Mises' seminar in Vienna.

17. Independently from Husserl's work, the writings of Michael Polanyi (1958) have also demonstrated the extent to which adhering to the standards of science amounts to following a strict moral code.

18. This shows up in shortcomings of the interpretive social science work which took Husserl as its inspiration. Alfred Schütz's profound contribution to sociology attempts to wed Husserl's philosophy with the work of Max Weber, but never gives a satisfactory account of the nature of intersubjectivity. The scholar seems forced to toggle between a participatory study of the subjective level, that is, the "biographical situation" of the agent under examination, and an observational study of the objective level, that is, the "scientific situation" of the neutral observer. The social scientist is supposed to participate in the subjective life-world of the agent, and yet is supposed to take on a neutral, value-free standpoint. What remains unclear is the relationship between participation and observation. Schützian sociology seems to lapse into the very relativism which Husserl was striving to avoid. These criticisms of Schütz are elaborated by Dallmayr and McCarthy (1977).

19. Indeed the very issue of what the state-of-the-art of knowledge is within a profession will tend to be an issue that is always in contention to some extent.

20. I have elaborated why I think that research and education ought to be understood as interconnected in Lavoie (1994).

21. My own favorite candidate for such condemnation would be most of neoclassical economics.

REFERENCES

Anderson, M. 1992. *Impostors in the Temple.* New York: Simon & Schuster.

Bartley, W. W. 1990. *Unfathomed Knowledge, Unmeasured Wealth: On Universities and the Wealth of Nations.* La Salle, IL: Open Court.

Bloom, A. 1987. *The Closing of the American Mind: How Higher Education Has Failed Democracy and Impoverished the Souls of Today's Students.* New York: Simon & Schuster.

D'Souza, D. 1991. *Illiberal Education: The Politics of Race and Sex on Campus.* New York: Free Press.

Dallmayr, F. R., and T. A. McCarthy (eds.). 1977. *Understanding and Social Inquiry.* Notre Dame, IN: University of Notre Dame Press.

Dobb, M. H. 1933. "Economic Theory and the Problems of a Socialist Economy." *Economic Journal*, 43: 588-98.

Edmundson, M. (ed.). 1993. *Wild Orchids and Trotsky: Messages from American Universities.* New York: Penguin.

Ermarth, M. 1978. *Wilhelm Dilthey: The Critique of Historical Reason.* Chicago: University of Chicago Press.

Evangelauf, J. 1994. "A New 'Carnegie Classification.'" *The Chronicle of Higher Education*, 40 (31).

Gadamer, H.-G. 1986/1992. "The Idea of the University." Address given in Heidelberg, translated in *Hans-Georg Gadamer on Education, Poetry, and History: Applied Hermeneutics*, edited by D. Misgeld and G. Nicholson. Albany: State University of New York Press.

________ . 1963/1987. "The Problem of Historical Consciousness." Reprinted in *Interpretive Social Science: A Second Look*, edited by Rabinow and Sullivan. Berkeley: University of California Press.

________ . 1960/1989. *Truth and Method.* Revised translation by J. Weinsheimer and D. Marshall. New York: Crossroad.

Habermas, J. 1970. "A Review of Gadamer's Truth and Method." Pp. 251-90 in *Zur Logic der Sozialwissenschaften.* Reprinted in *Understanding and Social Inquiry*, edited by F. R. Dallmayr and T. A. McCarthy. Notre Dame: University of Notre Dame Press.

Hirsch, E. D., Jr. 1967. *Validity in Interpretation.* New Haven: Yale University Press.

Kirzner, I. M. 1992. *The Meaning of Market Process: Essays in the Development of Modern Austrian Economics.* New York: Routledge.

Lavoie, D. 1994. "Higher Education, Socialism, and the Future of Democracy." Unpublished paper presented at the Mont Pelerin Society meetings, Cannes, France.

Madison, G. B. 1991. "Getting Beyond Objectivism: The Philosophical Hermeneutics of Gadamer and Ricoeur." Pp. 34-58 in *Economics and Hermeneutics*, edited by D. Lavoie. London: Routledge.

Mises, L. von. 1949/1966. *Human Action: A Treatise on Economics.* Chicago: Henry Regnery Company.

Polanyi, M. 1958. *Personal Knowledge: Towards a Post-Critical Philosophy.* Chicago: University of Chicago Press.

Powell, J. 1994. "Review of *The Fall of the Ivory Tower* by George Roche." *Laissez Faire Books*, April.

Sowell, T. 1993. *Inside American Education: The Decline, the Deception, the Dogmas.* New York: The Free Press.

Sykes, C. J. 1988. *ProfScam: Professors and the Demise of Higher Education.* New York: St. Martin's.

Warnke, G. 1987. *Gadamer: Hermeneutics, Tradition and Reason.* Cambridge: Polity Press.

Weber, M. 1904/1977. "/'Objectivity' in Social Science and Social Policy." From *The Methodology of the Social Sciences*, reprinted in *Understanding and Social Inquiry*, edited by F. Dallmayr and T. McCarthy. University of Notre Dame Press

Weinsheimer, J. C. 1985. *Gadamer's Hermeneutics: A Reading of Truth and Method.* New Haven: Yale University Press.

A DIFFICULT DISTINCTION

Hans F. Sennholz

During the summer of 1993 I had the opportunity to meet a number of Russian professionals visiting the Georgia Institute of Technology in Atlanta and Duke University in Durham, North Carolina. They had come to the United States eagerly seeking knowledge about the functioning of democratic institutions and the working of a market order. Having experienced first hand that Marxism and Leninism do not work, they were searching for the secrets of American prosperity and for what they had to do to be successful in the new market order of Russia.

The Russian move to capitalism since 1991, as they described it vividly, is bearing fruit slowly and painfully. The old economic structure is in disarray and the new is barely discernible in the maze of confusion and disorder. Moving aimlessly between the market order and the command system, between capitalism and communism, large sectors of the economy are crumbling and output is plummeting. While many privatized or newly founded enterprises in trade and commerce are flourishing—primarily with imported products—the large State conglomerates manage to survive without much production for the market merely by consuming their meager capital resources and with the help of generous government credits. Most consumer products, which were decontrolled in January 1992, are readily available at soaring prices. With the

Advances in Austrian Economics, Volume 2B, pages 405-413.

ISBN: 1-55938-531-6

budget deficit of the Russian government exceeding 10 percent of GNP, the central bank is preoccupied with printing money to finance it all. The annual inflation rate is well over 1,000 percent.[1] Feeling beaten down by life's daily punishment, the mood of many Russians has turned nasty, to which the December 1993 election returns clearly attest. The political situation shows signs of becoming explosive.[2]

The poverty and despair of millions of Russians contrast sharply with the conspicuous life styles of some *nouveaux riches* who frequent exclusive resorts from the beaches of Yalta to the mountains of St. Moritz. Many of these are ex-communists who, as managers of the new enterprises, parlayed their know-how into personal fortunes. They are accustomed to fraud and bribery which are efficient lubricants in every kind of command system. Now, liberated from the tyranny of the communist party and the terror of the Gulag, they feel free to engage in all sorts of graft, creating large personal fortunes (Edwards 1993). These *nouveaux riches* frequently compete in their fashion with an emerging class of genuine entrepreneurs who are the driving force of the market system. Countless Russians are miraculously transforming their own lives, creating functioning businesses and a viable enterprise order.

On first glance, it may be simple to distinguish between the entrepreneurs who are busily adjusting the complex production activities to the radically changed data of institutional setting and numerous swindlers who are taking advantage of the people's confusion, desperation, and trust. Upon further reflection, however, the distinction may be obscured by considerations of legality and morality. Entrepreneurial activities may be declared illegal and, therefore, by the laws of the country, punishable. Both the thief and the entrepreneur may earn the wrath of the judges and be incarcerated together. If judges and juries treat criminals and entrepreneurs alike, it is unlikely that the public will view them in a different light.

Wherever entrepreneurial activity is declared illegal it may descend to the underground economy. After all, legislators and regulators cannot for long impose their will on human nature. Entrepreneurs become black marketeers who simply ignore the price edicts. Thieving officials are likely to join them in the underground economy and engage in valuable entrepreneurial activity, adjusting the production to the changes in conditions. It is a specific entrepreneurial function to determine the employment of the factors of production, to withdraw them from one line of business and employ them in another where they serve consumers better. To withdraw materials and supplies from State enterprises that waste them in inefficient production on needless goods or do not use them at all; to convert a store, shop, or factory from a State institution that is sovereign unto itself to an enterprise serving the public; or to shift the ownership of the means of production from the hands of those who waste and mismanage them to those of more efficient producers—all these are entrepreneurial activities. The fact that they are accomplished in violation of a law or regulation does not negate the function although it does raise serious ethical questions. Though entrepreneurial activity and moral disciplines are guided by their own principles in their own spheres, the former nevertheless depends on the latter which in the end tend to prevail.

The common inability to distinguish between the activities of the manipulators and the labors of genuine entrepreneurs is giving "democracy" and "capitalism" a bad name and casting serious doubt on the future of the reform. This is not to imply that anyone will ever want to restore the soviet command system. On the contrary, the market order has won. Even high officials of the former soviet system readily admit the superiority of the capitalistic system. We doubt, however, that the future system in Russia and several of its empire satellites will be democratic. Guided by the example of China in its introduction and enforcement of market reforms, it sooner or later may turn openly antidemocratic which would have chilling effects on Russia's relationship with the democratic West, especially the United States.

It is difficult to read the future by the past. But we do know that *in an unhampered market order* the differences between the entrepreneurial activities of businessmen and the fraudulent practices of charlatans and swindlers are easily seen and defined. Entrepreneurs employ goods and money, continuously reshuffling the factors of production, reacting to perceived discrepancies between the prices of the complementary factors of production and the future prices of the final products. The discrepancies are the very source of their profits and losses. There are no other means of acquiring wealth than through successful service to consumers. Although entrepreneurs often err, they are the leaders of the market order, always pointing the way to material progress.

Charlatans and swindlers are malefactors who inflict harm on their fellow men. They may commit larceny, which, in its broadest sense, is the taking and carrying away of the property of another person, depriving the owner of its use. Grand larceny is distinguished from petty larceny by the value of the property stolen. They may engage in embezzlement, breaking a relationship of confidence and trust as employees, agents, trustees, and civil servants charged with the safekeeping of other people's property. They may defraud customers by selling defective merchandise or rendering services inferior to representation and advertisement. In every case they are easily distinguishable from genuine entrepreneurs. The former help to populate the prisons; the entrepreneurs occupy honored positions in society.

In a market economy chafing under a heavy burden of economic laws and regulations, the distinction between entrepreneurial activity and swindle may still be clear to an economist although economic legislation and regulation may seek to obscure it by making much entrepreneurship illegal and punishable. The brilliant entrepreneur who produces valuable goods and services under onerous conditions may intentionally or unintentionally violate one or several government mandates such as compulsory licensing and rate-making, inspection and label laws, labor laws, export and import controls, government regulations pertaining to money and banking, government edicts on energy production and distribution, environmental matters, and countless others. He may meet all the conditions of the entrepreneurial function but run afoul of a law or regulation designed to prevent him from acting as entrepreneur; he may violate a law designed to hamper or prohibit a needed service or preempt it for legislators, regulators, or another privileged social class. The law may discriminate flagrantly against some people and favor others. In short, the law or regulation itself may be grossly immoral and entrepreneurial activity proper and ethical, yet the criminal code of the land may prosecute great entrepreneurs and send them to prison.

The case is similar *in a command system of the fascist variety* building on economic laws and regulations without formally expropriating the means of production. In such an order entrepreneurship may always be criminal and the distinction between entrepreneurial and criminal activity completely obscured. Legislators and regulators set prices and wages, and judges and juries denounce and condemn entrepreneurs for violations of the wage-price edicts, which they call "black marketeering," and punish them like thieves and embezzlers. Under the influence of government pronouncements and thoughtless media repetitions, the public may view both as one and the same. It may condemn entrepreneurs and applaud their imprisonment for having violated an edict although they merely sought to use their property to satisfy the most urgent needs of consumers.

In a command system of the soviet type the scope for entrepreneurial activity as we know it is minuscule. After all, the means of production, which entrepreneurs may use to coordinate the production of goods and services, are owned by government and controlled by its officials and agents. Government enterprises are sovereign unto themselves and not accountable to the public. Yet black markets do develop despite all the brutal laws designed to suppress them. But these black markets differ significantly from those in the hampered market order or even in the command system of the controls variety in which the goods bought and sold are privately owned by the traders and have come into their possession through honest work or exchange. In the black markets of the soviet type, the goods coming to the market usually are stolen, embezzled, or plundered from government stores and warehouses. The markets are black, black markets or "criminal markets" as I would like to call them. The "criminal marketeers" deal in stolen goods only. According to the code of Judeo-Christian morals, no one can ever acquire the ownership in a stolen good, neither the criminal who commits the larceny nor the black marketeer who handles it, nor the ultimate buyer who uses it. The stolen good remains stolen property until it is returned to its rightful owner.

Three types of people make up the criminal markets: the thieves who purloin the state property, the black marketeers who knowingly handle it, and the buyers who knowingly acquire it. All three are guilty under God's law and man's criminal law. Under a brutal command regime, the first may be punished for grand larceny and economic crimes against society and suffer the death penalty; the second may be sent to a Siberian Gulag; and the third be fined and forced to make restitution.

In the new Russia free markets, black markets and criminal markets exist side by side, interconnected and interacting, keeping in close touch with the public sector that continues to be an important source of supplies. The most honest markets undoubtedly are the street markets in which countless traders peddle used household wares, second-hand clothing, and imported consumer products. Made legal in 1992 they have made Moscow streets a great bazaar and given rise to a kind of "sidewalk capitalism." And yet, even in these markets it is difficult to distinguish between the goods that were acquired honestly and those obtained through thievery, especially by crooked State store managers. The Russians call these markets "tolkuchki" or "push markets" because the streets are crowded and nearly impassable; I prefer to call them "suitcase markets" because most goods arrive in suitcases, valises, and traveling bags (Edwards 1993, pp. 13-16).

The budding capital market is kept in a continuing state of confusion and commotion not only by the bungling and half-hearted official efforts at privatization but also by much deception and outright fraud. The *New York Times* laments fake lotteries and phony investment schemes. Fictitious companies advertise nonexistent services. Real estate brokers trick owners into selling their apartments and sell apartments that are not for sale. Investment companies promise cash and bonuses and then disappear. Some use advertising that is deceitful and morally wrong but lawfully unprosecutable. The only guardian of the truth in many cases is the press drawing attention to false advertising. It is no wonder that many Russians don't believe in anything any more—not in the government, not in politicians, and not in what they believe to be capitalism (Bohlen 1994b).

The issue of privatization vouchers in early 1992 laid the cornerstone of the capitalistic order: the stock market. Carrying a nominal value of 10,000 rubles, the vouchers could be sold in voucher markets, used to buy stock of State enterprises sold at auctions, or be entrusted to some 657 registered investment companies. As of the beginning of 1994 only one half of all privatization vouchers had been invested in corporate stock or investment company shares. The unused vouchers have become subject to a feverish scramble by the investment companies that vary greatly in size, managerial ability, and credibility. They are a natural attraction for all swindlers who seek to persuade their victims to part with their vouchers. Many Russians are easy victims because much of this is beyond the comprehension of the average citizen who has never heard about shares, stock markets, and investment companies (Bohlen 1994b, pp. 1, 16).

The privatization process is mired in confusion, politics, and crime. Surely, there are many reassuring voices who are urging us not to write off the Russian reforms despite the dramatic events of the last three years: a couple of coup d'etat, three prime ministers, and five economic ministers. After all, there are hundreds of thousands of new businesses throughout Russia, 86,000 privatized companies, a widespread banking system, commodity and stock exchanges, and market prices (Fyodorov 1994a). Robert Krieble of the Krieble Institute, which supports some forty reform teams throughout the former Union, reports that in the Moscow region alone some 1,000 small enterprises have been sold to employee partnerships, another 1,000 at over 100 public auctions. Some seventy percent of the retail businesses and forty percent of medium manufacturing firms are estimated to be in private hands, that is, with one million stockholders who chose to exchange their vouchers for shares (Council for National Policy 1993, p. 52). *The Wall Street Journal Europe* (1994) reassures its readers that Prime Minister Viktor Chernomyrdin, although he managed to purge all those in government who wanted genuinely free markets, has no intention to halt the market reform. He is merely reluctant to close down unprofitable enterprises and bring about mass unemployment. Being mindful that the Russian people are tired of what they erroneously perceive to be the results of capitalism, he would like to restore some measure of stability. Yet it is doubtful that the continuing support of State enterprises with newly printed rubles can actually achieve the desired stability. A thousand-percent rate of inflation destabilizes not only the economic situation but also the social, political, and moral conditions of a country. It casts doubt on the future of reforms that may falter in an orgy of hyperinflation. With the ruble nearly worthless and the markets permeated by theft and deception, it is not surprising that violent crime stalks city streets.

In the fall of 1990 when the soviet command system was faltering visibly, this writer suggested five steps of reform that needed to be taken promptly (Sennholz 1991, pp. 165-166). Today, nearly four years later, the main steps toward a market order have not yet been taken. The Russian government has not relinquished its control over the people's money. On the contrary, clinging to its money monopoly, it has issued and continues to issue legal-tender money at hyperinflationary rates. It has not relinquished its control over financial markets but rather engages in deficit spending that continues to consume whatever liquid capital is left. Although some means of production have been privatized, the vast holdings of the defense-related industries continue to be in bureaucratic hands. And, finally, import and export restrictions continue to maintain old trade barriers. In medieval fashion, the Russian government limits exports in order to safeguard domestic supplies and restricts imports in order to protect its foreign exchange reserves.

President Boris Yeltsin undoubtedly had an opportunity to pursue a consistent reform program. In November 1991 the Russian Parliament granted him great emergency powers to introduce market reforms by decree. But by the summer of 1992 his team had abandoned its initial "policy of breakthrough" or "shock therapy" and instead sought a "more orderly transition" to the market system. The new policy signalled the end of urgently needed micro-reforms such as the constitutional rights of man, the protection of his property, and the laws of contract. And it meant the end of macro-reforms aiming at monetary stability and budgetary balance. It left the Russian economy floating rudderlessly in the ocean of politics and corruption (Aslund 1992; Hewett 1992; Smith 1993; Fyordorov 1994b). According to a December 1993 opinion poll by the All-Russian Central Institute of Public Opinion, 47 percent of the people polled considered "getting rid of mafia and corruption" (*The Economist* 1994) as the most important task in 1994. Tired of instability and corruption, fifteen million Russians casting their votes on December 12, 1993, in the referendum on a new constitution, voted for an extreme nationalist, Vladimir Zhirinovsky. Their votes bode ill for the future of democracy in Russia.

Entrepreneurs cannot be expected to correct the blunders of government policies and explode the errors in economic thought. That is the task of scholars and writers. Entrepreneurs cannot rebuild the foundation of an ethical order that provides answers to questions such as why and when an economic act is "good" or "bad," "right" or "wrong." That is the task of philosophers and theologians. Schooled in economic thought and entrepreneurial theory they should be able to distinguish between entrepreneurial activity and fraudulent behavior. Without an explanation by philosophers and theologians, it is unlikely that the public will ever comprehend it.

Many of the difficulties of reform in the former Soviet Union stem from the lack of a moral code that permits the development of a market order. The old code continues to reject individual behavior for pursuing market objectives. And the old legal system, although having lost its cruel and arbitrary characteristics, is slow to adjust to the requirements of a market order.

Most Russians and their foreign advisers may now agree that the market order would provide satisfactory standards of living for many people, but they are quick to question the fairness and equity of the system.[3] To them, the market economies present an insoluble dilemma: they efficiently provide goods and services but also breed selfishness, greed, and profit-seeking which are morally repugnant. Having denounced and vilified the capitalistic order for a generation or two, and in transition facing deception and corruption on a large scale, it is well-nigh impossible suddenly to embrace it for its productivity. Having been subjected to uninterrupted indoctrination on all levels of information and education, it can hardly be surprising that old thoughts and perceptions linger on. Most doctrines of Karl Marx and V. I. Lenin live on although the soviet world has disintegrated.

Many Russian intellectuals still see Marxism as a valid response to nineteenth-century conditions. They are now turning to Marx's more psychological and ethical writings which speak of moral evils and social alienation in capitalistic countries. They give rise to a militant sense of Marxian justice which remains a powerful attraction in many parts of the world. The Russians I met in Houston, Atlanta, and Durham politely defended the value system of the Marxian body of thought. To them, communism was still a noble experiment diametrically opposed to fascism although corrupt individuals had betrayed the ideals. The history of society was still an inexorable "history of class struggle," and the exploitation theory a valid explanation of income allocation in capitalistic countries.

Theory is the guide to policy, and policy the ratification and application of theory. A common knowledge of the catallactic theory of entrepreneurship, as it was developed so sagaciously by Professor Israel Kirzner, would go a long way toward redirecting the Russian people toward the market order.

NOTES

1. See Uchitelle 1992. Russia's Central Bank officials are arguing against credit restraint fearing economic collapse; cf. also Quinn-Judge,
2. See Bohlen 1994a. The delegates of the Russian Liberal Democratic Party, meeting at its Fifth Congress, voted to confer full powers to control all party affairs on their leader until 2004; cf. also Sloane 1994; Kaplan 1994.
3. See Haitt 1994; Sachs 1990; Winiecki 1991; Williamson 1991; Anderson 1992; Peck and Richardson 1992.

REFERENCES

Anderson, A. 1992. *The Ruble Problem: A Competitive Solution.* Stanford: The Hoover Institution.

Aslund, A. 1992. *Post-Communist Economic Revolutions: How Big the Bang?* Washington, DC: Center for Strategic and International Studies.

Bohlen, C. 1994a. "Zhirinovsky Cult Grows: All Power to the Leader." *New York Times*, April 5.

———. 1994b. "A New Russia: Now Thrive the Swindlers." *New York Times*, March 17: A16.

Council for National Policy. 1993. "Boris Yeltsin's Russia: Freedom at Last?" *Policy Council*, Washington, DC.

The Economist. 1994. (London), January 29-February 4: 25.

Edwards, M. 1993. "A Broken Empire." *National Geographic* (March): 3-20. Fyodorov, B. G. 1994a. "Russian Reform Has Been Weakened from Within and Without." Fankfurt, *International Herald Tribune*, February 16.

———. 1994b. "Moscow Without Mirrors." *New York Times*, April 1: A27.

Hewett, A. E. 1992. *Open for Business: Russia's Return to the Global Economy*. Washington, DC: Brookings Institution.

Hiatt, F. 1994. "Divergent Western Advice Floods Russia." *Washington Post*, March 30: A26.

Kaplan, F. 1994. "Moscow Awash in Rumors of Coup." *Boston Globe*, March 20: 2.

Peck, M. J., and T. J. Richardson (eds.). 1992. *What Is To Be Done? Proposals for the Transition to the Market*. New Haven: Yale University Press.Quinn-Judge, P. 1992. "Harvard Adviser Hits Russia's Fiscal Policies."

Boston Globe, January 16.

Sachs, J. 1990. "What Is To Be Done?" *The Economist*, January 13: 19-24.

Sennholz, H. S. 1991. "Transforming the Command Economies." *The Freeman*. Irvington-on-Hudson, NY: The Foundation for Economic Education.

Sloane, W. 1994. "Ultranationalist Zhirinovsky Resists Joining Opposition Bloc." *Christian Science Monitor*, March 31: 7.

Smith, A. 1993. *Russia and the World Economy: Problems of Integration*. London: Routledge.

Uchitelle, L. 1992. "Russia's Central Bank Resists Cuts in Lending." *New York Times*, February 16.

The Wall Street Journal Europe. 1994. Brussels, January 26.

Williamson, J. 1991. *The Economic Opening of Eastern Europe*. Washington, DC: Institute for International Economics.

Winiecki, J. 1991. *Resistance to Change in the Soviet Economic System, A Property Rights Approach*. London: Routledge.

SECTION II

BOOK REVIEWS

POWER, THE ORGANIZATION OF INQUIRY AND THE ACHIEVEMENT OF "SPONTANEOUS" ORDER:

A REVIEW ESSAY

Warren J. Samuels

There is now a substantial literature on the history, operation, and putative effects of the major private foundations that have helped fund the leading social science research organizations and many scholarly projects. The book reviewed here, Donald Fisher's *Fundamental Development of the Social Sciences* (1993), examines the role of Rockefeller philanthropy, especially that of the Laura Spelman Rockefeller Memorial (LSRM), in creating and funding the Social Science Research Council (SSRC), commencing in 1923, carrying the story to about 1945.[1] Fisher examines the intentions of the funding foundations and the enormous impact they seem to have had on the conduct and direction of research in the social sciences[2] during the last three-quarters of a century. I say "seem to have had" because, while they surely reinforced certain trends, it is likely that these trends would have transpired even without their resources—although perhaps not quite as strongly.[3] Among these trends are

Advances in Austrian Economics, Volume 2B, pages 417-426.

ISBN: 1-55938-531-6

professionalization and scientism in general and empiricism and quantification in particular, including formalization. Readers of this publication will be interested to find that SSRC facilitated the rise and role of the social science expert and thereby the deliberative, or constructivist, elements in the achievement of so-called spontaneous order.

I. ROCKEFELLER PHILANTHROPY AND THE SSRC

As Fisher tells the story, the formation in 1923 of SSRC was the work of the eminent political scientist, Charles E. Merriam, president of the American Political Science Association in 1921 and from 1923 the chair of the Department of Political Science at the University of Chicago, and Beardsley Ruml, the 26-year-old director of the Laura Spelman Rockefeller Memorial—and, at the time of World War II, creator of income tax withholding. Numerous other leading figures in each of the social sciences were also active in varying capacities. Among the economists with principal roles were Wesley C. Mitchell (whose National Bureau of Economic Research had been founded in 1920), Edwin F. Gay, Frederic Dewhurst, Edmund E. Day, Edwin G. Nourse, Harry Jerome, Walter F. Wilcox, Harold G. Moulton, Walter W. Stewart, John V. Van Sickle, J. H. Willits, and Sumner H. Slichter. Eminent academicians from other disciplines included Ernest W. Burgess, Raymond B. Fosdick, Lawrence K. Frank, John M. Gaus, Harold D. Lasswell, Robert S. Lynd, Howard W. Odum, William Fielding Ogburn, Robert Redfield, Stuart A. Rice, Edward Sapir, Arthur M. Schlesinger, James T. Shotwell, and Edwin B. Wilson. Many social scientists, leading and non-leading, were, of course, beneficiaries of SSRC grants.

Fisher tells the SSRC story, which is also that of Rockefeller philanthropy and, to a lesser but growing extent, that of the federal government, in four chapters: Chapter 2 deals with creation and early organization of SSRC, 1923-1927; Chapter 3, with the gilded age of expansion and growth, 1927-1930; Chapter 4, consolidation and retrenchment, 1930-1936; and Chapter 5, self-criticism, reconstruction, and planning, 1937-1945. Chapter 6 explores the impact of SSRC on the social sciences in North America, especially the boundary changes; and Chapter 7 presents conclusions. Needless to say, the organizational history is one of different and changing relationships among organizations and individuals, including changes in SSRC organization (and the Rockefeller philanthropies) and of personnel.

Among the diverse and conflicting motivations of the principals were: greater opportunity for and greater scientificity of research in the social sciences; the breakdown of barriers between disciplines; greater prestige and greater correlation and coordination as science, that is, structural legitimation both of each discipline and the social sciences as such; attention to social problems

in order to sustain the status quo: the conduct of social control and social change through scientific social research, that is, the development of a problem-solving mentality involving constructivist deliberative policy over non-deliberative policy-making; greater clarity of demarcation between social science and everyday knowledge; creation of a superdiscipline of a new science of society, an integrated social science; the transmission and internalization of the ideology of the ruling class as the "common sense of society" (p. 19); the creating of a bargain, a convergence of interests (p. 28), between academics and the ruling institutions of society; and, implicit in much of the foregoing, the formation and enhancement of the role of the expert in the making of policy as one of the social roles of the person of knowledge. The tensions are obvious: Social sciences en mass were to be promoted and individual disciplines were to have clearer and specialized identities, yet barriers between disciplines were to be broken down and a superdiscipline encompassing all of the social sciences was to be formed. Social scientists were to have the status of objective scientists, but they were also to be policy activists. Deliberative policy-making was to be supported by problem-solution oriented social research; and a transcendental agenda of sustaining the systemic if not also the institutional status quo. Such tensions are deep and significant though probably no more serious than any major venture with multiple objectives.

Dissatisfaction and conflicts developed between those who wanted to disperse resources among a larger number of projects and those who wanted to concentrate resources on a relatively few strategic objectives. Tensions arose over conflicts of interests by decision makers who also proposed projects. Other tensions related to the conflict of objectives between social engineering and social science, though this could be resolved relatively easily.

Among the research fields deliberately promoted by SSRC, typically by specific committees, were: human migration, mechanization of industry, prohibition, industrial relations, agriculture, unemployment (well before 1929), personality and culture, industry and trade, consumption and leisure, pressure groups and propaganda, social statistics, scientific methods in the social sciences, public administration, international relations, interracial relations, national resource and other planning, and community organization. Major interdisciplinary programs in public administration, including the administrative development of TVA, and social security were supported during the 1930s. Larger and more systemic objectives are suggested by the areas coming under the aegis of the famous Seven Numerals committees: (I) improvement of research organization; (II) development of research personnel; (III) enlargement, improvement, and preservation of research materials; (IV) improvement of research methods; (V) dissemination of methods and results of investigation; (VI) facilitation of research work; and (VII) enhancement of the public appreciation of the significance of the social sciences (pp. 92ff and passim). Together with the Rockefeller organizations, SSRC promoted a number of universities as regional social science research centers: Chicago, Columbia, Harvard, North Carolina at Chapel Hill, Stanford, Texas at Austin, Virginia, and Yale (p. 93). The totality of Rockefeller-SSRC social science resources were thus broadly but selectively and intensively targeted to promote both general and specific objectives. The specific means included fellowships, grants-in-aid, conferences, special projects. Over 93 percent of SSRC disbursements were financed by Rockefeller sources (p. 208).

This was the period of the perceived threat of a viable Bolshevik alternative to capitalism, the aftermath of the Red Scare. That LSRM chose to support the social sciences in order to promote conservation of the reigning order is made clear by both evidence and interpretation (by Fisher and other writers). Fisher writes that, "The transformation Ruml envisaged did not encompass a challenge to the current socioeconomic structure. Social science was going to help solve the problems faced by capitalist systems, not contribute to their downfall" (p. 32; see also pp. 9, 11 and passim).

The involvement of Rockefeller-SSRC interests and resources with the federal government was, over time, substantial and complex. Particularly instructive is the Rockefeller Foundation funding President Herbert Hoover's Research Committee on Social Trends, which produced the highly influential report, *Recent Social Trends in the United States* (1933) (pp. 96ff and passim). This project was entirely consistent with Rockefeller interests, for it, too, sought the "scientific study of the social problems facing American society" (p. 99). SSRC was made the fiscal agent for the Rockefeller Foundation funds (p. 102). Notwithstanding fears that the change in administration in 1933 "might render the report and the recommendations useless...[a]s it turned out, the report was destined to have a major impact on the SSRC, the government, and the relation between government and the social sciences" (p. 111). Whatever one may think about conservative versus liberal approaches to the interpretation of the federal government in the 1930s, Fisher insists that the objective of the Rockefeller Foundation and SSRC was "to serve the reorganization of the political and social orders" through programs "designed as means for preventing the collapse of liberal, democratic capitalism in the United States" (p. 112). These were "'sophisticated conservatives' who wished to make the status quo more stable" (p. 65), in the process seeking to improve it (p. 66), according to their lights.

Not all beneficiaries of SSRC grants became apologists, but the funding policies of SSRC (and other organizations) channeled the allocation of research resources and affected the choice of problems and professional careers of individual scholars. More important, "Rockefeller philanthropy facilitated and pushed the social control ideology...[and itself] exercised a fair amount of control over the bridging that occurred between social scientists and government and facilitated the emergence of a new form of cultural hegemony" (p. 112).

But "Rockefeller" came with a certain baggage of suspicion in many quarters, a consequence of the business and labor practices and legal history of the firms whose profits ultimately were the sources of Rockefeller philanthropy. As Fisher puts it:

> If controversy was to be avoided, then it was essential that Rockefeller interest in, and utilization of the SSRC, be kept secret. Yet while anonymity was important so was control. In order to achieve these dual objectives, a new structure was needed that as Louis Wirth noted [in a major report on the SSRC] would preserve the 'forms of democracy without some of its substance' (p. 46).[4]

The results, according to Fisher, were mixed; certainly not everyone's objectives were fulfilled, but these were contradictory from the start. (1) SSRC "led the movement away from fundamental science to concrete studies of practical concern" (p. 165). "The main accomplishment of the Council had been the improvement of research competence, not fundamental progress" (p. 236). "Prior to the creation of the SSRC it is fair to say that research was isolated, specific, and for the most part humanistic.... SSRC not only substantially increased the amount of social research conducted in the United States but also pushed and pulled researchers in an empirical direction" (p. 205). (2) The status and activity of both social science in general and the individual social science disciplines were promoted, not an integrated social science (p. 224). His verdict is "that many social scientists were more interested in furthering their own careers, institutions, and disciplines rather than the development of integrated social science" (p. 241). (3) "The alliance between the ruling class and the State was mediated by philanthropy and social scientists" (p. 165).

Several questions arise: (1) Was there no fundamental theoretical development in the social sciences between 1923 and 1945? I think there was, even if SSRC et al. had little directly to do with it—and it is not clear that it did have little directly and indirectly to do with it. (2) How important was an integrated science of society to disciplinarians in the several social sciences? Fisher overstates how much this was an operative possibility in academia, the preferences of a few individuals aside. Even he recognizes the predominance of a "long-term structural trend toward an increasing division of labor" (p. 237) as well as careerism working to the contrary. (3) How much more important than SSRC and Rockefeller objectives was the simple availability of money for research, however much that research was skewed, if only in the writing of research proposals? Fisher quotes Ruml as thinking in 1951 that "the boys were more interested in getting the money than they were in the development of their subject matter on a fundamental basis" (p. 236). (4) Would not the methodological development of economics—specifically its greater empiricism, mathematicization, and formalism—likely have transpired even absent SSRC?[5]

II. SIGNIFICANCE

Several preliminary points:

First, prior to the foundation of SSRC in 1923, economists had been engaged in the pursuit of disciplinary and professional status as a science for quite some time, at least since the efforts of Alfred Marshall in England and the chairs of the major economics departments in the United States, in the late nineteenth century. SSRC and related activities abetted their success but that success would have been achieved even in the absence of SSRC. Correlative with this quest for the status of a science, economists sought both the social role of the expert and the position of having something serious to say about the economic role of government.

Second, most scholars favored capitalism and the institutional status quo, at least in general, in which respects they were like most people. At most they wanted to reform, not to destroy, the system. They wanted to perpetuate and to enhance liberal democratic capitalism in the United States. The argument was largely not whether capitalism was to be sustained but what form it would institutionally take.[6]

Third, the dominant ideology notwithstanding, government is fundamentally important for the organization and operation of the economic system. The operative question involves the determination of the uses to which government is to be put.

Fourth, substantially all economists have had a problem-solving orientation, some quite conspicuously, but most if not all, even those articulating a philosophy of laissez faire, had their own agendas for proper and sound government action. Economic theorists have almost always looked for the policy implications of their theories.[7]

Fifth, the approach to policy taken by Carl Menger and Friedrich von Hayek, when considered in nonideological terms, emphasizes the combined working of deliberative and nondeliberative forces. Even those institutions and arrangements which evolve more or less organically, spontaneously and nondeliberatively are held susceptible to critical intelligence and deliberative reform. This view, so stated, is not incompatible with the ideas of Thorstein Veblen and John R. Commons.

Fisher's study shows how the SSRC facilitated the rise and role of the social science expert and thereby the deliberative, or constructivist, elements in the achievement of so-called spontaneous order. In doing so, SSRC and Rockefeller philanthropy contributed to or reinforced movements and activities which were more broadly and more fundamentally based.

According to Fisher, "The social sciences had been molded to fit in with changes in the relation between the private and public sectors." Indeed, "Through the SSRC, Rockefeller philanthropy played a critical role in changing the public/private relation" (p. 230). Moreover, "The shift that occurred was away from basic research and fundamental development of the social sciences, toward the practical social welfare activities that later characterized postwar federal contract research. It was a shift from pure and purposive research toward explicitly applied research. Rather than independent critics of government or foundations, social scientists had become scientific servants of the State." In all these respects, "the resources, the prestige, and, necessarily, the power of Rockefeller philanthropy" were placed "behind these efforts." At bottom was social control under a changing cultural hegemony: "That part of the ideology that emphasized social control linked scientific social research to the major social problems that faced society in the United States" (p. 230). The changing cultural hegemony signifies for Fisher that:

> The alliance that emerged in the 1930s between the State, Rockefeller philanthropy, and social scientists involved a dramatic shift within the SSRC from fundamental development to an almost exclusive emphasis on practical service.... Social scientific knowledge was promoted because of its ability to legitimize planning and control. As it involved the SSRC, this process of mutual legitimation was funded, guided, and to some extent controlled by Rockefeller philanthropy (pp. 231-232).

Social scientists drawn into the public arena—and any social scientist whose work was important tended to be so—"were involved in a process of mutual legitimation... In exchange for their objectivity and scientific disinterestedness, these academics received from the State public recognition of their status as experts working for the social good" (p. 8). Fisher finds that "the cooperation of philanthropy and the State in the bargaining process is indicative of the increasing interpenetration of political and civil society during the period" (p. 8; on the distinction between political and civil society, see p. 7). In addition, through the formation of social science knowledge, "the ideology of the ruling class is internalized and made into the common sense of society" (p. 19).

The question of criticism is extremely meaningful for Fisher:

> The SSRC, it appeared, had missed a unique opportunity to establish a science of society.... Legitimacy and cognitive authority were attached to those disciplines and fields like economics, statistics, and public administration that would through their science contribute directly to the maintenance of the social order. The bargain that had been struck between social scientists, the State, and Rockefeller philanthropy deemphasized intellectual and critical functions in favor of technical investigations whose aims were the preservation of the status quo (p. 234).

One danger of an integrated social science likely would have been the raising of critical, fundamental questions about the status quo. And as for the "bargain," Fisher writes that "another major implication of this work is that the State institutions that were developed in the post-Second World War era like NSF and the National Institute of Education were modeled on the foundations and took over the primary role of agents for the ruling class" (p. 248)—no fundamental criticism likely emanate from those sources either.

Fisher's approach to the study of SSRC and Rockefeller philanthropy emphasizes the social construction of the social sciences and a non-Whig approach to their history. Apropos of change, he focuses on both the motivations and processes internal to disciplines, including professionalization, and external factors and forces, especially:

> the exchange of power and resources between the academy, the economy, and the State. As universities have become more industrial and technical, so academics have become more dependent and, therefore, more vulnerable to role definitions imposed from outside the profession and the academy. The most significant resource holders... were the philanthropic foundations (p. 3).

This encompasses the development of modern social science contemporaneously with the "emergence of the modern welfare State and the place of social scientific research in this structure" (p. 6), as the expertise of social scientists was required in orchestrating, operating, and assessing the institutions of the welfare state.

If one has a predisposition to organic spontaneous nondeliberative decision making, the foregoing may appear anathema. If one recognizes, perhaps affirms, the critical role of constructivist deliberative decision making, the foregoing will be unsurprising. But one can interpret Rockefeller philanthropy and SSRC to have been participants in the process of organic spontaneous nondeliberative decision making. That approach to social order and change does not rule out deliberative decisions by participants. And that is precisely what Ruml and all the others associated with Rockefeller and SSRC policy were involved in: the making of private decisions as contributions to the allocation of resources with regard to social change. One would have to rule out of analytical and normative bounds collective private action to reach a different conclusion. Moreover, that such collective private action can exist in a symbiotic relation with government is also suggestive: government can be seen, in part, as a mode of pursuing organically generated ends. All this is, of course, rather different from the views of those who have decried governmental activism, especially (though not solely) since the New Deal. What is in some sense true about all this, is, of course quite another matter. But Fisher's work gives us food for thought. What is unequivocal, however, is the contributory role of Rockefeller and other organizations, including governments, in the social construction of the system of U.S. research universities (see Geiger 1993; Wilson 1993).

NOTES

1. Fisher himself acknowledges grants from the Rockefeller Archive Center and the Social Sciences and Humanities Research Council of Canada, as well as from his employer, the University

of British Columbia (p. viii). Subsequent discussion will indicate that his interpretation of SSRC and Rockefeller philanthropy is an independent one. Fisher has written over nine books and journal articles on various aspects of U.S., British, and Canadian philanthropy and the social sciences, university education in general, and scientific medicine, as well as on the relation between power and knowledge. Both his own work and the other major literature in the field are listed in his extensive thirty-two page bibliography.

Full disclosure requires that I state that I have neither applied for nor received foundation grants for my own research. I have received small grants to finance data acquisition for a graduate student dissertation, a small Law and Society Association conference on law and economics, the travel by Ronald Meek to the United States for a history of economic thought conference, and the photocopying of research materials. The first two were from NSF; the third, from Ford; and the fourth, running several years in the 1960s, from Southern Bell.

2. By social sciences is generally meant anthropology, sociology, political science, economics, psychology, statistics, and history (p. 9), though at various organizational meetings not all disciplines were represented.

3. Fisher surely exaggerates when he writes that "It is fair to say that the story of the SSRC is just about the whole story of the changing nature of social scientific research in the United States in the interwar period" (p. 8).

4. This may seem strong, particularly with regard to any expectations as to anonymity of funding, but anonymity of control was indeed critical. Thus the powerful Problems and Policy Committee (PPC) of SSRC was formed in 1925 as a means of high-level control. As Wirth also said in his report, PPC was "in part a response to the dependence of the Council upon support from foundations" (p. 47). As Fisher puts it, "In line with its own practices, the LSRM had created a self-perpetuating elite to run the affairs of the SSRC" (p. 47), and, more broadly, "The ability to appoint advisory committees provided the ideal mechanism for masking Rockefeller involvement. Not only would the topic and the funding all be under the PPC heading but it could also be made to look as though the idea had come from the social scientists rather than from outside" (p. 50). A tension therefore inevitably developed "in the relationship between Rockefeller philanthropy and the social scientists because the Rockefeller side wanted the Council to appear to be an independent institution while, at the same time, the Rockefeller side wanted to maintain control" (p. 69). One early example of the means of control was that the Council had to apply to LSRM for funds "that were already guaranteed by the memorial" (p. 69), thus according the memorial the opportunity for detailed oversight. An early report of the Executive Committee and Director of SSRC, dated November 22, 1927, indicated that the LSRM was through the SSRC "able to promote lines of work in social science which clearly need to be done but which could not possibly be undertaken wisely by the Memorial itself" (pp. 72-73). The reader has, of course, the option of emphasizing either nefarious intentions or having to live down the Rockefeller past; either way, it seems clear that the Rockefeller philanthropists were not radicals—unless one considers Rockefeller philanthropy to have abetted, perhaps even fomented, the new cultural hegemony of which Fisher writes.

5. For a critical review of Fisher's theses, see Bulmer (1993).

6 Fisher goes beyond this point in arguing that it developed that "social scientists should become the technical servants of power, and that, as servants, they should produce disciplined knowledge that would increase social control and thereby maintain the status quo" (p. 242). This may sound extreme, but surely it applies to those who accept and work for such institutions as the Federal Reserve System and International Monetary Fund as if they were ontologically given elements of the economic system, whereas in fact they are part of the power structure of the existing order with no special ontological or epistemological status.

7. Fisher also focuses on the demarcation of social science knowledge from other knowledge:

> The focus is on the social construction of a boundary that separates social science knowledge from everyday knowledge.... The assumption is that neither science nor social science is

separate or distinctive in and of itself. What is of interest are the efforts made by practitioners and their patrons to convince themselves and others that this is the case. It is instructive therefore to focus on boundary work not because the boundaries are "real" but rather because the people involved put a great deal of effort into the creation and maintenance of the boundary between social science and other knowledge (p. 4).

REFERENCES

Bulmer, M. 1993. "Ventures in Patronage." *Science*, 262: 259-260.

Fisher, D. 1993. *Fundamental Development of the Social Sciences: Rockefeller Philanthropy and the United States Social Science Research Council.* Ann Arbor, MI: University of Michigan Press.

Geiger, R. L. 1993. *Research and Relevant Knowledge: American Research Universities Since World War II.* New York: Oxford University Press.

President's Research Committee on Social Trends. 1933. *Recent Social Trends in the United States.* Washington, DC.

Wilson, D. A. 1993. "Academic Paragons." *Science*, 262: 771.

THE ECONOMICS OF FRIEDRICH HAYEK

Bruce Caldwell

Friedrich A. Hayek's writings span seven decades. His *Collected Works*, now being edited, will reach (and probably exceed) twenty volumes. The secondary literature grows like topsy. How does one get a handle on all of this? Where does an economist start, who wants to understand Hayek's many contributions to knowledge? Even more difficult: where might one advise a student to begin?

Gerry Steele's recent book, *The Economics of Friedrich Hayek*, is certainly a viable candidate. Steele sympathetically summarizes Hayek's contributions to economics, and situates those writings within the broader scheme of his social thought. The exposition is admirably concise and clear, yet still faithful to the subtleties of Hayekian analysis. Given the scope of Hayek's vision, Steele's book is an admirable achievement. It is not wholly without weaknesses, however, a point to which I will return.

Steele employs a logical rather than a chronological approach to explaining Hayek's ideas. A brief introduction is followed by a chapter entitled "Liberty and Law" in which Hayek's writings about how individual intentional actions can produce unintended spontaneous orders are highlighted, then linked to notions of liberty. His ideas are contrasted with those of constructive rationalists, who believe that, if they are to yield the proper outcomes (those consistent with "social justice," a favorite Hayekian weasel-word), social

Advances in Austrian Economics, Volume 2B, pages 427-431.

ISBN: 1-55938-531-6

institutions must be consciously designed. Hayek's preference for the common law over legislation is examined, together with his insistence that just laws be "abstract, general, prospective, known, certain and equitable" (p. 46). His consequentialist justification of democracy is taken up next (democracy was preferred by Hayek principally because it helped to ensure the orderly tranfer of political power), as well as his warnings of the dangers of majoritarian politics, especially egalitarianism. His antidotes (commonly shared notions of right and wrong, education, and a separation of powers under a strong constitution) are then outlined, as well as some of the specific proposals for reform that are contained in *The Constitution of Liberty*.

Chapter Three examines Hayek's ideas on the proper scope of state intervention in the economy. After first identifying the crucial necessity of the protection of property rights for the establishment of an order, Steele then moves to a discussion of Hayek's position on a number of the standard issues of public finance: how to deal with neighborhood effects (externalities), the role of the government in providing a "safety net" of welfare legislation, and his preferred forms of taxation. Hayek favored proportional taxation on the grounds that it would be easier for taxpayers to assess just how much each government program was costing them; elements of progressivity under his scheme could always be introduced via the allocation of the funds. Steele concludes the chapter by briefly noting the dependence of utilitarianism (the ultimate consequentialist doctrine) on omniscience. Unless one possessed the latter trait, how would one be able to tell the full consequences of one's actions, particularly in matters in which complex phenomena are involved?

The next chapter deals with Hayek's contributions to methodology. It begins with his later work on the theory of complex phenomena and the related doctrine that pattern prediction is often the best that we can do when dealing with such phenomena. Next comes Hayek's assertion that the structure of the human mind is everywhere the same, a position that finds its justification in his psychological work in *The Sensory Order*. Steele then very briefly takes up Hayek's most extended explicit discussion of methodology, the "Scientism" essay, focusing his attack on historicism. (I emphasize "explicit" because Hayek managed to inject methodological points into virtually everything he wrote.) The last part of the chapter contains an excellent summary of Hayek's brief against equilibrium theory.

Chapters Two through Four, then, contain Hayek's broader social, political, and philosophical vision, as found in his methodological writings and such works as *The Constitution of Liberty* and *Law, Legislation and Liberty*. Chapters Five through Ten concern Hayek's contributions to economics proper. This manner of approach helps the reader to see the coherence of Hayek's project, and to appreciate just how comprehensive an undertaking it was.

Chapter Five concerns the socialist calculation debate, and Steele sagely follows Lavoie's (1985) now classic revisionist account (*Rivalry and Central*

Planning: The Socialist Calculation Debate Reconsidered). He correctly notes that the market socialists had their task made easier by other economists: "Paradoxically, both classical long-run analysis and neoclassical (Walrasian) general equilibrium had given an exaggerated idea of the efficacy of market capitalism in producing cohesion, and this was exploited by Oskar Lange in his construction of socialist counterarguments" (p. 112). The Austrian analysis of the market process is not utopian; there is no guarantee of coordination. What it does claim is that a system in which prices are free to adjust to reflect relative scarcities is one in which coordination is least likely to be hindered. (Or, to put it obversely, systems which do not give adequate recognition to the role of freely adjusting prices are likely to hinder the coordination of economic activity.) This is a crucial Austrian insight, one which the neoclassical emphases on equilibrium models (which obscures the way that markets help to create "common knowledge," and hence to assist coordination) and on efficiency (which provides grounds for intervention to "correct" for deviations from the ideal of perfectly functioning markets) can miss. Mainstream analysis is not always wrong in these matters, of course. Prisoner's Dilemma problems do emerge in certain social settings, particularly when questions of externalities arise, and Austrians have not always been very good at addressing them. But the use of models in which it is plain that the necessary "marginal conditions" are not likely to be met naturally set up the analyst to look for corrections for "market failures," remedies that can end up being worse than the disease they purport to cure.

Returning to the book: Steele's presentation of the calculation debate, in which the economic case against planning was made, is followed by an exposition of Hayek's ethical arguments against socialism. Here the author draws principally on *The Road to Serfdom*, but also mentions an earlier pamphlet (*Freedom and the Economic System*, published in 1939) in which Hayek first started to develop the themes.

Chapter Six is entitled "Neutral Money and Monetary Policy." It covers a topic that critics of Hayek never seem to get right. As Steele shows, Hayek is no monetarist. Just as price controls keep relative prices in goods markets from performing their signalling function, so does monetary policy that is aimed at securing a constant aggregate price level muck up another set of relative prices, and in particular those that influence the formation of the capital stock. The policy skepticism that is a key element of the Austrian vision is due both to our ignorance about the "correct" size of the money supply ("neutral money" is not an operational concept) and to its essential endogeneity. For some reason, particularly in Britain, critics seem to think that Hayek is a monetarist. It may be because monetarism is associated with Thatcher there, and Thatcher used to claim Hayek as a kindred spirit. But whatever its origins, the belief is wrong: Hayek comes much closer to Kaldor (whose thought he influenced) than to Friedman in his discussions about the prospects for monetarism. Kaldor and Hayek differed, of course, in their response to the limitations of our knowledge regarding money. Kaldor castigated monetarism in order to rehabilitate other forms of intervention in markets. He somehow forgot that the sort of ignorance that makes monetary policy difficult to get right is even more of a problem for schemes that require more detailed intervention, be it an incomes policy, or a scheme for the social planning of investment, or something else.

Chapters Seven and Eight deal, respectively, with Hayek's capital and business cycle theories. In addition to being areas where Hayek's thinking evolved over time, his writings on capital and the cycle are undoubtedly the most difficult parts of his work in economics. These are topics, then, where Steele's obvious gift as an expositor would yield the greatest benefits. Unfortunately, it is just here that the author changes his approach. Steele has published articles in professional journals on these topics, and his chapters reflect his earlier and quite original contributions. Thus he argues that Austrian concepts of capital come quite close to standard business conceptions, then shows that modern investment appraisal techniques can be employed to buttress arguments made by Hayek in the capital theory debates and his battles against Keynes and his Cambridge followers. These chapters will be of considerable interest to those who are already familiar with Hayek's arguments. Furthermore, one can get some idea from them about what Hayek thought about the cycle and capital. But particularly in comparison to the chapters that precede and follow them, these two will be of less help to those who are dipping into Hayek's ideas for the first time.

Steele gets back on track in Chapters Nine and Ten, which deal with Hayek's proposals regarding the international monetary order and the privatization of money. The first draws principally on his work in the late 1930s, when Hayek was very much responding to the crises of his day. He argued then that the time was not right for a return to the gold standard (which would have required more international cooperation than could be achieved in a world on the brink of war), but neither could he stomach the sort of "monetary nationalism" being advocated by Keynes and others. After outlining the probable effects of various regimes, Hayek ended up endorsing one that was truly international, but also clearly utopian. His exercise was a theoretical one, and (as Steele notes) not without elements of constructive rationalism. It was not until some forty years later that Hayek came to endorse the denationalization of money, a radical proposal that marked the full integration of Hayek's monetary thought with the rest of his economics. The pernicious effects of attempts to manage the money supply are outlined by Steele in the first half of Chapter Ten; Hayek's proposals regarding its privatization follow.

The final chapter is titled "Hayek's Legacy," and Steele begins it with a quote from a work by Norman Barry. In my opinion the quotation perfectly captures both the essence of Hayek's message, and the reason why it failed for so long to be heard: "A doctrine that tells us more of the limitations on our ability to manage social affairs than of the possibilities of controlling the course of social and economic development is not likely to be popular in an age of scientism" (Barry 1979, p. 202, in Steele, p. 228).

Steele's book is a fine contribution to the secondary literature, and with the caveat mentioned regarding Chapters Seven and Eight on Hayek's capital and business cycle theories, it would be a fine starting point for students.

There are two additional limitations, however, that should be noted regarding Steele's approach. As I have repeatedly emphasized, the author is a virtuoso at concisely summarizing Hayek's ideas. This poses an obvious problem, though, for areas in which Hayek's ideas changed over time. How does one reconcile, for example, Hayek's insistence in *Monetary Theory and the Trade Cycle* that an acceptable theory of the cycle must be consistent with the results of equilibrium theory, with his post-1937 writings that spotlight the limitations of equilibrium theory? In general, Steele's approach though useful for many purposes is not very suitable for tracing the historical embeddedness and evolution of Hayek's ideas. Secondly, Steele does not go into much detail about the controversies that have surrounded Hayek's contributions. There are, of course, good reasons for this, not the least of which is to keep the book to a reasonable length. But even his admirers do not accept all of Hayek's ideas, and the critical assessment of a person's ideas is often made easier by a rehersal of some of the debates already existing in the literature.

These last two limitations really come down to the unreasonable complaint that no book can do everything and still be kept to a reasonable length. This is why courses on a subject typically require more than one text. If you are thinking about teaching a course on Hayek (May there be many of you in this category!!), or are simply looking for a book to recomend to a student, Gerry Steele's *The Economics of Friedrich Hayek* is a very good place to start.

REFERENCES

Barry, N. P. 1979. *Hayek's Social and Economic Philosophy*. London: Macmillan.
Hayek, F. A. 1933. *Monetary Theory and the Trade Cycle*. London: Jonathan Cape.
———. 1939. *Freedom and the Economic System*. Edited by H. Gideonse. Public Policy Pamphlet no. 29. Chicago: University of Chicago Press.
———. 1944. *The Road to Serfdom*. Chicago: University of Chicago Press.
———. 1952. *The Sensory Order*. Chicago: University of Chicago Press.
———. 1960. *The Constitution of Liberty*. Chicago: University of Chicago Press.
———. 1973-1979. *Law, Legislation and Liberty*. Chicago: University of Chicago Press.
Lavoie, D. 1985. *Rivalry and Central Planning: The Socialist Calculation Debate Reconsidered*. Cambridge: Cambridge University Press.

THE RECLAMATION OF INTERWAR MONETARY ECONOMICS:

A REVIEW ESSAY OF HAYEK AND THE KEYNESIAN AVALANCHE BY BRIAN J. McCORMICK

William N. Butos

I. INTRODUCTION

It is often claimed that Keynes is the great intersection of monetary economics in the twentieth century and that no appreciation of the relevance, analytical strengths and weaknesses, complexity, and diversity of economics can be gained without recognizing and accepting this fact. During the past few years, a succession of studies have dealt specifically with Keynes and the interwar period in England.[1] These works, of which Brian McCormick's *Hayek and the Keynesian Avalanche* is a recent addition, all find that several theorists of the period in addition to Keynes provided substantial insights into a host of questions in monetary theory, economic dynamics, trade cycles, and macro policy. Thus, one striking conclusion seems unavoidable: the success of Keynesianism after World War II must be reckoned against its neglect of pre-

Advances in Austrian Economics, Volume 2B, pages 433-446.

ISBN: 1-55938-531-6

1936 monetary economics. On this account, readers are in debt to McCormick for demonstrating that, indeed, the interwar period produced a great deal of path-breaking work often overlooked by contemporary economists.

II. OVERVIEW

McCormick aims, first, to examine the debates between Hayek and Keynes in the context of the research being pursued at the London School of Economics (LSE) and Cambridge from the 1930s through the post-World War II neoclassical synthesis and, second, to trace Hayek's later social and political thought. This expansive coverage is rather ambitious for a book of less than 300 pages. Not surprisingly, notable gaps in the story and inadequately explained ideas and linkages detract from the book. The emphasis on secondary players and issues at times tends to pull the book off focus and to distract the reader from the main storyline. These difficulties are compounded by problems with the books's pedagogy, lack of attention to detail, and poor editing.[2] In some instances they are so severe that I wonder if the book's effectiveness could have been improved substantially by another read-through by the author.

McCormick's book, it turns out, might best be considered a history of the activity during the 1930s and afterward at the LSE and Cambridge University. McCormick includes fascinating LSE course reading lists,[3] which help the reader understand intellectual activity during the 1930s, and provides insightful commentaries on luminaries such as Robbins, Hicks, Lerner, and Kaldor and on lesser appreciated players such as Gilbert and Durbin. Unfortunately, this breadth directs attention away from Hayek and Keynes. Although McCormick always keeps his protagonists on stage, the precise ways they fit into the story are not always clear. This is especially problematic for McCormick's discussion of post-World War II developments.

III. McCORMICK'S THESIS

The basic outline of McCormick's argument runs as follows: (1) Hayek's work during the 1930s, while provocative and at times even brilliant, was nonetheless flawed or irrelevant; (2) Keynes and his followers swept Hayek away because they had a more relevant "vision"; (3) Hayek did not recover from the Keynesian avalanche because he could not explain the slump phase of the cycle; (4) the response to *The General Theory* resulted in a neoclassical synthesis that contained certain Hayekian elements; and (5) the reemergence of Hayek during the 1970s primarily reflects his enduring contributions in social theory, not technical economics.

McCormick explicates and defends points (1) through (3) in the first eight of twelve chapters. Here, McCormick examines the main analytical areas intersecting the works of Keynes and Hayek, including trade cycle theory, the monetary theories of Hawtrey and Robertson, the nature of monetary equilibrium and neutral money, the Hayek-Knight capital controversy, the socialist calculation debate, and open economy issues. Chapters 9 and 10 address point (4) and Chapter 11 point (5).

Aside from the difficulties noted above, there are substantive questions that need to be raised concerning the robustness of McCormick's analysis of the "avalanche" and his interpretation of the development of Austrian economics following World War II. These difficulties, it seems to me, reflect McCormick's somewhat more basic disposition to not fully explore or appreciate the role subjectivism has played in the evolution of Austrian thinking since the 1930s. These difficult and complex matters can only be highlighted in this paper. Consequently, my discussion of necessity will be selective and mainly illustrative of these more general considerations.

IV. THE KEYNESIAN AVALANCHE

McCormick expends considerable effort presenting the interwar period's monetary economics. Although it is not clear exactly what significance McCormick actually gives to the role of analytical economics in accounting for the Keynesian avalanche,[4] his treatment in any case is uneven and his conclusions sometimes misleading or not fully substantiated.

McCormick argues that Keynes' economics was better than Hayek's for the circumstances of the 1930s. The evidence he marshals to demonstrate this, however, is unconvincing. Pieces of *The General Theory*'s economics are scattered throughout the book, but McCormick nowhere subjects the *The General Theory* to a systematic presentation or provides an argument that demonstrates its superiority. The reader is not given a good sense of which interpretation out of several possible ones McCormick believes represents the "real" Keynes.

McCormick does provide, however, an extended discussion (pp. 55-61) of Keynes' *A Treatise on Money*. His treatment warrants a brief comment. First, McCormick's presentation of Keynes' "fundamental equations," which attempt to relate price level movements to differences in saving and investment, is incorrect. Careless errors make following the equations and surrounding discussion on pages 56-57 very difficult. Second, although McCormick correctly emphasizes the significance to the *Treatise* of the "excess bearishness" factor, he does not stress that this was not a widely contested belief at the time. What made Keynes' treatment controversial was his notion that there was "no automatic mechanism in the economic system" to restore equilibrium (Keynes

1973, p. 251). According to Keynes, if "bears" keep the rate of interest above its equilibrium value, the resulting excess of savings over investment will depress income and profits. In the *Treatise*'s model this implies a corresponding increase in entrepreneurs' saving, thereby intensifying the disequilibrium.[5] The unorthodox definitions used in the *Treatise*, the impotence of equilibrating mechanisms, and the absence of an identifiable theory of capital formed the basis for fairly widespread criticism by such heavyweights as Robertson and Hayek. (See Robertson 1931, 1933; Hayek 1931-1932.) It is perhaps understandable that Keynes, eager to make his mark as a leading theorist (Dimand 1988, p. 23), would respond to this onslaught by moving on to a new project. Yet, the controversy over the *Treatise* involved disputes about fundamental matters of theory. McCormick's remark that the debate got "bogged down in terminological debates about...savings and investment" (p. 60) is more than just a bit wide of the mark.

That more than terminology was involved is seen by considering the reaction to *The General Theory* by Keynes' 1920s collaborator and former student, Dennis Robertson. Although Robertson had worked very closely with Keynes during the 1920s, especially on *Banking Policy and the Price Level* (1949/1926), he became increasingly critical of Keynes following the publication of *A Treatise on Money* in 1930. Robertson's real over-investment cycle theory related expansion of capital goods production during the upswing to "automatic-lacking" or what Hayek referred to as "forced saving." Keynes purged this concept from the final draft of the *Treatise*, to Robertson's great disappointment. For Robertson, forced saving could play a positive role during the upswing by financing "warranted investments"; for this to happen, the (commodity) price level had to rise in the wake of bank credit expansion. Keynes, however, believed that the "objective of price stability" was more important than accommodating "the demand for circulating capital during the boom" (Presley 1979, p. 115).

At bottom, however, the dispute over forced saving concerned differing analytical approaches. Robertson's "step-by-step" analysis, which he contended had failed to get "under his [Keynes'] skin" (Robertson 1949, p. xi), underpinned and gave coherence to the dynamic forced saving process. Yet, during the 1930s Keynes continued to develop a comparative static analysis, in effect compelling him in *The General Theory* to reject forced saving as one of "the worst muddles of all" (Keynes 1936, p. 183). In *The General Theory*, the multiplier achieves the equality between saving and investment since any excess of investment over saving is satisfied via the increase in voluntary savings induced by the generation of income. Keynes' claim that "the logical theory of the multiplier, which holds good continuously, without time-lag, at all moments of time" (1936, p. 122) elicited a strongly negative reaction from Robertson. Thus, for example, in the "New Introduction" to the 1948 edition of *A Study of Industrial Fluctuations*, Robertson observed that "Keynes's final attempt in his *General*

Theory to deal with the savings-investment complex in terms of a theory of static and stable equilibrium was bound to seem a step backwards" (p. xvi).

Robertson's break with Keynes also carried over to the theory of interest. In *The General Theory*, Keynes argued that changes in income brought savings and investment into equality, but this left the interest rate undetermined. To fill the breach, Keynes offered the liquidity preference theory of interest, a purely monetary approach based upon the demand and supply of money. Only later and prodded by Robertson did Keynes concede that investment demand could affect the interest rate via the "finance demand." (See, for example, Keynes 1937b; Liang 1984.) Robertson, who objected in general to the static quality of Keynes' theory, focused his criticism specifically against its failure to relate real factors—productivity and thrift—to the determination of the interest rate (Robertson 1936, especially pp. 175-91, 1937).

McCormick seems receptive to Robertson's criticism of Keynes' interest theory and approvingly invokes Robertson's famous "grin without a cat" metaphor of the disembodied interest rate existing apart from the "organ which secretes it" (Robertson 1937, p. 433). McCormick, however, interprets this to mean that liquidity preference theory severs the prevailing interest rate from a "normal rate of interest" (p. 217). But Keynes, in fact, did ground the rate of interest in terms of what speculators believe is the normal rate of interest. Robertson's criticism was that because the rate of interest needed to be based on "other categories of money besides the 'speculative'," productivity and thrift must play a role. This point is also implicit in Robertson's observation of Keynes' "curious inhibition against visualizing more than two margins at once (Robertson 1937, p. 431). McCormick also fails to note that Robertson did not accuse Keynes of not employing a normal rate of interest but for leaving speculators' "normal" rates of interest undetermined, a problem resolvable by basing such rates on productivity and thrift. Even though after 1936 Keynes yielded considerable ground to his critics on the relation between productivity and interest, it was not until the Hicksian IS/LM model, to which Keynes gave his blessings, that investment (productivity) and saving (thrift) and money demand and supply were reconciled by the simultaneous determination of the interest rate and income.[6]

The widespread acceptance of IS/LM after World War II represented more than just an artful resolution of alternative theories of interest. Although IS/LM nudged the theory of interest toward the Robertsonian approach, it accomplished this reformulation of Keynesian theory by settling on a framework of static general equilibrium. The Hicksian approach infused Keynesian economics with certain "classical" tenets; yet, the vehicle for this transformation was an "un-classical" Walrasianism that was clearly more in tune with post-World War II developments than with the monetary economics of the 1920s and 1930s. Thus, the Keynesian avalanche that apparently overwhelmed Hayek was itself partially affected by those like Robertson and

Pigou who criticized *The General Theory* from a prewar perspective; more importantly, however, the avalanche was also reformulated, transformed, and ultimately co-opted by those like Hicks and others who turned monetary-macroeconomics into a branch of general equilibrium analysis.

In explaining the Keynesian avalanche, McCormick places considerable emphasis on Keynes' and Hayek's respective "visions," by which he means Schumpeter's pre-analytic vision. His basic point is that in contrast to Keynes, Hayek "asked the wrong questions and therefore put the wrong answers to the problems...in the 1930s" (p. 4). McCormick intimates that many economists during the late 1920s and the 1930s became increasingly impatient with the idea that the economy "must be left to unwind" and that intervention should be avoided "lest further distortions be created" (p. 60). High and chronic unemployment induced many leading economists (in addition to Keynes) to propose public spending programs and restrictive trade policies, and to question the desirability of Britain remaining on the gold standard (which it returned to in 1925 at prewar parity, with disastrous results, and then left in 1931). In general, the air seems to have been pregnant with policies at variance with those suggested by Hayek's diagnosis and analysis of the cycle. Many of the major players (e.g., Robertson, Pigou) shared policy views similar to those Keynes promulgated in popular articles, as an influential member of the Macmillan Committee under Ramsey MacDonald's Labor Government, in the *Treatise*, and later in *The General Theory*. During this time, then, a significant aspect of the prevailing milieu was one in which interventionist policies were accepted. (See Clarke 1988 for a detailed discussion of these matters.) That Hayek's views would be swept aside by the Keynesian avalanche is perhaps as much a consequence of widely held views as it was of any special significance of Keynes' analytical economics, a point McCormick does not explore. In a sense, Hayek may have already lost the policy battle long before the appearance of *The General Theory*.

Even if this point were granted, it would still remain a crucially important task to identify the analytical arguments used to defend different "visions" (Boettke 1992). It is mainly in this connection that McCormick's explanation of the Keynesian avalanche loses much of its force. I think there is little question that the "general circumstances" of the 1930s worked to Hayek's disadvantage and Keynes' advantage. But an important dimension to such circumstances, in addition to a vague "pre-analytic vision" or some "general disposition" toward certain policies, is the special kind of "vision" (if I may use this word) associated with the conceptual-analytical frameworks used by the scientific community. Such frameworks need to be understood because they are integral to understanding and assessing the growth of scientific knowledge.[7] Unfortunately, McCormick's treatment of the analytical propositions in Hayek's and Keynes' economics is not adequately developed. As a result, while the reader may agree with McCormick that Keynes' vision better suited the

1930s than Hayek's, the reader is not likely to have a clear sense of what analytical propositions might have made that so.

There are two general problems with McCormick's treatment of Hayek that interfere with the reader gaining an adequate understanding of his analytical economics. The more important one, arising from McCormick's neglect of the role of subjectivist economics and from his characterization of Keynes' and Hayek's approaches to methodology, will be deferred to section V below. The other concerns the conclusions McCormick draws from his treatment of Hayek's economics. The reader is told, for example, (1) that Hayek failed to respond to Sraffa's criticism that "disturbances might arise from the real side of the economy" (p. 84), (2) that "money seemed to play no important part in *Prices and Production*" (p. 96), and (3) that Hayek failed "to develop a monetary economy as a prelude to his analysis of the trade cycle"[8] because he failed "to appreciate the difference between Vienna, Lausanne, and Cambridge" (p. 96).

Each of these criticisms contains an element of validity. Yet, each also tends to mislead. McCormick is not careful to document his claims or explain them in ways that allow important nuances to be brought out. Thus, it is not strictly incorrect when McCormick asserts that Hayek's cycle theory did not address disturbances originating from the real side, but it is misleading. After all, Hayek had already analyzed real theories of the cycle in *Monetary Theory and the Trade Cycle* (1928, English ed. 1933, chapter II) and presented arguments against them.[9] The second criticism is a true statement: the model in *Prices and Production* is a barter one. However, Hayek primarily aims in the University of London lectures to analyze the effects of a monetary disturbance on the structure of production, which required him to make simplifying assumptions about the role of money. Hayek (1966, p. xiii) acknowledged "how small a section of monetary theory is treated in this book" and realized that the argument needed to be incorporated "into the body of monetary theory," a "task which has yet to be undertaken." Hayek openly conceded that deficiencies of the model in *Prices and Production* needed to be addressed. Yet, the real point of the model and virtually all of Hayek's work during the 1930s on the trade cycle (and, by implication, in the theory of capital) was to contest the claim that unemployment was primarily due to aggregate demand insufficiency. Unfortunately, McCormick neglects to give this claim the central place it deserves.

McCormick's third criticism of Hayek comes in two parts. The first part, which claims that Hayek's cycle theory lacked an underlying monetary theory, is more difficult to evaluate because McCormick simply fails to explain himself. Perhaps he is referring to the absence of money in Hayek's 1928 intertemporal price model (Hayek 1984, chapter 4) or perhaps to the fact that Hayek himself does not treat the general theory of money, preferring, instead, sometimes to direct the interested reader to Mises' *Theory of Money and Credit*, a treatise that was widely used on the Continent.

The second part of McCormick's third criticism, which claims that Hayek did not understand differences between modern schools of thought, is similarly difficult to fathom. McCormick twice claims that Hayek did not recognize differences between Austrians and Walrasians; in each instance McCormick does so without either documentation or elucidation. But there is a sense in which the statement is correct. As Kirzner (1992, p. 101) observes, among Austrians, Marshallians, and Walrasians during the early part of the century a "superficial shared understanding of markets...submerged important distinctions that would become important only much later." These distinctions centered on the market process tradition of the Austrians in contrast to the strict equilibrium view of the Walrasians. Significantly for the problem at hand, Kirzner goes on to argue that as a result of the calculation debate, Hayek and Mises refined their conception of the market process, inspired in part by the failure of their equilibrium oriented critics to understand the Austrian critique of socialism. Thus, while McCormick's claim is plausible, his failure to go beyond assertion prevents him from drawing out potentially relevant and insightful analytical points.

My discussion is meant to illustrate how McCormick's criticisms of Hayek's economics are not persuasive. Elements of truth inhere in them, but McCormick seems hesitant to carefully explain his viewpoint or to attempt to evaluate their analytical merit. I wish to point out, however, that in two important areas of Hayek's economics, the capital controversy with Knight and the Ricardo effect, McCormick's treatment is effective and largely on target. These areas, perhaps more than others, have sowed considerable confusion over the years; for that reason, McCormick's discussion is worth reading. Yet, the very success of his discussion raises, in turn, another question. On the strength of McCormick's treatment of Hayek's theory of capital, the reader is left to ponder the basis for McCormick's claim that Hayek was unable to respond to Keynes because he did not have at hand a theory of capital.[10] To be sure, McCormick points out that Hayek failed to write the planned second volume of *The Pure Theory of Capital* that was to deal with dynamics. Nonetheless, and despite whatever lacking Hayek's theory evidenced, it is probably no exaggeration to say that it represented the most thoroughly worked out account of a capital-using economy then available. For McCormick to claim that Hayek failed to respond to *The General Theory* because he "failed to produce a theory of capital" (p. 245) trivializes the refinement of that theory in the course of the capital controversy with Knight and ignores Hayek's belief that the appropriate long run strategy for analyzing the cycle required a systematic elaboration of the theory of capital. It might be argued that Hayek used a poor strategy to deal with the Keynesian avalanche; yet, it may also be argued that the subject area has not advanced much beyond where Hayek and later Lachmann (1956) left it.[11] Thus, McCormick's claim in this respect rings a bit hollow.

The lead essay in *Profits, Interest and Investment* (1939), in which Hayek presents the Ricardo effect, specifically attempted to show how "cyclical fluctuations...tend to become self-generating" (p. 6) and to analyze how the economy moves through the phases of the cycle. Together with "Economics and Knowledge" (1937), this was Hayek's most important publication in the years immediately after the publication of *The General Theory* and may on that account represent something of a response to Keynes' mature work. McCormick's treatment of the Ricardo effect correctly notes that criticisms of it, such as Kaldor's, failed to comprehend its dynamic features. Trying to understand Hayek's model from a comparative static perspective, as Blaug (1993) now admits to having done in the first edition of *Economic Theory in Retrospect*, inhibits seeing it as a restatement of an Austrian cyclical process under special assumptions.[12] Interestingly, McCormick quotes Robertson's generally approving comments on the Ricardo effect; equally interesting is that McCormick does not take the opportunity here to remind the reader that Robertson all along had been primarily concerned with dynamics and that his criticism of Keynes centered on the static qualities of Keynes' works.

V. AFTER THE AVALANCHE

The post-World War II period witnessed the entrenchment (though some might say entrapment) of Keynesian ideas in the neoclassical synthesis. But it is not particularly useful to claim, as McCormick does, that certain elements of Hayek's economics may have survived in that synthesis. What matters more for understanding Hayek is that his conceptual-analytical framework became increasingly at odds with that of the mainstream. Hayek's distancing from Walrasianism and aggregative economics and his continued refinement and extension of subjectivist economics passes virtually unnoticed by McCormick. Because McCormick fails to take account of the evolution of modern Austrian economics, he is prevented from providing a useful analysis of Hayek's reaction to Keynes and of Hayek's influence on modern economics. The essential flaw in McCormick's book is his failure to understand the importance of subjectivism to Austrian economics. McCormick does not recognize that the Keynesian avalanche buried not only Hayek's trade cycle theory but, more importantly, the Austrian subjectivist research program as well. The unfortunate consequences of this lacuna may be illustrated by briefly considering Hayek's relation to (modern) Walrasianism and the similarity McCormick insists exists between Hayek and Keynes in their approaches to methodology.

An inherent tension exists between subjectivism and modern Walrasian general equilibrium analysis. This is especially evident in the respective kinds of questions and approaches each uses to understand how markets work.[13] The

Walrasian emphasis on equilibrium states contrasts with the subjectivist emphasis on the market process associated with individuals' pursuing plans under uncertainty.[14] The ability of Walrasian models to incorporate adequately money, time, and expectations and to treat the institutional framework of decentralized systems seems precluded by an analytical framework in which the passage of time does not matter and problems of incomplete knowledge are solved costlessly by a fictitious auctioneer.[15] This ongoing elaboration of subjectivist economics has induced Austrians to go beyond Walrasian general equilibrium models in order to treat more effectively the market process.[16]

Contemporary Austrians have pointed to the importance of the socialist calculation debate as a reflection of subjectivist versus Walrasian approaches and as a mainspring for "improved self-understanding" of subjectivism for Mises and Hayek (Kirzner 1992, p. 102). Hayek's railing against Keynes' emphasis on aggregate economics, his critique of socialist calculation and interventionist policies, and his response to the Keynesian avalanche comprise elements of an underlying subjectivism, which itself was being refined. McCormick's failure to realize this means that his storyline is necessarily incomplete and often misleading. His claim that the post-World War II influence of Hayek's economics is mainly found in the economics of the neoclassical synthesis is merely another facet of this lacking.

The ways Keynes and Hayek differed or were similar is crucial for understanding the Keynesian avalanche. Their areas of disagreement are well known; McCormick, however, also claims that they held essentially similar methodological views, as evidenced by their positions on testing, modeling, and prediction. But appearances can be deceiving. Here, McCormick's failure to recognize the varieties of subjectivism results in his not finding decisive dissimilarities.

Hayek and Keynes represent two different philosophical traditions: anti-rationalist and Cartesian rationalist, respectively.[17] For Keynes, knowledge is justified true belief that is obtained by proof. This is explained in *A Treatise on Probability*. But suppose the Cartesian ideal of rational (i.e., justified) belief cannot be attained. What happens if genuine knowledge is not possible, say, for future asset prices? In such cases Keynes holds that animal spirits, the "spontaneous urge to action" (Keynes 1936, p. 161), will be vented on stock markets. Keynes in *The General Theory* was especially concerned that long-term expectations, which rest on no "adequate or secure foundation" (Keynes 1937a, p. 218), may turn to excess bearishness, resulting in interest rates that are too high and prospective profits from new investment that are too low to bring about full employment. For Keynes the impossibility of rational calculation and prediction is evaluated against the criterion of justified true knowledge as obtained by Cartesian rationalism. In this sense long-term expectations are second best beliefs. They are not hooked into the market process, but instead assumed by Keynes to be exogenous. As Keynes emphasizes in Chapter 12 of *The General Theory*, these expectations are prone to carry particularly perverse implications for the efficient functioning of modern organized financial markets and, thus, for the economy as a whole.

Hayek's brand of subjectivism is very different from Keynes'.[18] In rejecting the philosophical tenets of Cartesian rationalism and other justificationist enthusiasms, Hayek is not required to hold our knowledge accountable to some higher and unattainable criterion. Rather, Hayek's subjectivism leads him to examine the process by which knowledge is produced and distributed. For Hayek, knowledge and expectations are embodied in the rules governing action. They inhere in the routines, norms, and traditions that individuals follow in executing plans. The error correcting character of such rules (which is virtually absent in *The General Theory*) is essential in Hayek's scheme because it ensures that the rules individuals use to guide their activities under uncertainty will ordinarily be coherent, well behaved, and endogenous to the market process. Provided the institutional framework within which individuals act is itself rule governed, stable, and not subject to arbitrary interference, the interaction of individuals on markets will tend to generate a reasonably well-ordered process.[19] Even though individuals function under certainty, there is no a priori suggestion within Hayek's system that their actions, unlike Keynes' actors, are likely to generate perverse or incoherent market outcomes.

VI. CONCLUSIONS

Hayek and the Keynesian Avalanche treats a fascinating topic in economics. McCormick conveys a real sense of the diversity and excitement that occurred in economics at the LSE and Cambridge during the 1930s and brings to the reader's attention his considerable knowledge of the literature of that period. There are flashes of insight and suggestive leads sprinkled throughout the book. In short, there is value to be gained from the book by those interested in the history of twentieth century monetary-macroeconomic thought.

Yet, the book has its problems, some of which are severe. The execution of the author's plan, as I noted in the first paragraph of section II, really does make the book difficult to read. But even if this lack of attention to detail and editing were resolved, the author's interpretations are not in every case convincing. There is, to be sure, room here for differences among scholars, particularly in an area as controversial and complex as this. Nonetheless, I believe large gaps mar McCormick's account of the development of Austrian economics after World War II and his treatment of how and why and to what Hayek succumbed in the late 1930s. Despite these shortcomings, however, the important lesson the astute reader of *Hayek and the Keynesian Avalanche* may learn is that the success of the revolution in economics after 1936 came at a very high price in terms of its neglect of Keynes' fellow economists of the interwar years. McCormick's book is one attempt to deal with this. But his is not the full story; hopefully, others will follow.

NOTES

1. See, for example, Presley 1979; Gilbert 1982; Fletcher 1987; Clarke 1988; Dimand 1988; Meltzer 1988.

2. These difficulties include: claiming in the Introduction that in Chapter 3 he will trace Hayek's trade cycle to Schumpeter, despite not mentioning Schumpeter once in that chapter (p. 5); giving wrong chapter numbers (pp. 6-7) and date (p. 40); omitting a key word, probably "outlay" (p. 51); providing incorrect equations for the price level in Keynes' "fundamental equations" (p. 56); labeling a crucial coordinate in Fig. 5.2 incorrectly, that is, B" should be B' (p. 104); claiming that the flow of inputs from Fig. 5.2 is AA'C'BB'when it is AA'CC'BB' (p. 105); providing incorrect citations for quotations (p. 137, 137-138, 171); misspelling Morgenstern's name throughout the book. Some of these mistakes are innocuous; others, unfortunately, interfere with understanding the text.

3. McCormick provides reading lists for the following courses:
Robertson, Session 1930-31, Principles of Currency
Gregory, Session 1930-31, Theory of Banking and the Money Market
Robbins, Session 1934-35, Disputed Problems in the Methodology of Economics
Robbins, Session 1934-35, General Principles of Economic Analysis
Robbins, Session 1938-39, General Principles of Economic Analysis
Hayek, Session 1930-31, Principles of Currency
Hayek, Session 1933-34, Theory of Value
Hayek, Session 1934-35, Theory of Value
Hayek, Session 1936-37, Industrial Fluctuations
Durbin, Session 1937-38, Modern Trade Cycle Theory
Durbin, Session, 1938-39, Economic Planning in Theory and Practice
Thomas, 1934-35, Neo-Wicksellian Fluctuation Theory in Sweden
Hicks, 1929-30, Theory of Risk and Profit
Hicks, 1931-32, Problems of Industrial Fluctuations
Hicks, 1933-34, The Foreign Exchanges and International Trade
Hicks, 1934-35, Theory of Value
Hicks, 1934-35, Economic Dynamics
Kaldor, Session 1937-38, Capital and Interest
Kaldor, Session 1938-39, Advanced Problems of Economic Theory (Statics and Dynamics

4. This point is discussed later in section IV.

5. See Keynes 1971, p. 125. *A Treatise on Money* alters the conventional meaning of saving (the excess of money income over consumption) in a way that defines equilibrium as the equality of investment expenditures with saving (in the ordinary sense) plus ex post windfall profits/losses. Keynes defined windfalls as the discrepancy between actual and "normal" income received by entrepreneurs. According to Keynes, entrepreneurs' saving is inversely related to windfall profits. These definitions provide the basis for Keynes' controversial "Danaid jar" and "widow's cruse" examples. Robertson (1931 p. 407) pointed out that according to Keynes' definitions "if an entrepreneur spends his 'profits' on the purchase of new machines, he is not 'saving,' while if he refrains from spending on consumption a normal income he has never received, he is deemed to be 'saving'." Robertson probably expressed the sentiments of many theorists when he said: "I do not think there is any question that this terminology is extremely confusing" and "liable to lead even practised thinkers into error" (p. 407). Also see Hayek 1931-1932, especially Section XIII).

6. Keynes held that the "classical" theory of interest was indeterminate, a claim that Robertson successfully redirected at Keynes' own theory. See Keynes 1936, pp. 183, 242-440; Robertson 1937.

7. "Thus it was not just ideology... that drove economists into the Keynesian camp" but that "Keynes had caught a measure of substantive truth about the workings of an economic system" (Blaug 1991, p. 188).

8. I presume McCormick may mean that Hayek failed to develop a theory of a monetary economy or perhaps that Hayek failed to develop a monetary theory as a prelude to his trade cycle analysis.

9. Hayek responded to Sraffa's criticism by stating that in *Prices and Production* he had attempted to show how "monetary factors may bring about a kind of disequilibrium in the economic system—which could not be explained without recourse to those monetary factors" (1931, p. 238).

10. A critical evaluation of Keynes from the perspective of the Austrian theory of capital is provided by Garrison 1985.

11. More recent work in the Austrian theory of capital includes Kirzner 1966 and the chapter by Garrison in O'Driscoll and Rizzo 1985.

12. On the Ricardo effect, see O'Driscoll 1977; Moss and Vaughn 1986.

13. It should be emphasized that Austrians have had a long standing interest in understanding the evolution and role of social institutions, areas to which the formalism of general equilibrium models is not hospitable.

14. A good overview of the Austrian subjectivist approach is found in O'Driscoll and Rizzo 1985.

15. Rosner and Winckler (1989) provide an interesting discussion of the early Austrian reaction, especially of Morgenstern's, to Walrasian general equilibrium analysis.

16. This is no better seen, perhaps, than in Kirzner's work on entrepreneurship. See, for example, Kirzner 1973.

17. This view of Keynes is developed by O'Donnell 1989; also see Hayek 1967, pp. 89-90.

18. This point is developed in detail by Butos and Koppl 1994. See Vanberg 1994 for a detailed treatment of rules and institutions.

19. A good overview of Hayek in this area is found in Streit 1993. A Hayekian theory of expectations is developed by Butos and Koppl 1993.

REFERENCES

Blaug, M. 1991. "Second Thoughts on the Keynesian Revolution." *History of Political Economy*, 23 (2): 171-192.

———. 1993. "Hayek Revisited." *Critical Review*, 7 (1): 51-60.

Boettke, P. J. 1992. "Analysis and Vision in Economic Discourse." *Journal of the History of Economic Thought*, 14 (1): 84-95.

Butos, W. N., and R. G. Koppl. 1993. "Hayekian Expectations: Theory and Empirical Applications." *Constitutional Political Economy*, 4 (3): 303-329.

———. 1994. "The Varieties of Subjectivism: Keynes and Hayek on Expectations." Photocopy.

Clarke, P. 1988. *The Keynesian Revolution in the Making, 1924-1936*. New York: Oxford University Press.

Dimand, R. W. 1988. *The Origins of the Keynesian Revolution*. Stanford, CA: Stanford University Press.

Fletcher, G. A. 1987. *The Keynesian Revolution and its Critics*. New York: St. Martin's Press.

Garrison, R. W. 1985. "Intertemporal Coordination and the Invisible Hand: An Austrian Perspective on the Keynesian Revolution." *History of Political Economy*, 17 (2): 309-321.

Gilbert, J. C. 1982. *Keynes's Impact on Monetary Economics*. London: Butterworth Scientific.

Hayek, F. A. 1931-1932 (August, February). "Reflections on the Pure Theory of Money of Mr. J. M. Keynes." *Economica*, 11, 12: 270-295, 22-44.

———. 1932. "Money and Capital: A Reply." *Economic Journal*, 42 (July): 237-249.

———. 1937. "Economics and Knowledge." *Economica*, 4(February): 33-54.

———. 1939. *Profits, Interest and Investment*. London: George Routledge & Sons.

———. 1966/1931. *Prices and Production* (2nd ed.). New York: Augustus M. Kelley.

———. 1967. "Kinds of Rationalism." Pp. 82-95 in *Studies in Philosophy, Politics and Economics* Chicago: University of Chicago Press.

———. 1975/1933. *Monetary Theory and the Trade Cycle*. Clifton, NJ: Augustus M. Kelley.

———. 1984. *Money, Capital, and Fluctuations: Early Essays*. Edited by R. McCloughry. Chicago: University of Chicago Press.

Keynes, J. M. 1936. *The General Theory of Employment, Interest and Money*. New York: Harcourt, Brace & World.

———. 1937a. "The General Theory of Employment." *Quarterly Journal of Economics*, 51 (February): 209-23.

———. 1937b. "Alternative Theories of the Rate of Interest." *Economic Journal*, 47 (June): 241-52.

———. 1971. *The Collected Writings of John Maynard Keynes* (Volume 5) *A Treatise on Money, v. 1: The Pure Theory of Money*. London: Macmillan.

———. 1973. *The Collected Works of John Maynard Keynes* (Volume 13) *The General Theory and After: Part 1, Preparation*. London: Macmillan.

Kirzner, I. M. 1966. *An Essay on Capital*. New York: Augustus M. Kelley.

———. 1973. *Competition and Entrepreneurship*. Chicago: University of Chicago Press.

———. 1992. *The Meaning of Market Process*. New York: Routledge.

Lachmann, L. M. 1956. *Capital and its Structure*. London: Bell & Sons.

Liang, M.-Y. 1984. "Keynes's Errors in the Liquidity Preference versus Loanable Funds Controversy." *Journal of Macroeconomics*, 6 (2): 215-27.

McCormick, B. 1992. *Hayek and the Keynesian Avalanche*. New York: St. Martin's Press.

Meltzer, A. H. 1988. *Keynes's Monetary Theory: A Different Interpretation*. New York: Cambridge University Press.

Moss, L. S., and K. I. Vaughn. 1986. "Hayek's Ricardo Effect: A Second Look." *History of Political Economy*, 18 (4): 545-66.

O'Driscoll, G. P. 1977. *Economics as a Coordination Problem: The Contributions of Friedrich A. Hayek*. Kansas City: Sheed Andrews and McMeel.

O'Driscoll, G. P., and M. J. Rizzo. 1985. *The Economics of Time and Ignorance*. New York: Basil Blackwell.

Presley, J. R. 1979. *Robertsonian Economics*. New York: Holmes and Meier.

Robertson, D. H. 1931. "Mr. Keynes' Theory of Money." *Economic Journal*, 41 (September): 395-411.

———. 1933. "Saving and Hoarding." *Economic Journal*, 43 (September): 399-413.

———. 1936. "Some Notes on Mr. Keynes' General Theory of Employment." *Quarterly Journal of Economics*, 51 (November): 168-91.

———. 1937. "Alternative Theories of the Rate of Interest." *Economic Journal*, 47 (September): 428-36.

———. 1948/1915. *A Study of Industrial Fluctuations*. London: University of London.

———. 1949/1926. *Banking Policy and the Price Level*. New York: A. M. Kelley.

Rosner, P., and G. Winckler. 1989. "Austrian Economics of the 1920s and 1930s." *Research in the History of Economic Thought and Methodology*, 6: 19-31.

Streit, M. 1993. "Cognition, Competition, and Catallaxy: In Memory of F.A. Hayek." *Constitutional Political Economy*, 4 (2): 223-62.

Vanberg, V. 1994. *Rules and Choice in Economics*. London: Routledge.

DISCOVERY, TRANSACTION COSTS, AND GROWTH:

ESSAY ON DOUGLASS C. NORTH'S *INSTITUTIONS, INSTITUTIONAL CHANGE, AND ECONOMIC PERFORMANCE*

Charles N. Steele

I. INTRODUCTION

Some economies prosper, others stagnate and decline. Lucas (1988) has argued that persistent disparities among economies pose a central puzzle for economics, and an entire field—growth theory—is devoted to answering questions of differing performance. The general consensus seems to be that economic success is explained by some aspect of human capital (Lucas 1993).

Douglass North (1990) dissents from this view, and argues that economic performance is a function of the institutions, or rules, followed by a society. Institutional frameworks determine (in part) the constraints and incentives faced by economic actors, which in turn determine their behavior, which in

Advances in Austrian Economics, Volume 2B, pages 447-459.

ISBN: 1-55938-531-6

turn generates the economic performance of a society. The actual challenge for economists, North argues, is to develop a theory of institutions which will clearly explain the variety of economic performances seen across countries and throughout history.

North develops such a theory, albeit in incomplete form, in his book *Institutions, Institutional Change, and Economic Performance* (1990). North grounds his theory in a set of behavioral assumptions and positive transaction cost theory (i.e., property rights economics), and goes on to develop arguments as to why institutions are important, how they influence economic performance, and how economic behavior in turn alters institutions and directs their evolution. In doing so he relaxes several neoclassical assumptions concerning the information available to economic actors, and attempts to describe a process by which institutions change. I will argue that although he has made important strides he is not fully successful, and his theory would benefit from incorporating concepts of ignorance and discovery similar to those employed by Kirzner (1973) in describing the market process. This would eliminate certain internal inconsistencies from the theory, and would particularly contribute to the development of the theory of institutional evolution.

Section II of this paper summarizes the theory North presents in his book. In section III, I discuss an apparent problem in North's approach, and suggest a solution. Section IV concludes.

II. A SURVEY OF NORTH'S THEORY OF INSTITUTIONS

North's objective is to explain why different societies generate very different, persistent patterns of economic growth. North finds modern growth theory, with its reliance on such factors as human capital, inadequate to the task. As he has argued elsewhere (North and Thomas 1973) the accumulation of human capital cannot be used to explain economic growth, because human capital accumulation is itself an example of economic growth. The puzzle remains why some economies grow, while others do not.

> To put it simply...in a zero transaction cost world, increases in the stock of knowledge and its application (both physical and human capital) provide a key to the potential well-being of human beings in society. What was left out of the analysis was why the potential was not realized, and why there is such an enormous gap between the rich countries and the poor countries when the technology is, for the most part, available to everyone. The gap in the real world is paralleled by the gap in the theories and model building of economists....Surely this neoclassical formulation has...begged all the interesting questions. To put the issue starkly, recent neoclassical models of growth built around increasing returns (Romer 1986) and physical and human capital accumulation (Lucas 1988) crucially depend upon the existence of an implicit incentive structure that drives the models (pp. 133-134).[1]

In other words, while human interaction and cooperation can lead in some cases to economic growth, why is it that in other cases they yield stagnation and decline? North points to the incentives faced by individuals in a society as the explanation. These shape human action, and channel it in particular directions and away from others. The incentives facing individuals depend crucially upon the constraints they face, and the essential set of constraints—those which can explain sustained differences across societies and throughout history—are the manmade constraints.

These constraints, the rules or institutions followed by a society, make up the framework (along with technological and resource constraints) under which economic choice occurs. This institutional framework includes both formal rules (e.g., constitutions, laws, etc.) and informal rules (e.g., social conventions and customs, norms, self-imposed ethical codes, etc.) North's book addresses three particular issues: the nature of an institutional framework, the effects of an institutional framework on economic performance, and how an institutional framework changes and evolves.[2]

A. The Nature of an Institutional Framework

Positive transaction costs are a central feature of North's theory, and would seem to be essential to any theoretic treatment of institutions. Transaction costs are those costs associated with defining, protecting, and exchanging property rights. They can be interpreted as the costs of measuring the attributes of assets, that is, as information costs (Barzel 1986). In a zero transaction cost world, information is costless. The assumption of costless information is commonly thought to imply perfect information. It follows that in such a world, institutions are irrelevant, since perfect information implies that resources will be allocated optimally regardless of the initial distribution of property rights.[3]

Conversely, in a world where information is costly, information will be imperfect, and property rights (i.e., de facto property rights, or control over attributes of assets) will not be completely delineated, and exchange and cooperation will be costly. Institutions are relevant in such a world. Different institutional structures can yield very different sets of transaction costs, and can thus determine, in part, the kinds and complexity of exchanges (economic and otherwise) which individuals will find it worthwhile to pursue. Thus positive transaction costs are a necessary component of North's theory.

Other essential components of North's theory are his assumptions about individual human behavior. He places particular emphasis on two deviations from the neoclassical hypothesis of rational maximization: first, concerning the motivations of actors, he argues that the assumptions of preference stability and wealth-maximization are inadequate to account for many important phenomena—factors such as ideology and self-imposed ethics can be important in shaping behavior. Second, he challenges the assumed abilities of individuals to decipher their environment according to correct models. On this second point, North argues that in general individuals interpret the incomplete information they receive according to imperfect, often subjective models or theories. Although models of learning predict that feedback and repetition should allow individuals to improve their theories so that they converge to the truth, this assumes reliable feedback mechanisms and sufficiently similar situations. These conditions are not necessarily given, North argues. In large part they depend upon the institutional framework.

In sum, North models individuals as having incomplete information, which they evaluate according to imperfect, perhaps incorrect, theories; thus individuals act subject to uncertainty. Such actors do not qualify as neoclassical maximizers, obviously. Instead, they appear to be much more akin to Kirzner's (1973) "pre-Robbinsian" decision makers. (Note that North's assumptions do not imply that actors are non-rational: they still consistently pursue their objectives to the extent of their limited abilities. This seems similar to Mises' (1966) concept of rationality.) Institutions are a means by which actors reduce this pervasive uncertainty with respect to human interactions, by providing a framework which guides actions, and in this way reducing (some) transaction costs.[4]

Institutions can be categorized in a variety of ways, and North devotes some effort to analyzing such categories. For example, rules of conduct can be either formal or informal—formality being, in fact, a matter of degree. In the case of informal rules, they may be internally enforced (as in following one's own ethical code), or self-enforcing (in the sense of Nash equilibrium play), or enforced by third parties. Also, such institutions may or may not be consciously designed; they may not even be consciously recognized.

Formal institutions include such things as constitutions, laws, and legally encoded property rights, such as contracts. These sorts of institutions seemingly always include some explicit enforcement mechanism. North points out that a formal institutional framework forms a hierarchical structure. For example, laws may be written and adapted to fit under a constitution, and contracts, which are rules of a quite narrow scope, will be written to conform to the overall legal structure.

Also, there is linkage between formal and informal rules. Formal rules often codify previously accepted informal rules. Similarly, informal rules may arise or be modified in response to a formal rule. A contract, for example, may be written to conform simultaneously to formal and informal rules, for example, contract law and business traditions. (North does not assume that the institutions in a society necessarily dovetail; rules may conflict.) Clearly, the nature of the formal and informal rules followed by a society will crucially affect the kinds of actions individuals will undertake.

B. Economic Performance

How does all of this relate to explaining differential performances of economies? North argues that the uncertainty faced by individuals leads to multiple equilibria (pp. 24, 94). Also, the neoclassical maximization model will be a poor predictor of human behavior when outcomes are uncertain, feedback is poor, and individuals follow self imposed rules. All of these conditions depend crucially upon the kind of institutional framework functioning in a society. It is important to realize that while neoclassical models such as a static general equilibrium or a rational expectations equilibrium may for some purposes be adequate representations of economies where rules provide for clear delineation, enforcement, and ease of transfer of property rights, they implicitly assume such institutions, and are not well suited for describing situations where institutions are quite different.[5] For example, if no third party enforcement of contracts exists, exchange will in general be costlier than with such enforcement, and resulting general patterns of exchange will be less complex with fewer of the potential gains from trade realized. Similarly, a society which includes effective rules to strictly constrain the abilities of political leaders to transfer property rights will likely see a different employment of resources than one without such limits, where rent-seeking will likely be more common. In such ways institutions can affect economic performance.

C. Institutional Change

The non-neutrality of institutions on economic outcomes is only part of the explanation for differences among economies. Differences persist: some economies exhibit dynamic change while others do not, some economies grow while others seem to be caught in growth traps. If the institutional framework is a fundamental factor in economic performance, why don't societies with structures which are channeling them into undesired consequences simply change frameworks, particularly in cases where there exist examples of more successful frameworks? And why do some societies exhibit growth, perhaps after a long period of stagnation, while others do not, sometimes for millennia? To answer these questions one needs a theory of institutional change. North develops such a theory, which includes two fundamental themes: the tendency of an institutional framework to remain in place, and the processes of gradual change which frameworks undergo.

North argues that an institutional framework is subject to increasing returns, such that once a framework is in place, it is difficult to dislodge or replace it. North points out four likely sources of such self-reinforcement: (1) large initial setup costs, for example, as in adopting a constitution, (2) learning effects as individuals and organizations invest in skills in order to respond to the opportunity set provided by the institutional framework, (3) coordination effects through contracting and among actors as channeled by institutions, and (4) adaptive expectations where use of a rule increases expectations that it will be followed in the future. (These categories obviously overlap.) These self-reinforcing effects shape the knowledge of actors, limiting the range of possible choices perceived. They also give rise to organizations with vested interests in maintaining the status quo. Thus an institutional structure is subject to lock-in, that is, once an institutional solution is in place, it is very difficult to exit from it. It follows that institutional frameworks exhibit path dependency, that is, the institutional structure and the resultant choice set faced by actors at any given time is dependent upon the previous institutional structure, and decisions involve a degree of irreversibility. History matters.

If all institutional structures gave rise to low transaction cost markets with effective feedback to actors, then the long-run paths of institutions and economies would tend to converge. But when transaction costs are high and feedback is poor, the subjective models of actors will shape the path, and path dependence will be likely. And with path dependence, economies can become locked-in to high, low, or no growth paths.

How, then, do institutional frameworks change? North argues that the driving force is changes in relative prices,[6] either from exogenous origins or endogenous, that is, originating in human action[7] (p. 64). As relative prices change, actors alter their exchange patterns and renegotiate contracts. If formal rules constrain actors from making desired adjustments, they may devote resources to changing the rules. In the case of informal rules, such as norms, actors may simply ignore a rule which prevents adjustment, and if a rule is ignored frequently enough it will erode, and the new behavior pattern will replace it as the rule. Thus the process of institutional change is almost entirely incremental, North argues, as actors tinker at the margins.

For example, consider a relatively drastic rule change, such as the adoption of a new constitution. The overall institutional framework into which these new rules are introduced includes customs, traditions, and so forth, which remain in place. Thus the overall framework will still tend to exhibit a degree of stability despite the major change. And of course, most rule changes are of a far less sweeping scope than introduction of a new constitution.

North also briefly considers the issue of discontinuous change such as revolution. He argues that revolution may be more likely in gridlock situations, where very widespread recontracting (in response to relative price changes) is called for, but the institutional framework prevents it. He also maintains that revolutionary change "is seldom as discontinuous as it appears on the surface (or in the utopian visions of revolutionaries)" (p. 90). The complex hierarchical nature of the network of rules makes rapid, sweeping change unlikely.

D. Summary

North's book is an attempt to develop a theory of institutions and their role in economic activity. His theory employs information costs and the subjectivity of individuals' theories. Given these, actors find it difficult to acquire and process information, and thus to interact. Rules arise, either spontaneously or by design (or by some combination of the two), which in some way reduce certain transaction costs and thus simplify decision making, by helping to define the choice set available to actors. Once in place, rule structures tend to persist, as actors invest resources, form organizations, and adapt their expectations according to the existing structure. Wholesale change becomes prohibitively costly. And without sufficient feedback, alternative solutions may remain unknown.

Institutional change occurs incrementally, as actors push at the margins in response to relative price changes. The direction of the evolution of the institutional framework depends on how the subjective models of actors induce them to behave, given the choices offered by the framework, as well as on the interplay among competing actors and organizations. The result is that institutional paths may diverge, and economies may grow, stagnate, or decline.

III. A COMMENT ON NORTH'S THEORY

North's theory is designed to explicitly integrate institutions into economic theory in a coherent, consistent fashion. The payoff is a richer economic theory, better able to explain the wide variation observed across countries and throughout history. North's efforts appear to be quite valuable. His results, while incomplete, seem an excellent start on sorting out the complicated issues surrounding institutional structure. His starting point—the actions of individuals operating with subjective models and costly, incomplete information—is well considered and keeps the theory firmly grounded in microfoundations. For North, these starting points are synonymous with the property rights approach. While this paradigm is a source of strength for his arguments, it also leads him into a trap, in which the assumptions of the modeling strategy render the theory incapable of addressing many of the puzzles it is designed to solve.

In property rights theory, the costliness of information implies that individuals act with less than perfect information. However, as maximizers they are economizing on all margins at all times, given all costs. Also, the costliness of information is assumed to be the sole source of its incompleteness. The result is that the world is always in a unique wealth-maximizing equilibrium (Barzel 1989, p. 9). This implies the following for any observed economic phenomenon or outcome: it could have been no other way, and it is efficient (Barzel 1989, p. 107).

North explicitly wishes to escape from these two implications while preserving the core of the property rights approach (costly transacting and the explicit recognition of economizing over margins other than price and quantity). He does so by arguing that incomplete information leads to multiple equilibria; from this he is able to generate diverging institutional and economic paths.[8] However, he is explicit that information is imperfect for one reason: it is costly (pp. 107-108). This, I argue, leads North into the following equilibrium trap.

If the incompleteness of information is dictated entirely by costs, then individuals' actions always yield equilibrium, since they conform to all relevant constraints—including information constraints—and are otherwise perfect. Any resulting equilibrium must necessarily be efficient, as all constraints are based upon cost. Further, it appears that the equilibrium is thus given (i.e., determined by the initial conditions), and unique (unless one allows for game theoretic mixed strategies, in which case the ex post outcome is not given). If this were not so, that is, if there were, say, two possible equilibria, one of which yielded more total wealth than the other, then it would pay actors to agree (contract) to play the higher-wealth equilibrium, *unless the costs of transacting were too high*. But in that case, whichever equilibrium ultimately results will be determined by the information held by actors, and hence by costs. And thus it would seem to be unique.

Similarly, if everything is driven by the costliness of information, then the institutional path, as it unfolds, must be uniquely determined. (Again, with the qualifier that if actors play mixed strategies, an element of randomness enters into determination of the outcome.) In other words, if one assumes that everything is driven by cost, then one must conclude that individual action and overall outcomes are uniquely determined and efficient.[9]

Uniqueness of equilibrium does not itself necessarily prevent the theory from saying anything about disparities in economic performance. Suppose two societies exhibit entirely different institutional and economic paths. Even if we must conclude that both could have turned out no other way, given all relevant constraints, still we may now be able to say a great deal more about why they evolved differently, and about the initial conditions which gave rise to the disparities.[10] (North himself notes that incorporating institutions into static neoclassical analysis should be relatively simple, involving modifying existing theory by specifying and incorporating the additional constraints.)

However, North's primary objective is to provide an account of how economies evolve and change, a dynamic theory of the unfolding of the path. Unfortunately, the use of a property rights equilibrium framework makes analysis of change problematic. This is the trap. The theory lacks a means of explaining how individuals adjust their actions in response to changing conditions, and posits that they do so automatically and instantaneously, since they are by assumption maximizers.

> [Individuals] are in equilibrium with regard to their rights over assets. At any time, then, their rights are so well defined that they do not wish to change them. Economic conditions, however, are constantly changing, and with them the equilibrium property rights delineation is changing as well (Barzel 1989, p. 74).

It would seem reasonable that adjustment to exogenous change requires specification of some sort of learning process on the part of actors, something apart from costly intentional search. The property rights paradigm provides no such theory and simply assumes that cost is the sole source of information imperfections. This seems equivalent to replacing the Walrasian auctioneer of the zero transaction cost world with a Barzelian puppeteer, who pulls individuals' strings such that their behavior adjusts instantaneously on the proper least cost margins, so preserving equilibrium. Since North explicitly desires to explain economic *change* and processes of feedback and learning, the property rights equilibrium framework assumes too much to be useful.[11]

However, the trap is not inescapable. There seems no particular reason why North requires an equilibrium assumption in his theory at all. Dropping this assumption would allow one to focus attention directly on the crucial problems of learning and coordination which are essential for understanding dynamics, problems from which an equilibrium approach necessarily abstracts. The omnipresence of equilibrium in property rights models seems to arise from an implicit assumption of the paradigm, that costliness is the *only* reason why information is incomplete. Kirzner (1973) has shown that zero information cost is not a sufficient condition for information to be perfect; there must also be a noticing, or discovery. Incorporating Kirzner's ideas of discovery and ignorance into North's theory would seem to overcome the equilibrium trap posed earlier, and allow one to begin modeling the (disequilibrium) processes of discovery, learning, and feedback in different institutional settings. In North's theory, the path seems to be a sequence of static equilibria, thus he argues that "[D]evising a model of economic change requires the construction of an entire framework, because no such model exists" (p. 112). But Austrians *already have* successfully developed a clear account of economic change within the market setting, in Kirzner's theory of entrepreneurship and market process. Formulating an analogous process view of the path, applicable to more general institutional settings, would seem to be a useful step in developing the dynamic framework North seeks.[12] Also, incorporating Austrian concepts of ignorance and discovery and their role in information imperfection would yield a measure of open-endedness to the theory, bringing back the possibility of multiple outcomes (no longer equilibria). This is a plus if hysteresis and strict determinism are thought intellectually unappealing. It is a minus if one desires theory to provide perfectly (completely) specified predictions. In sum, it appears that incorporating Austrian insights into North's theory would give it the dynamic and subjective elements he seeks, but hasn't quite obtained.[13]

However, there exist some important difficulties to be overcome in implementing this proposed solution. Market process theory obviously applies to a particular institutional environment, and appeals to this environment for the price signals and profit incentives which drive the process. When the institutional environment is not given but is endogenous, the constraints on the process become quite different. For example, one cannot rely on competition to eliminate institutions which do not satisfy actors. Similarly, one cannot generally appeal to competition among political "entrepreneurs" to establish sets of formal institutions conducive to economic growth. More generally, the forces that direct an institutional process are not necessarily those which guide a market process, and are much less well identified. The process of institution formation and evolution, and the forces that impinge upon it, must be carefully worked out.[14] North has made important steps in this regard.

A key aspect of this problem concerns the role of coercion. Market theories are theories of voluntary exchange. Applying them directly to involuntary exchanges does not seem to be a good way to analyze such phenomena; certainly transfering any welfare, equilibration, coordinative, or stability properties associated with voluntary exchange assumes far too much. If the possibility of involuntary exchange and coercion is included in an institutional process theory, as it certainly must be, then the theory cannot simply be a copy of market process theory.

Another issue concerns the acceptance and utilization by economists of an institutional process theory. Such a theory might well prove to be a rigorous logical implication of individual action, and even a useful tool for the economic historian.[15] But as theory it will likely have difficulty making inroads against more common neoclassical approaches, unless it can be shown that it entails observable implications which differentiate it from other explanations of the same phenomena. North states that his own formulation of institutional theory does not have testable implications, at least as it stands, and defends the theory on the basis that it is the only existing theory that can account for the wide variety of observed phenomena and is simultaneously grounded in marginalist economic theory. If an institutional theory, process, or equilibrium, is to be further developed, it will be important to derive observable implications, even if one believes that failure of an implication to be observed cannot falsify the theory itself.

This requirement is perhaps not as serious an obstacle for a broad, open-ended theory as it might at first seem. The theory, if adequate, should be capable of pattern prediction in the widest variety of settings; and it is broad, general empirical success under many differing circumstances, not failure to be rejected by a single tightly constructed hypothesis test, which is most persuasive (Summers 1991).

These considerations are difficulties to be overcome in developing a more complete theory of institutions, not arguments against the possibility of such a theory. Certainly a consistent and rigorous theory of institutional evolution can be developed, and it should prove to be a tool useful in understanding economic phenomena. North has made some extremely important steps along this path.

IV. CONCLUSION

I would like to leave the reader with three points. First, North has made a strong case for the role of institutions in determining economic performance. His arguments linking rules to economic outcomes are well constructed and persuasive, and he shows that the resulting theory can illuminate observed historical experiences.

Second, his theory addresses a number of extremely difficult and complicated issues. The foundations of individual behavior, the interconnectedness of formal and informal rules, and the influences of rules and economic behavior on each other combine to pose a very messy problem for analysis. North does an admirable job in sorting out these strands.

Finally, the shortcomings in North's work appear to arise from applying the property rights equilibrium approach to a task for which it is ill-suited: modeling processes characterized by ignorance on the part of actors. These difficulties might be overcome by retaining the property rights ideas of positive transaction costs and action on non-pecuniary margins, while adopting an Austrian view of knowledge, ignorance, and discovery.

ACKNOWLEDGMENT

The author gratefully acknowledges useful comments given on an earlier draft by Professors Israel Kirzner, Peter Boettke, and Mario Rizzo of New York University, and Professor Ronald Johnson of Montana State University.

NOTES

1. Here, and throughout this chapter, page numbers without further identification refer to North (1990).

2. This approach thus falls squarely into the New Institutional Economics outlined by Langlois (1986): it is economic theory informed by the existence of institutions, and is also a theory *of* institutions.

3. This argument abstracts from the issue of entrepreneurial discovery. Even if information is costless someone must notice it (Kirzner 1973). This issue is raised subsequently.

4. Although North also raises the issue of the motivations of the actors, the question is problematic, and for the most part he sidesteps it in this work. North (1994) presents some thoughts on how to begin tackling this matter.

5. These models also might *not* be adequate for depicting market economies, for example, for addressing questions where one cannot sensibly abstract from institutions (as in the theory of the firm) or for describing adjustment processes in an economy (as in the theory of entrepreneurship).

6. North defines these relative price changes as shifts in the relative availabilities of land, labor, and capital. I suggest that to call these "prices" is a metaphor which may be misleading, as the concept of price assumes a market, in turn suggesting various analytic results which may not be applicable such as equilibration or efficiency. It may be better to think of these changing "prices" as changing resource availabilities, or opportunities.

7. North also argues that changes in preferences may play an important role, but although he devotes some discussion to this, he makes little headway and notes that there remains much work to be done. Obviously, preference changes would also be reflected in changes in relative prices.

8. North's subsequent work includes doubts about the assumption of individual rationality, and invokes this as a possible reason for divergence (North 1994).

9. See Barzel (1989) for a similar argument that individual maximization implies that all observed outcomes are necessarily unique and efficient.

10. But note that North's criticism of endogenous growth theory might be turned upon him as well here: appealing to an exogenously given cost structure at the beginning of history may not be so different from appealing to initial endowments of human or physical capital.

11. None of this is meant to disparage the extremely valuable insights of property rights economics for *static* analysis. It is simply that for questions where dynamics are essential, the assumption of equilibrium is an obstacle to understanding.

12. North himself now doubts that a dynamic theory can ever be developed (North 1994).

13. Market process theory itself likely has much to contribute to North's framework. Certainly discovery and entrepreneurship are crucial for economic growth, implying that attention should be directed to understanding the effects of institutions on these phenomena. Also, recognition of the disequilibrium setting of Kirznerian entrepreneurship (as opposed to Schumpeterian entrepreneurship, which occurs in equilibrium) dispels the supposed conflict between allocative efficiency and adaptive efficiency, at least within the market setting, a tension with which North wrestles unsuccessfully (North 1990, pp. 80-82, 1995).

14. The process is ultimately rooted in the actions of individuals, so in one sense the basic sources of change are known. What remains to be worked out is the interplay of individual action.

15. It is perhaps worth noting that North is an economic historian rather than a pure theorist, and as such is more interested in developing explanations for observed phenomena than in engaging in impressive mathematical exercises.

REFERENCES

Barzel, Y. 1989. *Economic Analysis of Property Rights*. Cambridge: Cambridge University Press.

Kirzner, I. M. 1973. *Competition and Entrepreneurship*. Chicago: University of Chicago Press.

Langlois, R. N. 1986. "The New Institutional Economics: An Introductory Essay." In *Economics as a Process: Essays in the New Institutional Economics*, edited by R. N. Langlois. Cambridge: Cambridge University Press.

Lucas, R. E., Jr. 1993. "Making a Miracle." *Econometrica*, 61 (2): 251-272.

________. 1988. "On the Mechanics of Economic Development." *Journal of Monetary Economics*, 22: 3-42.

Mises, L., von. 1966. *Human Action: A Treatise on Economics* (3rd edition). Contemporary Books.

North, D. C. 1995. "Privatization, Incentives, and Economic Performance." In *The Privatization Process: A Worldwide Perspective*, edited by T. L. Anderson and P. J. Hill. Lanham, MD: Rowman and Littlefield Publishers, Inc.

———. 1994. "Economic Performance Through Time." *American Economic Review*, 84 (3): 359-368.

———. 1990. *Institutions, Institutional Change, and Economic Performance*. Cambridge: Cambridge University Press.

North, D. C., and R. P. Thomas. 1973. *The Rise of The Western World: A New Economic History*. Cambridge: Cambridge University Press.

Romer, P. M. 1986. "Increasing Returns and Long-Run Growth." *Journal of Political Economy*, 94 (5): 1002-1037.

Summers, L. H. 1991. "The Scientific Illusion in Empirical Macroeconomics." *Scandinavian Journal of Economics*, 93 (2): 129- 148.

SECTION III

BIBLIOGRAPHY

PUBLICATIONS OF ISRAEL M. KIRZNER

Compiled by Peter J. Boettke

BOOKS

The Economic Point of View (Princeton, NJ: Van Nostrand, 1960) [Reprinted, Kansas City: Sheed and Ward, 1976].

Market Theory and the Price System (Princeton, NJ: Van Nostrand, 1963).

An Essay On Capital (New York: A.M. Kelley, 1966).

Competition and Entrepreneurship (Chicago: University of Chicago Press, 1973) [Spanish edition, 1975], [German edition, 1978], [Paperback (English) edition, 1978] [Japanese edition, 1985] [Portuguese edition, 1986].

Perception, Opportunity and Profit: Studies in the Theory of Entrepreneurship (Chicago: University of Chicago Press, 1979) [German edition, 1988].

Discovery and the Capitalist Process (Chicago: University of Chicago Press, 1985).

Discovery, Capitalism and Distributive Justice (Oxford: Basil Blackwell, 1989).

The Meaning of Market Process, Essays in the Development of Modern Austrian Economics (London: Routledge, 1992).

Advances in Austrian Economics, Volume 2B, pages 463-471.

ISBN: 1-55938-531-6

BOOKS EDITED

Method, Process, and Austrian Economics: Essays in Honor of Ludwig von Mises (Lexington, MA: Lexington Books, 1982).

Subjectivism, Intelligibility and Economic Understanding: Essays in Honor of Ludwig M. Lachmann on his Eightieth Birthday (New York: New York University Press, 1986).

Classics in Austrian Economics: A Sampling of a Tradition, 3 volumes (London: William Pickering and Chatto, 1994).

ARTICLES AND CHAPTERS IN BOOKS

"Rational Action and Economic Theory," *Journal of Political Economy*, 70 (August, 1962).

"Rejoinder," *Journal of Political Economy*, 71 (February, 1963).

"The Premises of Growth Economics," *New Individualist Review*, (Summer 1963).

"What Economists Do," *Southern Economics Journal*, 31 (February, 1965).

"Divergent Approaches in Libertarian Economic Thought," *Intercollegiate Review*, (January-February, 1967).

"Methodological Individualism, Market Equilibrium and Market Process," *Il Politico*, 32 (1967).

"On Man-made Tightropes," *National Review* (February 27, 1968).

"The 'Power' Problem on Campus," *Intercollegiate Review* (Spring 1970).

"Entrepreneurship and the Market Approach to Development," in *Toward Liberty: Essays in Honor of Ludwig von Mises* (Menlo Park: Institute for Humane Studies, 1971).

"Advertising," *The Freeman* (September 1972).

"Altruism, Social Responsibility, and the Market Economy," *The Hillsdale Report*, Vol. 11, no. 4 (1972).

"Tribute to Von Mises: On the Market," *National Review* (November 9, 1973).

"Advertising," in T. Machan (ed.) *The Libertarian Alternative: Essays in Social and Political Philosophy*, (Chicago: Nelson-Hall, 1974).

"The Ugly Market: Why Capitalism is Hated, Feared and Despised," in *The Freeman* (December 1974); reprinted in M. Hendrickson, ed., *The Morality of Capitalism* (Irvington-on-Hudson: Foundation for Economic Education, 1992).

"Capital, Competition, and Capitalism," in *Champions of Freedom, Ludwig von Mises Lecture Series* (Hillsdale: Hillsdale College Press, 1974).

"Producer, Entrepreneur, and the Right to Property" in S.L. Blumenfeld, ed., *Property in a Humane Economy* (La Salle, Illinois: Open Court, 1975).

"Ludwig von Mises and the Theory of Capital and Interest," in L.S. Moss, ed., *The Economics of Ludwig von Mises: Toward a Critical Reappraisal* (Kansas City: Sheed and Ward, 1976).

"On the Method of Austrian Economics" in E.G. Dolan, ed., *The Foundations of Modern Austrian Economics* (Kansas City; Sheed and Ward, 1976).

"Philosophical and Ethical Implications of Austrian Economics," in Dolan, *op. cit.*

"Equilibrium versus Market Process," in Dolan, *op. cit.*

"The Theory of Capital," in Dolan, *op. cit.*

"Discussion" in *The Economic System in an Age of Discontinuity: Long Range Planning or Market Reliance*? (New York: New York University Press, 1976).

"The 1975 Nobel Memorial Prize in Economics: Some Uncomfortable Reflections," in *The Freeman* (April 1976).

"Foreword" to new edition of L. Mises, *The Ultimate Foundation of Economic Science, An Essay on Method* (Kansas City: Sheed, Andrews and McMeel, 1978).

"Economics and Error, in L. Spadaro, ed., *New Directions in Austrian Economics*, (Kansas City: Sheed, Andrews, and McMeel, 1978).

"The Entrepreneurial Role in Menger's System," in *Atlantic Economic Journal* (September 1978).

"Entrepreneurship, Entitlement, and Economic Justice," in *Eastern Economic Journal*, Vol. 4, No. 1 (1978); also reprinted in J. Paul, ed., *Reading Nozick: Essays on Anarchy, State, and Utopia* (Totowa, NJ: Rowman and Littlefield, 1981).

"The Perils of Regulation: A Market Process Approach" Occasional Paper of the Law and Economics Center, University of Miami School of Law, February, 1979.

"Entrepreneurship, Choice and Freedom," in *ORDO Jahrbuch fur die Ordnung von Wirtschaft und Gesellschaft*, Band 30 [Festgabe fur F.A. von Hayek] (May 1979).

"X-Inefficiency, Error and the Scope for Entrepreneurship," in M. Rizzo, ed., *Time, Uncertainty and Disequilibrium: Exploration of Austrian Themes*, (Lexington, MA: Lexington Books, 1979).

"The Primacy of Entrepreneurial Discovery," in Institute of Economic Affairs, [Readings 23] *Prime Mover of Progress: The Entrepreneur in Capitalism and Socialism* (London: I.E.A., 1980).

"The Morality of Capitalist Success," Culver-Stockton College, Canton, MO, 1980.

"Policy Implications of Austrian Economics," in *Journal of Economic Affairs*, [London, England], Vol. 1, No. 3 (1981).

"Mises and the Renaissance of Austrian Economics," in *Homage to Mises: The First Hundred Years* (Hillsdale, MI: Hillsdale College Press, 1981).

"Mises on Entrepreneurship," in *Wirtschaftspolitische Blatter*, No. 4 (1981).
"The 'Austrian' Perspective," in Bell and Kristol, eds., *The Crisis in Economic Theory* (New York: Basic Books, 1981).
"The Theory of Entrepreneurship in Economic Growth," in *Encyclopedia of Entrepreneurship*, C.A. Kent, D.L. Sexton, K.H. Vesper, eds. (Englewood Cliffs, NJ: Prentice-Hall, 1982).
"Uncertainty, Discovery and Human Action: A Study of the Entrepreneurial Profile in the Misesian System," in Israel M. Kirzner, ed., *Method, Process and Austrian Economics: Essays in Honor of Ludwig von Mises* (Lexington, MA: Lexington Books, 1982).
"Competititon, Regulation, and the Market Process: An 'Austrian' Perspective," *CATO Institute Policy Analysis*, No. 18 (September 30, 1982).
"Entrepreneurship and the Future of Capitalism," in J. Backman, ed., *Entrepreneurship and the Outlook for America* (New York: Free Press, 1983).
"Entrepreneur and the Entrepreneurial Function: A Commentary," in J. Ronen, ed., *Entrepreneurship: Where Did It Come From, and Where Is It Going*? (Lexington, MA: Lexington Books, 1983).
"Die zentrale Bedeutung unternehmerischen Entdeckens," in *Zeitschrift fur Wirtschaftspolitik* (32 Jahrgang, Heft 3, 1983) [translation of "The Primacy of Entrepreneurial Discovery"].
"Incentives for Discovery," *Economic Affairs* (January 1984).
"Economic Planing and the Knowledge Problem," in *CATO Journal*, 4, (Fall 1984).
"Prices, the Communication of Knowledge, and the Discovery Process," in Kurt R. Leube and Albert H. Zlabinger, eds., *The Political Economy of Freedom: Essays in Honor of F.A. Hayek* (Munich-Vienna: Philosophia Verlag, 1984).
"The Entrepreneurial Process," in Calvin A. Kent, ed., *The Environment for Entrepreneurship* (Lexington, MA: Lexington Books, 1984).
"Rejoinder," in *Economic Affairs* (January-March, 1985).
"The Role of the Entrepreneur in the Economic System," Centre for Independent Studies, Syndney, Australia, Occassional Paper #10 (1985).
"Must Capitalism Yield to Socialism?," in *Economic Affairs* (April-June, 1985).
"Comment on R.N. Langlois, 'From the Knowledge of Economics to the Economics of Knowledge: Fritz Machlup on Methodology and on the "Knowledge Society," in Warren Samuels, ed., *Research in the History of Economic Thought and Methodology*, 3 (1985).
"Liberalism and Limited Government," in *The Freeman* (November 1985).
"Another Look at the Subjectivism of Costs," in Israel M. Kirzner, ed., *Subjectivism, Intelligibility and Economic Understanding* (New York: New York University Press, 1986).

"The Open-Endedness of Knowledge: Its Role in the F.E.E. Formula," in *The Freeman* (March, 1986).

"Ludwig von Mises and Friedrich von Hayek: The Modern Extension of Austrian Subjectivism," in Norbert Leser, ed., *Die Wiener Schule der Nationalkonomie* (Vienna and Cologne and Graz: Herman Bohlaus, 1986).

"Roundaboutness, Opportunity and Austrian Economics," in Martin J. Anderson, ed., *The Unfinished Agenda* (London: Institute of Economic Affairs, 1986).

"Individualistic Capitalism," in Donna C. Charron, ed., *Views on Individualism* (St. Louis: St. Louis Humanities Forum, 1986).

"Entrepreneurship and American Competitiveness" in S.M. Butler and W.J. Dennis, eds., *Entrepreneurship: The Key to Economic Growth* (Heritage Foundation and National Federation of Independent Business, 1986).

"Taxes and Discovery: An Entrepreneurial Perspective," in Dwight R. Lee, ed., *Taxation and the Deficit Economy; Fiscal Policy and Capital Formation in the U.S.* (San Francisco: Pacific Research Institute, 1986).

"Unternehmer: Finder von Beruf" in *Wirtschaftswoche* [the West German counterpart to *Business Week*] (January 9, 1987), [translated from English version written expressly for the occasion].

"The Economics of Errant Entrepreneurs" in *The Freeman* (August 1987).

"Spontaneous Order and the Case for the Free Market," in *Ideas on Liberty: Essays in Honor of Paul L. Poirot* (Irvington-on-Hudson: Foundation for Economic Education, 1987).

The following three articles in *The New Palgrave Dictionary of Economics* (New York: Macmillan, 1987):

i. "The Austrian School of Economics"
ii. "Friedrich Hayek" (co-authored article with Roger Garrison)
iii. "Economic Harmony"

"The Economic Calculation Debate: Lessons for Austrians," in *Review of Austrian Economics*, 2 (1988).

"Advertising in An Open-Ended Universe," Foreward to Robert B. Ekelund, Jr. and Daniel S. Saurman, *Advertising and the Market Process* (San Francisco: Pacific Research Institute, 1988).

"Welfare Economics: A Modern Austrian Perspective," in W. Block and L. H. Rockwell, eds., *Man, Economy and Liberty, Essays in Honor of Rothbard* (Auburn: Ludwig von Mises Institute, 1988).

"Some Ethical Implications for Capitalism of the Socialist Calculation Debate," in *Social Philosophy and Policy*, 6 (Autumn 1988).

"The Use of Labels in Doctrinal History: Comment on Baird," in *Cato Journal*, 9 (Spring/Summer 1989).

"Menger, Classical Liberalism, and the Austrian School of Economics," in Bruce Caldwell, ed., *Carl Menger and his legacy in Economics*, (Durham and London: Duke University Press, 1990).

"The Meaning of Market Process," in A. Bosch, P. Koslowski, and R. Veit, eds., *General Equilibrium or Market Process: Neoclassical and Austrian Theories of Economics*, (Tubingen: J.C.B. Mohr, 1990).

"The Market Process: An Austrian View" in K. Groenveld, J.A.M. Maks, and J. Muysken, eds., *Economic Policy and the Market Process, Austrian and Mainstream Economics* (Amsterdam: North Holland, 1990).

"Carl Menger und die subjektivistische Tradition in der Okonomie" (translated from original English text contributed expressly for this volume) in Horst Claus Recktenwald, eds., *Carl Mengers wegweisendes Werk* (Dusseldorf: Verlag Wirtschaft und Finanzen GMBM, 1990).

"Commentary" on S. Boehm "The Austrian Tradition: Schumpeter and Mises," in K. Hennings and W. J. Samuels, eds., *Neoclassical Economic Theory, 1870-1930* (Boston, Dordrecht, London: Kluwer, 1990).

"Self-Interest and the New Bashing of Economics" in *Critical Review*, 4 (Winter-Spring 1990).

"Knowledge Problems and Their Solutions: Some Relevant Distinctions," in *Cultural Dynamics*, 3 (1990).

"Discovery, Private Property, and the Theory of Justice in Capitalist Society," in *Journal des Economistes et des Etudes Humaines*, 1 (October 1990).

"The Driving Force of the Market," in R. Ebeling, ed., *Austrian Economics: Perspectives on the Past and Prospects for the Future* (Hillsdale, MI: Hillsdale College Press, 1991).

"F. A. Hayek, 1899-1992," in *Critical Review*, 5 (1991).

"Human Action, Freedom, and Economic Science," in J.W. Robbins and M. Spangler, eds., *A Man of Principle: Essays in Honor of Hans F. Sennholz* (Grove City, PA: Grove City College Press, 1992).

"Subjectivism, Freedom, and Economic Law, Ludwig Lachmann Memorial Lecture," in *South African Journal of Economics*, 60 (March 1992).

"The Morality of Pure Profit: The Logic and Illogic of a Popular Phobia," in *Journal des Economistes et des Etudes Humaines*, 4 (June-September 1993).

"The Pure Time Preference Theory of Interest: An Atttempt at Clarification," in J. M. Herbener, ed., *The Meaning of Ludwig von Mises: Contributions in Economics, Sociology, Epistemology, and Political Philosophy* (Boston: Kluwer Academic Publishers, 1993).

"The Limits of the Market: The Real and the Imagined," in W. Möschel, M. Streit and U. Witt, eds., *Marktwirtschaft und Rechtsordnung: Festschrift zum 70, Geburtstag von Prof. Dr. Erich Hoppmann* (Baden-Baden: Nomos Verlagsgesellschaft, 1994).

The following in *The Elgar Companion to Austrian Economics*, P. J. Boettke, ed. (Aldershot, UK: Edward Elgar Publishing, 1994):

i. "Value Freedom"
ii. "Entrepreneurship"

"A Tale of Two Worlds: Comment on Shmanske," in *Advances in Austrian Economics*, Vol. 1 (1994).

"The Entrepreneur in Economic Theory," in *The Dynamics of Entrepreneurship: Crafoord Lectures No. 5* (Malmö, Sweden: Lund University Press, 1994).

"The Ethics of Competition," in H. Siebert, ed., *The Ethical Foundations of the Market Economy* (Tübingen: J.C.B. Mohr, 1994).

"The Nature of Profits: Some Economic Insights and Their Ethical Implications," in R. Cowan and M. J. Rizzo, eds., *Profits and Morality* (University of Chicago Press, 1995).

"Hayek's Theory of the Coordination of Markets: A Commentary to Accompany the Facsimile Edition" in *Preise und Produktion* (Düsseldorf: Verlag Wirtschaft und Finanzen, 1995).

"The Subjectivism of Austrian Economics," in G. Meijer, ed., *New Perspectives on Austrian Economics* (London: Routledge, 1995).

BOOK REVIEWS

H. W. Briefs, *Three Views of Method in Economics*, in *Journal of Political Economy* (December 1963).

R. L. Smyth, ed., *Essays in Economic Methods*, in *Journal of Political Economy* (February 1964).

G. L. S. Shackle, *The Nature of Economic Thought*, in *Journal of Business* (April 1967).

D. Dewey, *Imperfect Competition, A Radical Interpretation*, in *Journal of Business* (October 1970).

H. Manne, ed., *Economic Policy and the Regulation of Corporate Securities*, in *Journal of Business* (October 1971).

Y. Brozen, ed., *Advertising and Society in Reason*, (November 1975).

J. R. Hicks, *Capital and Time, A Neo-Austrian Theory*; and J.R. Hicks and W. Weber (ed.), *Carl Menger and the Austrian School of Economics*, in *Libertarian Review*, (November 1975).

J. W. Markham, *Comglomerate Enterprise and Public Policy*; and J.F. Winslow, *Conglomerate Unlimited: The Failure of Regulation*, in *American Political Science Review* (March 1977).

J. K. Galbraith, *The Age of Uncertainty*, in *Libertarian Review* (September 1977).

L. Mises, *On the Manipulation of Money and Credit*, in *Reason Magazine* (April 1979).

F. A. Fetter, *Capital, Interest and Rent: Essays in the Theory of Distribution* (edited, with an introduction by M. N. Rothbard), in *Austrian Economics Newsletter* (Spring, 1980).

B. M. Friedman, ed., *New Challenges to the Role of Profit*, in *Public Choice* Vol.35/3.

H. Lepage, *Tomorrow, Capitalism: The Economics of Economic Freedom*, in *Inquiry* (April 1983).

G. J. Stigler, *The Economist as Preacher and Other Essays*, in *Inquiry*, (April 1983).

D. H. Hausman, *Capital, Profits and Prices: An Essay in the Philosophy of Economics*, in *International Philosophical Quarterly* (June 1983).

R. Hebert and A. Link, *The Entrepreneur*, in *Southern Economic Journal* (October 1983).

H. Frisch, ed., *Schumpeterian Economics*, in *Journal of Economic Literature* (December 1983).

M. Blaug, *The Methodology of Economics, or How Economists Explain*, in *Austrian Economics Newsletter* (Spring 1984).

G. Gilder, *The Spirit of Enterprise in Reason* (April 1985).

G. O'Driscoll and M. Rizzo, *The Economics of Time and Ignorance* in *Market Process* (Fall 1985); reprinted in P. J. Boettke and D. L. Prychitko, eds., *The Market Process: Essays in Contemporary Austrian Economics* (Aldershot, UK: Edward Elgar Publishing, 1994).

A. O. Hirschman, *Rival Views of Market Society and other Recent Essays*, in *Reason* (August-September 1987).

T. Alexander Smith, *Time and Public Policy*, in *The Freeman* (August 1989).

M. Currie and I. Steedman, *Wrestling with Time: Problems in Economic Theory*, in *Southern Economic Journal* (January 1991).

M. Skousen, *The Structure of Production*, in *Journal of Economic Literature* (December, 1991).

R. E. Cordato, *Welfare Economics and Externalities in an Open-Ended Universe: A Modern Austrian Perspective*, in *CATO Journal*, 13 (Spring/Summer 1993).

Mises: An Annotated Bibliography: A Comprehensive Lisiting of Books and Articles by and About Ludwig von Mises, compiled by B. Bien Greaves and R. W. McGee, in *The Freeman* (November 1993).

S. Ioannides, *The Market, Competition and Democracy: A Critique of Neo-Austrian Economics*, in *The Freeman* (January 1994).

B. Berger, ed., *The Culture of Entrepreneurship*, in *Advances in Austrian Economics*, Vol. 1 (1994).

D. Ramsay Steele, *From Marx to Mises: Post-Capitalist Society and the Challenge of Economic Calculation*, in *Economic Affairs* (April 1994).

J. Biner and R. Van Zijp, eds., *Hayek, Coordination and Evolution: His Legacy in Philosophy, Politics, Economics, and the History of Ideas* in *Southern Economic Journal* (forthcoming).